*Contents*

Fall: Thinking

Winter: Making

▓ Spring: Doing

Fall Thinking

SELECTED POEMS

SAPPHO

                           Love shook my heart
like the wind on the mountain
rushing over the oak trees

The moon has set,
and the Pleiades as well;
in the deep middle of the night
the time is passing,
and I lie alone.

Desire shakes me once again:
here is that melting of my limbs.
It is a creeping thing, and bittersweet.
I can do nothing to resist.

Sappho, when some fool

Explodes rage
in your breast
hold back that
yapping tongue!

THE CHARACTER SKETCHES (EXCERPTS)

Theophrastus

THE INSINCERE MAN

[Broadly speaking, insincerity would seem to be affectation of the worse in word or action.] When the insincere man meets a personal enemy, he is willing to make social conversation instead of showing his dislike. This is the kind of person, too, who praises you to your face after attacking you behind your back or who pointedly sympathizes when things have gone wrong. He also stands ready to pardon those who speak harsh words about him and to overlook what they say.

What's more, when people have been wronged because of him and are feeling angry, he talks with them as if nothing were the matter. And those who want to see him on urgent business are told to "come back later." Also, he never admits that he is actually doing anything; he claims he "has it under consideration." He pretends not to know what is going on, moreover: "I've only just arrived" is his excuse, or "I came late," or "I'm really not well." And to bill collectors or people who represent worthy causes he explains that he has no money; or if he is selling something he says he isn't, or the other way round. Once he has seen or heard anything he pretends that he hasn't; and after he makes a statement he claims he does not remember making it. In addition, to avoid taking a stand he will use a whole range of pretexts: for example, he "gave some thought to the matter"; he "doesn't know anything about it"; he's "surprised by what happened"; he "already came to the same conclusion himself." And he is a great one generally for expressions like "Why, I don't believe it!" "I can't understand it," "I'm absolutely staggered," or "From what you say, he must be a changed man," "That's not the way he told *me* the story," "I never would have thought it," "Tell that to somebody else," "I can't doubt your word, but I can't think ill of him either," "Don't be too quick to believe it!"

[That kind of empty formula and devious turn of speech characterizes the insincere man. He has a treacherous nature, and he is not straightforward. Stay clear of him—he is worse than any viper.]

Eirôneia: The Insincere Man

The Show-Off

Now, showing off would seem to be laying claim to advantages that one does not actually possess. The show-off is the kind of person who goes to the commercial pier down at the harbor and tells people from out of town that he's taking big investment risks in cargoes; or he will go on and on about the profits a man can make from marine insurance and the amounts he has made and lost personally. And in the middle of all this exaggeration about how much he is worth, he arrogantly orders his slave to stop at the bank—where his account totals one solitary drachma.

He is a great one, too, for imposing on anybody traveling with him: he will explain how he campaigned with Evander, and what Evander thought of him, and what a lot of jeweled cups he brought back—you don't find the workmanship here in Europe that you do in Asia, he argues. He acts as if he had the final inside word on anything along this line, when he has never been out of Attica in his life. He will even claim that he has three letters from Alexander's regent, Antipater, wanting him to come to Macedon; and that when the Macedonians tried to give him tax-free export rights on timber he turned them down, so that nobody could report him for being "too friendly to Macedon." Also—according to him—what he laid out during the famine came to more than five thousand in contributions to needy townspeople, but how could he say no? And even though the persons sitting nearby may all be strangers to him, he asks one of them to check his estimate. Then he lists a mass of figures—naming some recipient for each one to make the story more believable—and runs the total up as high as ten thousand. These were just his contributions, he goes on to point out: he isn't figuring in all his expenses on civic duties.

At horse auctions he tries to make the dealer think that he is in the market for a thoroughbred. In the same way, he will ransack the clothing stalls asking for things priced up to three figures, and then stage an argument with his servant for bringing only small change. He may be living in a rented house, moreover, but he tells anybody who doesn't know the facts that the place has been in the family for generations; and he will mention that he plans to put it on the market because he finds it too small for the entertaining he has to do.

Alazoneia: The Show-Off

THE STRAW, THE COAL, AND THE BEAN

THE GRIMM BROTHERS

In a village dwelt a poor old woman, who had gathered together a dish of beans and wanted to cook them. So she made a fire on her hearth, and that it might burn the quicker, she lighted it with a handful of straw. When she was emptying the beans into the pan, one dropped without her observing it, and lay on the ground beside a straw, and soon afterwards a burning coal from the fire leapt down to the two. Then the straw began and said: 'Dear friends, from whence do you come here?' The coal replied: 'I fortunately sprang out of the fire, and if I had not escaped by sheer force, my death would have been certain,—I should have been burnt to ashes.' The bean said: 'I too have escaped with a whole skin, but if the old woman had got me into the pan, I should have been made into broth without any mercy, like my comrades.' 'And would a better fate have fallen to my lot?' said the straw. 'The old woman has destroyed all my brethren in fire and smoke; she seized sixty of them at once, and took their lives. I luckily slipped through her fingers.'

'But what are we to do now?' said the coal.

'I think,' answered the bean, 'that as we have so fortunately escaped death, we should keep together like good companions, and lest a new mischance should overtake us here, we should go away together, and repair to a foreign country.'

The proposition pleased the two others, and they set out on their way together. Soon, however, they came to a little brook, and as there was no bridge or foot-plank, they did not know how they were to get over it. The straw hit on a good idea, and said: 'I will lay myself straight across, and then you can walk over on me as on a bridge.' The straw therefore stretched itself from one bank to the other, and the coal, who was of an impetuous disposition, tripped quite boldly on to the newly-built bridge. But when she had reached the middle, and heard the water rushing beneath her, she was after all, afraid, and stood still, and ventured no farther. The straw, however, began to burn, broke in two pieces, and fell into the stream. The coal slipped after her, hissed when she got into the water, and breathed her last. The bean, who had prudently stayed behind on the shore, could not but laugh at the event, was unable to stop, and laughed so heartily that she burst. It would have been all over with her, likewise, if, by good fortune, a tailor who was travelling in search of work, had not sat down to rest by the brook. As he had a compassionate heart he pulled out his needle and thread, and sewed her together. The bean thanked him most prettily, but as the tailor used black thread, all beans since then have a black seam.

Winter: Making

GERMANY FROM 1918 TO 1945

Encyclopaedia Britannica Online

THE WEIMAR REPUBLIC, 1918–33

The republic proclaimed early in the afternoon of Saturday, November 9, 1918, is often called the "accidental republic." When Friedrich Ebert, the leader of the so-called Majority Socialists, accepted the imperial chancellorship from Max von Baden, it was with the understanding that he would do his utmost to save the imperial system from revolution. Ebert believed that the only way to accomplish this would be by transforming Germany into a constitutional monarchy. Elections would have to be held for a constituent assembly, whose task it would be to draw up a new constitution.

DEFEAT OF REVOLUTIONARIES, 1918–19

Ebert, however, was faced with a precarious situation. The dangers confronting him were mounting all over the country. Four and a half years of seemingly futile combat and sacrifice had resulted in a disaffection with the war and discredited the imperial system, as well as its emperor. Shortages of food and fuel had rendered the population vulnerable to the influenza epidemic sweeping Europe. On October 18 alone Berlin authorities had reported 1,700 influenza deaths. Independent Socialists in Munich had forced the abdication on November 8 of Bavaria's King Louis III and proclaimed a Bavarian socialist republic. The port cities along the North Sea and the Baltic Sea were falling into the hands of sailors' and workers' and soldiers' councils (*Räte*) in the wake of the naval mutiny at Kiel in early November. Karl Liebknecht and Rosa Luxemburg, leaders of the radical Spartacus League, were eager to transform Germany into a republic of workers' and soldiers' councils (a *Räterepublik*) in imitation of the soviet republic being established by the Bolshevik leaders in Russia. As Ebert was accepting the reins of government in the Reichstag building on November 9, Liebknecht was proclaiming a socialist republic at a rally of his own followers in front of the deserted Royal Palace about a mile away. Many Marxist revolutionaries believed that the Bolshevik Revolution was merely the spark that would set off the worldwide proletarian revolution that Karl Marx had predicted. Inevitably, that revolution would have to spread to Germany. Given this ideologically charged scenario, Liebknecht confidently anticipated his destiny to become the German Lenin.

While the Liebknecht rally was proceeding in front of the Royal Palace, an angry crowd was gathering before the Reichstag building, the seat of the government. Because Ebert had just left the building, his friend and fellow Majority Socialist Philipp Scheidemann felt called upon to address the crowd. To meet its inevitable demands for change and to forestall whatever Liebknecht might be telling his followers, Scheidemann in his speech used the phrase "Long live the German republic!" Once made, the proclamation of a republic could not be withdrawn. Ebert was furious when he learned of Scheidemann's "accidental" proclamation, but he realized that there was no turning back. He spent the afternoon seeking partners to form a provisional government to run the newly proclaimed republic. By nightfall he managed to persuade the Independent Socialists, a party that in 1917 had split from the Majority Socialists over the continuation of the war, to provide three members of a provisional government. To gain their cooperation, Ebert had to agree to name the provisional government the Council of Peoples' Commissars and to transform Germany into a vaguely defined social republic. Despite this promise, Ebert still hoped that elections to a constituent assembly would lead to the creation of a moderate democratic republic. The Independent Socialists, however, though not as radical as Liebknecht, held to their vision of a socialist *Räterepublik.* They hoped that workers and soldiers would elect a multitude of councils across the entire country during the following weeks, assuming these would establish the foundation for a genuinely socialist republic.

For the time being, however, Majority and Independent Socialists jointly formed a provisional government for the defeated German nation, which everywhere seemed on the verge of collapse. Although the armistice of November 11 ended the fighting, it did not end the Allied blockade. The winter of 1918–19 brought no relief in the shortages of food and fuel, and the flu epidemic showed no signs of abatement. Soldiers returning from the military fronts by the hundreds of thousands were left stranded, jobless, hungry, and bitter—grist for the mill of revolution.

The push for revolution, led by an enthusiastic Liebknecht and a more reluctant Luxemburg, came on January 6, 1919, encouraged by Soviet Russia and further prompted by fear that Ebert's plans for the election of a constituent assembly, scheduled for January 19, might stabilize the German situation. The Spartacists, now officially the Communist Party of Germany, initiated massive demonstrations in Berlin and quickly seized key government and communications centres.

The events of "Spartacist Week," as the radical attempt at revolution came to be known, demonstrated that Germany was not nearly as ripe for revolution as leading radicals had believed. As Luxemburg had feared, mass support for communism did not exist among German workers; instead, most remained loyal to the Independent Socialists or to Ebert's more moderate and democratic vision of socialism. The German army, moreover, had recovered its nerve and was determined to prevent a further move to the left. In December the army had begun secretly to train volunteer units drawn from the sea of soldiers returning from the front. These so-called Freikorps ("Free Corps") units formed dozens of small right-wing armies that during the next years roamed the country, looking for revolutionary activity to suppress. The Spartacist revolt, which was confined largely to Berlin, was put down within a week by some 3,000 Freikorps members. When Liebknecht and Luxemburg were captured on January 15, they were both shot at the initiative of Freikorps officers. Although sporadic revolutionary activity continued elsewhere in Germany during the following months, its failure in Berlin clearly marked its doom. The proclamation on April 4, 1919, of a *Räterepublik* in Bavaria revived radical fortunes only briefly; Freikorps units put down the radical Bavarian republic by the end of the month.

The collapse of the Spartacist revolt greatly enhanced the chances for Ebert's vision of Germany's future to prevail. Moreover, the meeting of a national congress of workers' and soldiers' councils in mid-December 1918, upon which the Independent Socialists had pinned their own hopes for creating a socialist republic, proved to be far less radical than expected; it did nothing to interfere with Ebert's plans to elect an assembly to draw up a democratic constitution. The elections on January 19, 1919—the first German election in which women had voting rights—produced a resounding victory for Ebert's conception of democracy. Three of every four voters gave their support to political parties that favoured turning Germany into a democracy. After months of turmoil Germany was to become a democratic republic. The assembly began its deliberations on February 6, 1919, choosing to meet in Weimar, a small city that was considered less vulnerable to radical political interference than Berlin.

On January 18, 1919, representatives of the powers victorious over Germany began the deliberations in Paris that would establish a European peace settlement. Germany's new democratic leaders placed high hopes in the prospects for this settlement. U.S. President Woodrow Wilson's Fourteen Points seemed to promise Germans national self-determination as well as to encourage the efforts to transform Germany into a democracy. When the German constituent assembly met in Weimar for the first time, it immediately declared itself sovereign over all of Germany. It selected a provisional government—with Ebert as president and Scheidemann as chancellor—whose first major task was to prepare for the expected invitation to Paris to negotiate a peace treaty with the empire's former enemies.

But the invitation for a German delegation to come to Paris did not arrive until early April. Rather than being treated as a fellow—if fledgling—democracy, Germans soon learned that they were still viewed as the pariah of Europe. Wilson's idealism had been forced to yield to still-fresh wartime resentments being articulated by the leaders of the French, British, and Italian delegations. Instead of offering negotiations, the Allies forced Germany to sign the treaty with no alterations.

THE TREATY OF VERSAILLES

In its final form, the Treaty of Versailles contained many provisions that the Germans had fully expected. That Alsace-Lorraine was to be handed back to France was no surprise; nor were the small territorial adjustments along the border with Belgium. The plebiscite allowing the Danish population of northern Schleswig to choose between joining Denmark or remaining with Germany was unarguably consistent with the principle of national self-determination. But this principle, the Germans expected, would also justify a union between Germany and the Germans of what now remained of Austria after the collapse of the previous November. More serious to Germany was the stipulation that its coal-rich Saar region was to be taken over by the League of Nations and the coal given to France to aid its postwar reconstruction. Eventually a plebiscite was to allow Saarlanders to choose whether or not they wished to rejoin Germany.

On its eastern frontier Germany was forced to cede to the newly independent Poland the province of West Prussia, thereby granting Poland access to the Baltic Sea, while Germany lost land access to the province of East Prussia. Danzig was declared a free city under the permanent governance of the League of Nations. Much of the province of Posen, which, like West Prussia, had been acquired by Prussia in the late 18th-century partitions of Poland, was likewise granted to the restored Polish state. Also transferred from Germany to Poland, as the result of a later plebiscite, was a significant portion of coal-rich and industrially developed Upper Silesia.

Overseas Germany was compelled to yield control of its colonies. Although these colonies had proven to be economic liabilities, they had also been symbols of the world-power status that Germany had gained in the 1880s and '90s. More damaging were the treaty's commercial clauses that took from Germany most of its foreign financial holdings and reduced its merchant carrier fleet to roughly one-tenth of its prewar size.

The treaty's provisions for disarming Germany were to be, the Allied leaders promised, merely the first step in a worldwide process of disarmament. To ensure that Germany would not revive as a military power, its army was to be reduced to 100,000 men and would not be allowed to produce tanks, poison gas, or military planes. Moreover, Germany's frontier with France was to be permanently demilitarized; German military forces were to remain behind a line 31 miles (50 km) east of the Rhine. The treaty also called for the dissolution of the German general staff, the German army's military command structure that the Allies believed to be the engine of German aggression. The navy, too, was to be dismantled and limited to 15,000 men, a half dozen battleships, and 30 smaller ships, with an absolute prohibition on the building of submarines. Germany's compliance with the treaty's terms was to be assured by an Allied occupation of the Rhineland and the presence of the Inter-Allied Commissions of Control.

The terms of the Treaty of Versailles that the Germans most resented, however, were the so-called honour clauses: Articles 227 through 230 gave the Allies the right to try individual Germans, including the former emperor, as war criminals; Article 231, often called the war guilt clause, provided the justification for Article 232, which established a commission to collect reparation payments, the total of which was eventually set at 132 billion gold marks. German bitterness over these honour clauses was nearly universal. Almost no German believed that Germany was responsible for the outbreak of war in 1914. Technically, Article 231 did not declare Germany alone as guilty for causing the war; rather, Germany was branded as responsible "for causing all the loss and damage" suffered by the Allies in the war "imposed upon them by the aggression of Germany and her allies." Germans read it as an accusation of guilt, however, and interpreted it as the cynical product of victors' justice.

Upon learning of the full terms of the treaty, the German provisional government in Weimar was thrown into upheaval. "What hand would not wither that binds itself and us in these fetters?" Scheidemann asked, and he resigned rather than accept the treaty. Army chief Paul von Hindenburg did the same, after declaring the army unable to resume the war under any circumstances. Only an ultimatum from the Allies finally brought a German delegation to Paris to sign the treaty on June 28, 1919, exactly five years after the assassination of Archduke Francis Ferdinand.

THE WEIMAR CONSTITUTION

In the month following the signing of the treaty, the Weimar constituent assembly completed a draft constitution for the new republic, resulting in what was hailed as the most modern democratic constitution of its day. The Weimar constitution provided for a popularly elected president who was given considerable power over foreign policy and the armed forces. Article 48 also gave the president emergency decree powers to protect the republic from crises initiated by its opponents on either the left or the right. The president was empowered to nominate the chancellor, whose government required the confidence of the lower house of the parliament, the Reichstag, which was elected by universal suffrage through a system of proportional representation. An upper house, the Reichsrat, comprised delegates appointed by the governments of the federal states, the *Länder*.

The Weimar constitution's most modern features, the provisions for popular referendum and initiative, were designed to enable the electorate, by way of petition, to introduce bills into the Reichstag and to force the body to vote on them. If the bill was voted down, the constitution prescribed a national referendum to allow the electorate to pass the bill into law against the wishes of the Reichstag. Through these provisions, it was thought, the government would never be allowed to ignore the wishes of the voters.

The Weimar constitution was promulgated formally on August 11, 1919, ending the provisional status of government in Germany that had begun with Scheidemann's proclamation of a republic the previous November. In September the government, judging the situation sufficiently safe in Berlin, returned to the capital. But it did not yet consider it sufficiently safe to risk nationwide elections for president or for a Reichstag to replace the constituent assembly. Instead the assembly prolonged Ebert's provisional term as president for three years; elections for the Reichstag were delayed until June 1920.

Years of Crisis, 1920–23

In its early years the new German democracy faced continuing turmoil. The Treaty of Versailles, quickly labeled "the *Diktat*" by the German public, galvanized the resentment that had accumulated during the war, much of which was turned back on the republic itself. Its enemies began to blame the hated treaty on the republic's socialist and democratic progenitors, whom they accused of having undermined Germany's efforts in the final stages of the war. A revived and radicalized right wing asked whether the German army might not have been stabbed in the back by traitors on the home front. Racist circles took seriously the notorious *Protocols of the Learned Elders of Zion,* a fraudulent document fabricated in Russia in 1895 and published in Germany in 1920, which suggested that all of recent history, including World War I, resulted from a conspiracy of Jews seeking to control the world. Roving Freikorps units contributed to the brutalization of German political life. In March 1920 one of these units, under the command of the former naval captain Hermann Ehrhardt, succeeded in briefly seizing control of the government in Berlin. This so-called Kapp Putsch, named after the conservative politician Wolfgang Kapp, who had planned it, was thwarted not by the army but by a general strike of Berlin's socialist and communist workers. Threats by military figures succeeded in forcing the resignation of Bavaria's socialist government and its replacement by a conservative regime, however, and thereafter radical groups of the right found protection and a degree of nurture in this southern German state. By the end of 1922 there had been nearly 400 political assassinations, the vast majority of them traceable to rightists. The victims included prominent politicians such as Matthias Erzberger, who signed the armistice of 1918, and Walther Rathenau, the foreign minister.

The June 1920 elections to the first Reichstag reflected the difficulties in which the new democracy found itself. The Weimar coalition parties, the Social Democratic Party, the Centre Party, and the Democrats, which in January 1919 had together received more than 75 percent of the vote, this time managed to win only 43.5 percent. Contributing to the problems that the republic faced in the early 1920s was the escalating rate of inflation that was eventually to destroy the German mark. Although the inflation was rooted in the huge debt that Germany had amassed in financing its war effort, the hyperinflation of 1923 was triggered by the French-Belgian military occupation in January 1923 of the German industrial district in the Ruhr valley. The occupation occurred in retaliation for Germany's having fallen behind in its reparation payments and was intended to force German industry to provide compensation for the French and Belgian losses. Rather than accede quietly to the humiliation of occupation, the German government urged workers and employers to close down the factories. Idle workers were paid during the following months with a currency inflating so rapidly that printers gave up trying to print numbers on bills. By mid-1923 the German mark was losing value by the minute: a loaf of bread that cost 20,000 marks in the morning would cost 5,000,000 marks by nightfall; restaurant prices went up while customers were eating; and workers were paid twice a day. When economic collapse finally came on November 15, it took 4.2 trillion German marks to buy a single American dollar.

The social and political cost of the hyperinflation was high. Scholars note that the inflation did more to undermine the middle classes than the ostensibly socialist revolution of 1918. A lifetime of savings would no longer buy a subway ticket. Pensions planned for a lifetime were wiped out completely. Politically, the hyperinflation fueled radicalism on both the left and the right. The Communists, badly damaged by their failure in January 1919, saw greatly improved prospects for a successful revolution. In Munich the leader of the small National Socialist German Workers' (Nazi) Party, Adolf Hitler, used the turmoil to fashion an alliance with other right-wing groups and attempt a coup in November 1923—the Beer Hall Putsch—that sought to use Bavaria as a base for a nationalist march on Berlin. He hoped to overthrow the democratic system of Weimar that he believed was responsible for Germany's political and economic humiliation. Neither the radicals of the right nor those of the left succeeded in imposing their will. In the short run they did not succeed because of ineptitude and miscalculation; in the long run they failed because the government sponsored a currency reform that restabilized the mark and also decided to end its policy of passive resistance in the Ruhr in exchange for an end to the occupation and a rescheduling of the reparation payments that it owed to the Allies.

The Weimar Renaissance

Amid the political and economic turmoil of the early 1920s, Germany's cultural and intellectual life was flowering. The so-called Weimar Renaissance brought the fulfillment of the Modernist revolution, which in the late 19th century had begun to transform the European aesthetic sensibility. The Modernist rejection of tradition perfectly suited the need of many Germans for new meanings and values to replace those destroyed by the war. "A world has been destroyed; we must seek a radical solution," said the young architect Walter Gropius upon his return from the front in late 1918. In 1919 Gropius became the founder and first director of the Bauhaus school of design in Weimar, the most important institution in Germany for the expression of Modernism's aesthetic and cultural vision. Bauhaus artists believed that they were creating a new world through their painting, poetry, music, theatre, and architecture. The legacy of German Modernism in general, and of the Bauhaus in particular, is most immediately evident in the stark steel-and-glass high-rise buildings whose clear and clean lines have come to dominate the skylines of the world's cities. Moreover, the paintings and sculptures decorating them, as well as the designs of the furniture and the lighting fixtures, are heavily influenced by the aesthetic principles articulated in Weimar Germany during the 1920s.

Beyond the Bauhaus, painters such as George Grosz, Max Beckmann, and Otto Dix pursued an artistic approach known as Expressionism; they were interested in depicting their emotional responses to reality rather than reality itself. In music the rejection of tonality by composers such as Arnold Schoenberg, Anton von Webern, and Alban Berg broke a centuries-old tradition. At the juncture between popular and serious music, the composer Kurt Weill collaborated with the poet and dramatist Bertolt Brecht to create in 1928 *Die Dreigroschenoper* (*The Threepenny Opera*), a bitterly satiric musical play in which the world of modern capitalism was equated with that of underworld gangsterism. In films such as Robert Wiene's *Das Kabinett des Dr. Caligari* (1919; *The Cabinet of Dr. Caligari*) and Fritz Lang's *Metropolis* (1926), distorted sets and unusual camera angles probed for disturbing truths behind the surface appearances of reality.

Not everyone welcomed the Modernist attack on tradition. Angry audiences often interrupted opera performances and theatrical productions. Siegfried Wagner, the son of the composer Richard Wagner, deplored a Modernist version of his father's *Der fliegende Holländer* (1843; *The Flying Dutchman*), calling the production an example of "cultural bolshevism." Other artists—the novelist Thomas Mann, for example, winner of the 1929 Nobel Prize for Literature—chose to remain above the fray in the Olympian heights of German *Kultur*.

YEARS OF ECONOMIC AND POLITICAL STABILIZATION

The financial recovery that began with the restabilization of the German currency in late 1923 received a boost in 1924 when the Allies agreed to end their occupation of the Ruhr and to grant the German government a more realistic payment schedule on reparations. A committee of the Allied Reparations Commission headed by the American financier and soon-to-be vice president Charles Dawes had recommended these changes and urged the Allies to grant sizable loans to Germany to assist its economic recovery. The Dawes Plan marked a significant step in the upswing of the German economy that lasted until the onset of the Great Depression. The 800 million gold marks in foreign loans had by 1927 enabled German industrial production to regain its 1913 prewar high. That same year the Reichstag addressed the vital need for social and class reconciliation by voting for a compulsory unemployment insurance plan. Reconciliation on the political level seemed achieved in 1925 when the 77-year-old Hindenburg was elected to succeed the deceased Ebert as president. Although no democrat, the aged field marshal took seriously his duty to support the constitution and the republic.

The guiding spirit in German foreign policy from 1924 through 1929 was the foreign minister, Gustav Stresemann, who firmly believed that Germany was more likely to gain relief from the harshness of Versailles by trying to fulfill its terms than by stubbornly continuing to resist them. Stresemann's efforts ushered in what came to be known as "the era of fulfillment." It began in December 1925 when Germany signed the Pact of Locarno, in which it guaranteed to maintain the new postwar boundaries with France and Belgium and to submit to international arbitration any boundary disputes that might arise in the east with Poland or Czechoslovakia. Germany formally rejoined the family of nations by being granted membership in the League of Nations in September 1926. In 1928 Germany became party to the most dramatic symbolic gesture of postwar reconciliation, the Kellogg-Briand Pact, which promised to outlaw aggressive war; this agreement was signed by nearly all the world's major countries during the next year.

The May 1928 Reichstag elections seemed to reflect the economic and political stabilization of the Weimar Republic. The antirepublican parties of the left and right together received only 13 percent of the total vote, with the Communists receiving 10.6 percent and the Nazis taking only 2.6 percent. Germany's reintegration into the international political structure advanced with the decision in early 1929 by the Allied Reparations Commission to settle the reparations question. Owen D. Young, an American business executive, headed the committee appointed to make recommendations in this matter. The Young Committee proposed that German reparations be reduced to about 37 billion gold marks, less than one-third of the 1921 total, and that payments be stretched until 1988. It also called for the dissolution of the Reparations Commission and for an immediate end to what remained of the Allied occupation of the Rhineland.

The German government, seeing the obvious advantages in the Young Plan, officially accepted its terms in August 1929. However, right-wing opposition parties saw the plan as nothing less than a renewal of Germany's humiliation. Led by the German National Peoples' Party (DNVP) and its leader Alfred Hugenberg, the press and movie-industry lord, the nationalist opposition seized upon the constitutional processes for popular initiative and referendum in order to force the government to reverse its acceptance of the plan. To run the opposition's anti-Young Plan campaign, Hugenberg engaged Hitler, the leader of the apparently moribund Nazi Party. The objective was to force the German government to repudiate the reparations debt as well as the war guilt clause of Versailles upon which the debt rested. German signatories to the Young Plan, moreover, were to become liable to the charge of treason. The right wing's initiative did force the Reichstag into reconsidering its approval of the Young Plan but to no avail. The national plebiscite that necessarily followed found only 13.8 percent of the voters favouring the objectives of the right wing. The bitterness of the campaign, however, may have contributed to the illness and death of Stresemann during the campaign.

The End of the Republic

An unintended effect of the anti-Young Plan campaign was to give widespread public exposure to Hitler, who used his access to the Hugenberg-owned press empire and to its weekly movie newsreels to give himself and his Nazi movement national publicity. An additional assist to Hitler's career came on October 29, 1929, with the stock market crash on Wall Street, an event that signaled the onset of what quickly became a worldwide depression. The crash had an immediate effect in Germany as American investors, anxious about their financial position, began withdrawing their loans to Germany. German indebtedness to these investors had by 1929 reached nearly 15 billion marks. Prices on the German stock exchanges fell drastically during the last month of the year. Business failures multiplied. Early in 1930 Germany's second largest insurance firm collapsed. Unemployment rose to three million during the course of the year. By the winter of 1932 it reached six million. Germany's industry was working at no more than 50 percent of its capacity, and the volume of German foreign trade fell by two-thirds between 1929 and 1932.

The first critically important political effect of the economic crisis came in March 1930 when the government coalition fell apart over the rising cost of maintaining the unemployment program adopted in 1927. The Social Democratic Party, representing labour, and the Peoples' Party, representing business, were unable to agree on the size of the government's contribution to the fund, and their coalition dissolved. When a new coalition could not be formed, parliamentary democracy in Germany came to an end.

Political instability forced President Hindenburg to invoke his emergency powers (Article 48), which he used to appoint Heinrich Brüning of the Catholic Centre Party as chancellor. For the next two years, until May 30, 1932, Brüning governed without a parliamentary majority, deriving his authority from the powers residing in the office of President Hindenburg. However well-intentioned, Brüning's deflationary economic policies were unable to stem the tide either of the depression or of its social and political ravages. His fateful decision to call for Reichstag elections in September 1930, moreover, inadvertently opened the door for the enemies of Weimar democracy. Together the Nazis and Communists gained nearly one of every three votes cast. In comparison to 1928, the Nazis increased their share of the vote sevenfold to 18 percent, while the Communists won 13 percent, a slight gain from their 10 percent share.

Although bitterly opposed to each other, during the next two years the Nazis and Communists succeeded in mobilizing the political and economic resentments generated by the depression. Hitler's charismatic appeal and the youthful energies of his movement were attractive to large segments of a populace fearful of being ruined by economic and social disaster. Hitler's record as a war veteran lent authority to the hypernationalism he expressed in racist terms. His identification of the Jew as the enemy responsible for all of Germany's ills, be it the defeat of 1918, the Treaty of Versailles, the reparations, the inflation, or now the depression, seemed plausible to many eager to find a scapegoat. The power of Hitler's appeal was reflected in the party's growing membership lists—from 170,000 members in 1929 to 1,378,000 in 1932—and in the swelling ranks of the Nazi Party's paramilitary SA (Sturmabteilung), the infamous storm troopers.

Unlike Hitler, the Communists found it difficult to extend their support beyond the German working classes. Moreover, Stalin's increasing control over the Communists limited their political flexibility. Nonetheless, their self-confidence rose substantially because the depression seemingly confirmed their prediction of the inevitable collapse of capitalism. To the Communists, Hitler and National Socialism were perceived merely as products of the last phase of capitalism.

The depression reached its depths in the winter of 1931–32. Unemployment was still rising; the succession of business failures resembled rows of falling dominoes. Brüning, helpless in the face of these problems, was dubbed "the hunger chancellor" by his critics. Some hope of breaking the political impasse came with the series of critical state legislative elections scheduled for the spring of 1932 and with the presidential election required at the expiration of Hindenburg's first term. Hitler's opponents recognized that the 84-year-old Hindenburg, now fading into senility, was their only hope to prevent Hitler from winning the presidency, and, with great difficulty, they convinced Hindenburg, who wanted to retire, to seek a second term. The year 1932 was to be one of continuous election campaigning.

Although Hindenburg was eventually reelected, a runoff was necessary, and Hitler won 37 percent of the popular vote. His larger aim, however, had been to make himself the leading, or only, candidate for Brüning's position as chancellor. Hindenburg did choose to replace Brüning in May 1932 but named the political dilettante Franz von Papen rather than Hitler. Desperate to find a base in parliament, Papen called for Reichstag elections in July. The result was a disaster for Papen and another triumph for the Nazis, who took 37 percent of the vote, the largest total they were ever to acquire in a free election. The Communists won 15 percent of the vote. Thus the two parties dedicated to destroying German democracy held a majority in the Reichstag. Still, Hitler was not appointed chancellor. In November Papen called for another Reichstag election in the hope of gaining parliamentary backing. Again he failed, although the Nazi vote fell by 4 percent. By contrast, the Communist vote rose to nearly 17 percent. In early December, when Hindenburg decided to replace Papen, he again ignored Hitler, choosing instead a friend from the army, General Kurt von Schleicher.

In the Nazi camp there was bitter frustration at the end of 1932. The party was deeply in debt and demoralized by the year's endless campaigning. Putschist elements in the party, never persuaded that elections could bring the party to power, were growing increasingly restive. So deep was the frustration that on December 7 Gregor Strasser, second only to Hitler in the party, broke with the Nazis and retired from politics.

[Spartacus Manifesto]

First published as "Richtlinien für die Arbeiter—und Soldatenräte Deutschlands" in *Die Rote Fahne* (November 26, 1918).

PROLETARIANS! MEN AND WOMEN OF LABOR! COMRADES!

The revolution has made its entry into Germany. The masses of the soldiers, who for four years were driven to the slaughterhouse for the sake of capitalistic profits, and the masses of workers, who for four years were exploited, crushed, and starved, have revolted. That fearful tool of oppression—Prussian militarism, that scourge of humanity—lies broken on the ground. Its most noticeable representatives, and therewith the most noticeable of those guilty of this war, the Kaiser and the Crown Prince, have fled from the country. Workers' and soldiers' councils have been formed everywhere.

Proletarians of all countries, we do not say that in Germany all the power has really been lodged in the hands of the working people, that the complete triumph of the proletarian revolution has already been attained. There still sit in the government all those socialists who in August 1914 abandoned our most precious possession, the [Second] International [Workingmen's Association], who for four years betrayed the German working class and at the same time the International.

But, proletarians of all countries, now the German proletarians are speaking to you. We believe we have the right to appeal before your forum in their name. From the first day of this war we endeavored to do our international duty by fighting that criminal government with all our power, and by branding it as the one really guilty of the war.

Now, at this moment, we are justified before history, before the International, and before the German proletariat. The masses agree with us enthusiastically; constantly widening circles of the proletariat share the knowledge that the hour has struck for a settlement with capitalist class rule.

But this great task cannot be accomplished by the German proletariat alone: it can fight and triumph only by appealing to the solidarity of the proletarians of the whole world.

Comrades of the belligerent countries, we are aware of your situation. We know very well that your governments, since they have won the victory, are dazzling the eyes of many strata of the people with the external brilliance of this triumph. We know that they thus succeed through the success of the murdering in making its causes and aims forgotten.[. . .]

The imperialism of all countries knows no "understanding"; it knows only one right—capital's profits; it knows only one language—the sword; it knows only one method—violence. And if it is now talking in all countries, in yours as well as ours, about the "League of Nations," "disarmament," "rights of small nations," "self-determination of the peoples," it is merely using the customary lying phrases of the rulers for the purpose of lulling to sleep the watchfulness of the proletariat.

Proletarians of all countries! This must be the last war! We owe that to the twelve million murdered victims; we owe that to our children; we owe that to humanity.

Europe has been ruined through the infamous international murder. Twelve million bodies cover the gruesome scenes of the imperialistic crime. The flower of youth and the best men of the nations have been mowed down. Uncounted productive forces have been annihilated. Humanity is almost ready to bleed to death from the bloodletting. Victors and vanquished stand at the edge of the abyss. Humanity is threatened with the most dreadful famine, a halting of the entire mechanism of production, plagues, and degeneration.

The great criminals of this fearful anarchy, of this chaos let loose—the ruling classes—are not able to control their own creation. The beast of capital that conjured up the hell of the world war is not capable of banishing it again, of restoring real order, of insuring bread and work, peace and civilization, and justice and liberty to tortured humanity.

What is being prepared by the ruling classes as peace and justice is only a new work of brutal force from which the hydra of oppression, hatred, and fresh bloody wars raises its thousand heads.

Socialism alone is in a position to complete the great work of permanent peace, to heal the thousand wounds from which humanity is bleeding, to transform the plains of Europe, trampled down by the apocryphal horsemen of war, into blossoming gardens, to conjure up ten productive forces for every one destroyed, to awaken all the physical and moral energies of humanity, and to replace hatred and dissension with fraternal solidarity, harmony, and respect for every human being. [. . .]

Proletarians of all countries, when we now summon you to a common struggle, it is not done for the sake of the German capitalists who, under the label of "German nation," are trying to escape the consequences of their own crimes; it is being done for our sake as well as yours. Remember that your victorious capitalists stand ready to suppress in blood our revolution, which they fear as their own. You yourselves have not become any freer through the "victory," you have only become still more enslaved. If your ruling classes succeed in throttling the proletarian revolution in Germany, as well as in Russia, then they will turn against you with redoubled violence. Your capitalists hope that victory over us and over revolutionary Russia will give them the power to scourge you with a whip of scorpions and to erect the thousand-year empire of exploitation upon the grave of socialism.

Therefore the proletariat of Germany is looking toward you in this hour. Germany is pregnant with the social revolution, but socialism can be realized only by the proletariat of the world.

And therefore we call to you: "Arise for the struggle! Arise for action! The time for empty manifestoes, platonic resolutions, and high-sounding words has passed! The hour of action has struck for the International!" We ask you to elect workers' and soldiers' councils everywhere that will seize political power and, together with us, will restore peace.

Not David Lloyd George and [Raymond] Poincaré, not [Sidney] Sonnino, [Woodrow] Wilson, and [Matthias] Erzberger or [Philipp] Scheidemann; these must not be allowed to make peace. Peace is to be concluded under the waving banner of the socialist world revolution.

Proletarians of all countries! We call upon you to complete the work of socialist liberation, to give a human aspect to the disfigured world, and to make true those words with which we often greeted each other in the old days and which we sang as we parted: "And the International shall be the human race."

En Avant Dada: A History of Dadaism (1920)

Richard Huelsenbeck

Dada was founded in Zurich in the spring of 1916 by Hugo Ball, Tristan Tzara, Hans Arp, Marcel Janco and Richard Huelsenbeck at the Cabaret Voltaire, a little bar where Hugo Ball and his friend Emmy Hennings had set up a miniature variety show, in which all of us were very active.

We had all left our countries as a result of the war. Ball and I came from Germany, Tzara and Janco from Rumania, Hans Arp from France. We were agreed that the war had been contrived by the various governments for the most autocratic, sordid and materialistic reasons; we Germans were familiar with the book "*J'accuse,*" and even without it we would have had little confidence in the decency of the German Kaiser and his generals. Ball was a conscientious objector, and I had escaped by the skin of my teeth from the pursuit of the police myrmidons who, for their so-called patriotic purposes, were massing men in the trenches of Northern France and giving them shells to eat. None of us had much appreciation for the kind of courage it takes to get shot for the idea of a nation which is at best a cartel of pelt merchants and profiteers in leather, at worst a cultural association of psychopaths who, like the Germans, marched off with a volume of Goethe in their knapsacks, to skewer Frenchmen and Russians on their bayonets.

Arp was an Alsatian; he had lived through the beginning of the war and the whole nationalistic frenzy in Paris, and was pretty well disgusted with all the petty chicanery there, and in general with the sickening changes that had taken place in the city and the people on which we had all squandered our love before the war. Politicians are the same everywhere, flatheaded and vile. Soldiers behave everywhere with the same brisk brutality that is the mortal enemy of every intellectual impulse. The energies and ambitions of those who participated in the Cabaret Voltaire in Zürich were from the start purely artistic. We wanted to make the Cabaret Voltaire a focal point of the "newest art," although we did not neglect from time to time to tell the fat and utterly uncomprehending Zurich philistines that we regarded them as pigs and the German Kaiser as the initiator of the war. Then there was always a big fuss, and the students, who in Switzerland as elsewhere are the stupidest and most reactionary rabble—if in view of the compulsory national stultification in that country any group of citizens can claim a right to the superlative in that respect—at any rate the students gave a preview of the public resistance which Dada was later to encounter on its triumphant march through the world.

The word Dada was accidentally discovered by Hugo Ball and myself in a German-French dictionary, as we were looking for a name for Madame le Roy, the chanteuse at our cabaret. Dada is French for a wooden horse. It is impressive in its brevity and suggestiveness. Soon Dada became the signboard for all the art that we launched in the Cabaret Voltaire. By "newest art," we then meant by and large, abstract art. Later the idea behind the word Dada was to undergo a considerable change. While the Dadaists of the Allied countries, under the leadership of Tristan Tzara, still make no great distinction between Dadaism and "*l'art abstrait,*" in Germany, where the psychological background of our type of activity is entirely different from that in Switzerland, France and Italy, Dada assumed a very definite political character which we shall discuss at length later.

. . . In January 1917 I returned to Germany, the face of which had meanwhile undergone a fantastic change. I felt as though I had left a smug fat idyll for a street full of electric signs, shouting hawkers and auto horns. In Zurich the international profiteers sat in the restaurants with well-filled wallets and rosy cheeks, ate with their knives and smacked their lips in a merry hurrah for the countries that were bashing each other's skulls in. Berlin was the city of tightened stomachers, of mounting, thundering hunger, where hidden rage was transformed into a boundless money lust, and men's minds were concentrating more and more on questions of naked existence. Here we would have to proceed with entirely different methods, if we wanted to say something to the people. Here we would have to discard our patent leather pumps and tie our Byronic cravats to the doorpost. While in Zurich people lived as in a health resort, chasing after the ladies and longing for nightfall that would bring pleasure barges, magic lanterns and music by Verdi, in Berlin you never knew where the next meal was coming from. Fear was in everybody's bones, everybody had a feeling that the big deal launched by Hindenburg & Co. was going to turn out very badly. The people had an exalted and romantic attitude towards art and all cultural values. A phenomenon familiar in German history was again manifested: Germany always becomes the land of poets and thinkers when it begins to be washed up as the land of judges and butchers.

In 1917 the Germans were beginning to give a great deal of thought to their souls. This was only a natural defense on the part of a society that had been harassed, milked dry, and driven to the breaking point. This was the time when expressionism began to enjoy a vogue, since its whole attitude fell in with the retreat and the weariness of the German spirit. It was only natural that the Germans should have lost their enthusiasm for reality, to which before the war they had sung hymns of praise, through the mouths of innumerable academic thickheads, and which had now cost them over a million dead, while the blockade was strangling their children and grandchildren. Germany was seized with the mood that always precedes a so-called idealistic resurrection, an orgy à la Turnvater-Jahn, a Schenkendorf period.[1]

Now came the expressionists, like those famous medical quacks who promise to "fix everything up," looking heavenward like the gentle Muse; they pointed to "the rich treasures of our literature," pulled people gently by the sleeve and led them into the half-light of the Gothic cathedrals, where the street noises die down to a distant murmur and, in accordance with the old principle that all cats are gray at night, men without exception are fine fellows. Man, they have discovered, is good. And so expressionism, which brought the Germans so many welcome truths, became a "national achievement." In art it aimed at inwardness, abstraction, renunciation of all objectivity. When expressionism is mentioned, the first three names I think of are Däubler, Edschmid, and Hiller. Däubler is the gigantosaurus of expressionist lyric poetry. Edschmid the prose writer and prototype of the expressionist man, while Kurt Hiller, with his intentional or unintentional meliorism, is the theoretician of the expressionist age.

On the basis of all these considerations and the psychological insight that a turning-away from objective reality implied the whole complex of weariness and cowardice that is so welcome to putrescent bourgeoisie, we immediately launched a sharp attack on expressionism in Germany, under the watchword of "action," acquired through our fight for the principles of bruitism, simultaneity and the new medium. The first German Dadaist manifesto, written by myself, says among other things: "Art in its execution and direction is dependent on the time in which it lives, and artists are creatures of their epoch. The highest art will be that which in its conscious content presents the thousandfold problems of the day, the art which has been visibly shattered by the explosions of the last week, which is forever trying to collect its limbs after yesterday's crash. The best and most extraordinary artists will be those who every hour snatch the tatters of their bodies out of the frenzied cataract of life, who, with bleeding hands and hearts, hold fast to the intelligence of their time. Has expressionism fulfilled our expectations of such an art, which should be the expression of our most vital concerns? *No! No! No!* Under the pretext of turning inward, the expressionists in literature and painting have banded together into a generation which is already looking forward to honorable mention in the histories of literature and art and aspiring to the most respectable civic distinctions. On pretext of carrying on propaganda for the soul, they have, in their struggle with naturalism, found their way back to the abstract, pathetic gestures which presuppose a comfortable life free from content or strife. The stages are filling up with kings, poets and Faustian characters of all sorts; the theory of a melioristic philosophy, the psychological naïvety of which is highly significant for a critical understanding of expressionism, runs ghostlike through the minds of men who never act. Hatred of the press, hatred of advertising, hatred of sensations, are typical of people who prefer their armchair to the noise of the street, and who even make it a point of pride to be swindled by every small-time profiteer. That sentimental resistance to the times, which are neither better nor worse, neither more reactionary nor more revolutionary than other times, that weak-kneed resistance, flirting with prayers and incense when it does not prefer to load its cardboard cannon with Attic iambics—is the quality of a youth which never knew how to be young. Expressionism, discovered abroad, and in Germany, true to style, transformed into an opulent idyll and the expectation of a good pension, has nothing in common with the efforts of active men. The signers of this manifesto have, under the battle cry Dada!, gathered together to put forward a new art, from which they expect the realization of new ideals." And so on. Here the difference between our conception and that of Tzara is clear. While Tzara was still writing: "*Dada ne signifie rien*"—in Germany Dada lost its art-for-art's-sake character with its very first move. Instead of continuing to produce art, Dada, in direct contrast to abstract art, went out and found an adversary. Emphasis was laid on the movement, on struggle. But we still needed a program of action, we had to say exactly what our Dadaism was after. This program was drawn up by Raoul Hausmann and myself. In it we consciously adopted a political position:

What is Dadaism and What Does it Want in Germany?

1. Dadaism Demands

1) The international revolutionary union of all creative and intellectual men and women on the basis of radical Communism;

2) The introduction of progressive unemployment through comprehensive mechanization of every field of activity. Only by unemployment does it become possible for the individual to achieve certainty as to the truth of life and finally become accustomed to experience;

3) The immediate expropriation of property (socialization) and the communal feeding of all; further, the erection of cities of light, and gardens which will belong to society as a whole and prepare man for a state of freedom.

2. *The Central Council Demands*

a) Daily meals at public expense for all creative and intellectual men and women on the Potsdamer Platz (Berlin);

b) Compulsory adherence of all clergymen and teachers to the Dadaist articles of faith;

c) The most brutal struggle against all directions of so-called "workers of the spirit" (Hiller, Adler), against their concealed bourgeoisism, against expressionism and post-classical education as advocated by the Sturm group;

d) The immediate erection of a state art center, elimination of concepts of property in the new art (expressionism); the concept of property is entirely excluded from the super-individual movement of Dadaism which liberates all man-kind;

e) Introduction of the simultaneist poem as a Communist state prayer;

f) Requisition of churches for the performance of bruitism, simultaneist and Dadaist poems;

g) Establishment of a Dadaist advisory council for the remodelling of life in every city of over 50,000 inhabitants:

h) Immediate organization of a large scale Dadaist propaganda campaign with 150 circuses for the enlightenment of the proletariat;

i) Submission of all laws and decrees to the Dadaist central council for approval;

j) Immediate regulation of all sexual relations according to the views of international Dadaism through establishment of a Dadaist sexual center.

> The Dadaist revolutionary central council.
> German group: Hausmann, Huelsenbeck
> Business Office: Charlottenburg, Kantstrasse 118.
> Applications for membership taken at business office.

Notes

1. "Turnvater"—"gymnastic father," refers to Ludwig Jahn, the founder of the gymnastic societies which played an important part in the liberation of Germany from Napoleon.

November Group Manifesto

Published as "Manifest der Novembristen," *Zehn Jahre Novembergruppe: Zeitschrift für Kunst und Literatur* 3, nos. 1–3 (1928). First published in 1918.

We stand on the fertile ground of the revolution.

Our campaign slogan is:

FREEDOM, EQUALITY, FRATERNITY!

Our joining together is the result of the equivalence of a humane and an artistic way of thinking.

We regard it as our highest duty to devote our best energies to the moral cultivation of a young, free Germany.

We plead for excellence in every respect and dedicate all means at our disposal to the support of this way of thinking.

We demand that this view be lent unqualified expression and that one publicly declare one's position toward it.

We consider it our particular duty to gather together all abilities of value in the artistic sphere and to guide them toward the common good.

We are neither a party nor a class as such, but human beings—human beings who undertake to perform their work tirelessly from the places allotted to them by nature. Like any other kind of work that is to serve the common good, it must take account of general public interest and receive the respect and recognition of the whole.

WORK COUNCIL FOR ART MANIFESTO

First published as "Arbeitsrat für Kunst-Flugblatt" (March 1919).

In the conviction that the political revolution must be used to liberate art from decades of regimentation, a group of artists and art lovers united by a common outlook has been formed in Berlin. It strives for the gathering together of all scattered and divided energies which, over and above the protection of one-sided professional interests, wish to work resolutely together for the rebuilding of our whole artistic life. In close contact with associations with similar objectives in other parts of Germany, the Arbeitsrat für Kunst hopes in the not-too-distant future to be able to push through its aims, which are outlined in the following program.

In the forefront stands the guiding principle:

> Art and people must form a unity.
> Art shall no longer be the enjoyment of the few but the life and happiness of the masses.
> The aim is alliance of the arts under the wing of a great architecture.

On this basis six preliminary demands are made:

1. Recognition of the public character of all building activity, both state and private. Removal of all privileges accorded to civil servants. Unified supervision of whole urban districts, streets, and residential estates without curtailment of freedom over detail. New tasks: people's housing as a means of bringing all the arts to the people. Permanent experimental sites for testing and perfecting new architectural effects.

2. Dissolution of the Academy of Arts, the Academy of Building, and the Prussian Provincial Art Commission in their existing form. Replacement of these bodies, accompanied by a redefining of their territories, by others drawn from the ranks of productive artists themselves and free from state interference. The changing of privileged art exhibitions into exhibitions to which entry is free.

3. Freeing of all training in architecture, sculpture, painting, and handicrafts from state supervision. Transformation of all instruction in the arts and handicrafts from top to bottom. State funds to be made available for this purpose and for the training of master craftsmen in training workshops.

4. Enlivenment of the museums as educational establishments for the people. Mounting of constantly changing exhibitions made to serve the interests of the people by means of lectures and conducted tours. Separation of scientific material in specially-constructed buildings. Establishment of specially-arranged collections for study by workers in the arts and crafts. Just distribution of state funds for the acquisition of old and new works.

5. Destruction of artistically valueless monuments as well as of all buildings whose artistic value is out of proportion to the value of their material which could be put to other uses. Prevention of prematurely planned war memorials and immediate cessation of work on the war museums proposed for Berlin and the Reich.

6. Establishment of a national center to ensure the fostering of the arts within the framework of future lawmaking.

THE ART SCAB

JOHN HEARTFIELD AND GEORGE GROSZ

First published as "Der Kunstlump," *Der Gegner* 1, nos. 10–12 (Berlin; Malik Verlag, 1920), 48–56.

What is the worker supposed to do with the spirit of poets and philosophers, who, in the face of everything that constricts his life breath, feel no duty to take up battle against the exploiters?

Yes, what is the worker supposed to do with art? Have painters given their works the appropriate content for the working people's struggle for liberation, the content that would teach them to free themselves from the yoke of a thousand years of oppression?

No, despite this disgrace they have painted the world in a calming light. The beauty of nature, the forest with the twitter of birds and evening twilight! Do they show that the forest is in the oily hands of the profiteer, who declares it far and wide to be his private property, over which he alone disposes, who chops it down when his wallet requires it, but fences it in, so that freezing people cannot fetch wood.

Yet art remains detached. Look and see! [. . .]

That is why in works of art they preach escape for feelings and thoughts, away from the unbearable conditions of the earth, to the moon and stars, into heaven, vouchsafed by the machine guns of democracy, whose purpose is to send the dispossessed on a journey into the purer Beyond. That is why a weakling like the poet Rainer Maria Rilke, supported by the perfumed do-nothings, writes: "Poverty is a great radiance from within" [*Book of Hours*].

Workers! By presenting to you the ideas of the Christian churches, they wish to disarm you, in order to deliver you more easily to the state machine.

Workers! By representing things in their paintings that the bourgeois can cling to, things that give you a reflection of beauty and happiness, they sabotage your class consciousness, your will to power.

By directing you to art with the cry: "Art to the People," they wish to seduce you into believing in a common possession that you share with your oppressors, for the love of which you should cease the most just struggle the world has ever known. They once again wish to use the "spiritual" to make you submissive and to instill in you the awareness of your own smallness in relation to the wondrous works of the human spirit.

A swindle! A swindle!

The vilest betrayal!

No, art belongs in the museums, to be goggled at on the walking tours of petit-bourgeois tourists; art belongs in the palaces of the blood hounds, in front of the safes. [. . .]

Workers, you, who continually create the surplus value that allows the exploiters to hang their walls with this "aesthetic" luxury, you who thereby guarantee the livelihood of artists, which is nearly always more affluent than your own; workers, now listen how such an artist regards you and your struggle.

After the Kapp Putsch, in which you armed yourselves, to the irritation of the antimilitarists and pacifists [. . .] during these days a little art chap by the name of Oskar Kokoschka, republican Professor at the Dresden Art Academy, displaying the traditional cowardice of the intellectuals, directed the following pithy manifesto to the inhabitants of Dresden:

> *I urgently request all those who intend to use firearms in order to promote their political theories, whether of the radical left, the radical right or the radical center, to be kind enough henceforth to hold their combat exercises away from the Gemäldegalerie [art gallery] of the Zwinger—on the shooting ranges of the heath, for example, where works of human culture will not be in danger. On Monday, the 15th of March, a masterwork of Rubens was damaged by a bullet. [. . .] Certainly the German people will later find more joy and meaning in these preserved pictures than in the collected views of the politicized Germans of today. I do not venture to hope that my alternative proposal will find favor, whereby in the German Republic, as in classical times, feuds should be resolved by single combat between the respective political leaders—in the circus, perhaps—with the effect enhanced by the Homeric scorn of their parties. This would be less harmful and confused than current methods.*
>
> Oskar Kokoschka
> *Professor at the Academy of*
> *Fine Arts in Dresden*

We urgently request all who have not yet become such complete imbeciles as to concur with the snobbish statement of this art scab to oppose it publicly. We exhort everyone to whom it is inconsequential that bullets damage masterworks, since they tear human beings to pieces, to rescue themselves from the fangs of the bloodsuckers. [. . .]

The people would welcome it if, following the examples of Vienna, these pictures would be offered to the allies in exchange for food supplies. That would be doing more for the "poor people of the future" than leaving them the opportunity of standing, their legs crippled by rickets, in front of the unblemished masterpieces in the galleries. [. . .] The struggles of "the collected views of the politicized Germans of today" are the logical outcome of the will to survive and offer future generations conditions of existence other than those which make it possible only for the divinely illumined Kokoschka to eat his fill and wisecrack about the hungry. Sated people naturally need quiet for their digestion. [. . .] He who wishes his business with the brush to be regarded as a divine mission is a scab. Today the - cleaning of a gun by a Red soldier is of greater significance than the entire metaphysical output of all the painters. The concepts of art and artist are an invention of the bourgeoisie and their position in the state can only be on the side of the those who rule, i. e. the bourgeois caste.

The title "artist" is an insult.

The designation "art" is an annulment of human equality.

The deification of the artist is equivalent to self-deification.

The artist does not stand above his milieu and the society of those who approve of him. For his little head does not produce the content of his creation, but processes (as a sausage-maker does meat) the worldview of his public.

[. . .]

Kokoschka's statements are a typical expression of the attitude of the bourgeoisie. The bourgeoisie places a culture and its art higher than the life of the working class. This, too, leads to the conclusion that there can be no reconciliation between the bourgeoisie, its approach to life, and the proletariat.

Workers, we see the attempts of the Independents [the Independent Socialists or USPD] to preserve this culture and its mendacious views on art for the proletarian reconstruction of the world. We expect very shortly from Herr Comrade Felix Stössinger [editor of the USPD weekly newspaper *Freie Welt*], that he will soon illustrate for you works by the important painter Oskar Kokoschka and demonstrate to you their significance for the proletariat, just as he introduced to you the churchly rubbish of the Isenheim Altar [the work of Matthias Grünewald] or the individualistic artistic torments of a Van Gogh. Egocentric individualism went hand-in-hand with the development of capital and must fall with it.

With joy we welcome the news that the bullets are whistling through the galleries and palaces, into the masterpieces of Rubens, instead of into the houses of the poor in the working-class neighborhoods!

We welcome it if the open struggle between capital and labor takes place in the domain of this disgraceful culture and art, which consistently served to suppress the poor while edifying the bourgeois on Sunday, so that on Monday he could all the more calmly resume . . . his exploitation! [. . .]

We summon all to oppose the masochistic reverence for historical values, to oppose culture and art! [. . .]

We know, workers, that you will create your workers' culture entirely alone just as you have created your own organization for the class struggle.

Program of the Staatliches Bauhaus in Weimar

Walter Gropius

First published as "Programm des Staatlichen Bauhauses" (April 1919).

The ultimate aim of all visual arts is the complete building! To embellish buildings was once the noblest function of the fine arts; they were the indispensable components of great architecture. Today the arts exist in isolation, from which they can be rescued only through the conscious, cooperative effort of all craftsmen. Architects, painters, and sculptors must recognize anew and learn to grasp the composite character of a building both as an entity and in its separate parts. Only then will their work be imbued with the architectonic spirit that it has lost as "salon art."

The old schools of art were unable to produce this unity; how could they, since art cannot be taught. They must be merged once more with the workshop. The mere drawing and painting world of the pattern designer and the applied artist must become a world that builds again. When young people who take a joy in artistic creation once more begin their life's work by learning a trade, then the unproductive 'artist' will no longer be condemned to deficient artistry, for their skill will now be preserved for the crafts, in which they will be able to achieve excellence.

Architects, sculptors, painters, we all must return to the crafts! For art is not a "profession." There is no essential difference between the artist and the craftsman. The artist is an exalted craftsman. In rare moments of inspiration, transcending the consciousness of his will, the grace of heaven may cause his work to blossom into art. But proficiency in a craft is essential to every artist. Therein lies the prime source of creative imagination. Let us then create a new guild of craftsmen without the class distinctions that raise an arrogant barrier between craftsman and artist! Together let us desire, conceive, and create the new structure of the future, which will embrace architecture and sculpture and painting in one unity and which will one day rise toward heaven from the hands of a million workers like the crystal symbol of a new faith.

Walter Gropius

Program of the Staatliches Bauhaus in Weimar

The Staatliches Bauhaus resulted from the merger of the former Grand-Ducal Saxon Academy of Art with the former Grand-Ducal Saxon School of Arts and Crafts in conjunction with a newly affiliated department of architecture.

Aims of the Bauhaus

The Bauhaus strives to bring together all creative effort into one whole, to reunify all the disciplines of practical art—sculpture, painting, handicrafts, and the crafts—as inseparable components of a new architecture. The ultimate, if distant, aim of the Bauhaus is the unified work of art—the great structure—in which there is no distinction between monumental and decorative art.

The Bauhaus wants to educate architects, painters, and sculptors of all levels, according to their capabilities, to become competent craftsmen or independent creative artists and to form a working community of leading and future artist-craftsmen. These men, of kindred spirit, will know how to design buildings harmoniously in their entirety—structure, finishing, ornamentation, and furnishing.

Principles of the Bauhaus

Art rises above all methods; in itself it cannot be taught, but the crafts certainly can be. Architects, painters, and sculptors are craftsmen in the true sense of the word: hence a thorough training in the crafts, acquired in workshops and on experimental and practical sites, is required of all students as the indispensable basis for all artistic production. Our own workshops are to be gradually built up, and apprenticeship agreements with outside workshops will be concluded.

The school is the servant of the workshop and will one day be absorbed into it. Therefore there will be no teachers or pupils in the Bauhaus but masters, journeymen, and apprentices.

The manner of teaching arises from the character of the workshop:

Organic forms developed from manual skills.

Avoidance of all rigidity; priority of creativity; freedom of individuality, but strict study discipline.

Master and journeyman examinations, according to the Guild Statutes, held before the Council of Masters of the Bauhaus or before outside masters.

Collaboration by the students in the work of the masters.

Securing of commissions, also for students.

Mutual planning of extensive, utopian structural designs—public buildings and buildings for worship—aimed at the future. Collaboration of all masters and students—architects, painters, sculptors—on these designs with the object of gradually achieving a harmony of all the component elements and parts that make up architecture.

Constant contact with the leaders of the crafts and industries of the country.

Contact with public life, with the people, through exhibitions and other activities.

New research into the nature of the exhibitions, to solve the problem of displaying visual work and sculpture within the framework of architecture.

Encouragement of friendly relations between masters and students outside of work; therefore plays, lectures, poetry, music, fancy-dress parties. Establishment of a cheerful ceremonial at these gatherings.

RANGE OF INSTRUCTION

Instruction at the Bauhaus includes all practical and scientific areas of creative work.

1. Architecture,
2. Painting,
3. Sculpture, including all branches of the crafts.

Students are trained in a craft (1) as well as in drawing and painting (2) and science and theory (3).

1. Craft training—either in our own, gradually enlarging workshops or in outside workshops to which the student is bound by apprenticeship agreement—includes:
   a) sculptors, stonemasons, stucco workers, woodcarvers, ceramic workers, plaster casters;
   b) blacksmiths, locksmiths, founders, metal turners;
   c) cabinetmakers;
   d) scene painters, glass painters, mosaic workers, enamelers;
   e) etchers, wood engravers, lithographers, art printers, enchasers;
   f) weavers.
   Craft training forms the basis of all teaching at the Bauhaus. Every student must learn a craft.

2. Training in drawing and painting includes:
   a) free-hand sketching from memory and imagination;
   b) drawing and painting of heads, live models, and animals;
   c) drawing and painting of landscapes, figures, plants, and still lifes;
   d) composition;
   e) execution of murals, panel pictures, and religious shrines;
   f) design of ornaments;
   g) lettering;
   h) construction and projection drawing;
   i) design of exteriors, gardens, and interiors
   j) design of furniture and practical articles.

3. Training in science and theory includes:
   a) art history—not presented in the sense of a history of styles, but rather to further active understanding of historical working methods and techniques;

b) science of materials;

c) anatomy—from the living model;

d) physical and chemical theory of color;

e) rational painting methods;

f) basic concepts of bookkeeping, contract negotiations, personnel;

g) individual lectures on subjects of general interest in all areas of art and science.

DIVISIONS OF INSTRUCTION

The training is divided into three courses of instruction:

1. course for apprentices;
2. course for journeymen;
3. course for junior masters.

The instruction of the individual is left to the discretion of each master within the framework of the general program and the work schedule, which is revised every semester. In order to give the students as versatile and comprehensive a technical and artistic training as possible the work schedule will be so arranged that every architect-, painter-, and sculptor-to-be is able to participate in part of the other courses.

ADMISSION

Any person of good repute, without regard to age or sex, whose previous education is deemed adequate by the Council of Masters will be admitted, as far as space permits. The tuition fee is 180 marks per year (it will gradually disappear entirely with increasing earnings of the Bauhaus). A non-recurring admission fee of 20 marks is also to be paid. Foreign students pay double fees. Address enquiries to the secretariat of the Staatliches Bauhaus in Weimar.

April 1919
The Administration of the
Staatliches Bauhaus in Weimar
Walter Gropius

Art Is a Weapon!

Friedrich Wolf

First published as "Kunst ist Waffe!" in *Broschüre des Arbeiter-Theater-Bundes Deutschland* (Berlin, 1928), 105–108.

The writer as the conscience of the age!

The writer as prophet! Ever since Cassandra's political prediction of the fall of Troy, the writer's "voice of Cassandra" has usually been made light of and derided. "Writer," comes the response, "stick to your pen!"

Over and over, whenever the ashes of a historical turning point have glowed, whenever politics have become a manifest part of life, writers have joined in and put their shoulders to the wheel. In the states of North America it was a woman writer whose work securely guided the people through a sharp turn, who called forth a great political act with a literary work: Harriet Beecher Stowe! With her world-stirring *Uncle Tom's Cabin*! It was she who summoned public opinion in the northern states to oppose the slaveholding despotism of the South, who issued the first demand for the equality of the Negroes. It came to a battle and to the victory of the northern states, from which the United States emerged. [. . .]

Nor today can genuine dramatists continue to work in airless rooms or in the museum of the past; for them too "the scene becomes a tribunal!" [. . .] The stage becomes the court and conscience of the age! [. . .]

Or, as a well-known theatrical director recently put it in his playbill:

> *A lack of imagination leaves most people unable to experience even their own lives, not to mention their world. If it were otherwise, reading just a single page in the newspaper would cause humanity to rise up in revolt! So stronger tools are needed. One of them is [. . .] theater!*

The newspaper? As the material for a drama? The art dignitaries turn up their noses.

They do not know, or do not want to know what official statistics tell us: that of 510,219 schoolchildren under fourteen years of age in the state of Saxony, 93,936, or nearly 20 percent, are already working; that certain packaging factories enforce working hours for school children of "as long as eleven hours"; that in the Annaberg inspectoral district "children from eight years(!) on were found in the plants." They do not know that every year there are 20,000 certified cases in Germany in which mothers die in the dingy rooms of abortionists as the insane result of Paragraph 218; that none other than the Forty-fifth Conference of German Doctors, meeting in Eisenach in 1925, estimated the annual number of illegal abortions in Germany to be 800,000! How dire must be these women's need! They do not know that, according to the 1922 report of the municipal welfare office in Berlin, 34 percent of those suffering from tuberculosis have no bed of their own—that is, every third coughing tuberculosis patient has to sleep in the same bed with a healthy person for reasons of need! Please do not turn away in disgust and flee to [Goethe's play] *Iphigenia* or to the sublimity of a Gothic cathedral! The average number of inhabitants of a building in London is eight persons; in Paris it is thirty-eight, in Berlin, seventy-six! [. . .]

In all "eternity" there is only one tangible moment: that is the present! The writer who does not see the tragic conflicts of today on our streets, who is not seized by them and overpowered—he has no blood in his veins! He sees the world from his writer's studio or through the dusty windows of the church; but he does not forge ahead into hard, wild, crusty, unadorned life, of which art *today* is a part!

The writer of our present day, who brings to the stage the misery, the struggles, the faith, and defeat of the people on the street, in back houses, factories, and mines—he cannot pull in his claws and offer up sweet promises of the beyond; his thoughts will necessarily take the offensive, his words will be weapons! He will not flee into the past and speak of Charlemagne or the apostle Paul; he will present us with the tragedy of an unemployed worker, the desperate act of a sick, weakened mother carrying her seventh child, the oppression by the Western powers of the awakening colonial peoples, the new arms race in the struggle for oil; or the utter farce of the Lukutate swindle, the grotesque comedy of industrial espionage, the film projects of a high naval office. "Motifs" in masses!

Certainly, it falls far short of workers' theater to deliver steadfast cries of "Long live the world revolution!" to have the actors sing the "Internationale," and to have Lenin make repeated personal appearances on the stage. That is at most "the same old stuff" that very quickly bores workers in particular. A workers' play, precisely a workers' play must also be crafted! It must, in a word, be *good*! No well-intentioned, sensational shocker, but as vital and well-crafted a work as [Sergei] Eisenstein's *Potemkin*. Such a work bowls even its enemies over, opens a path to the future as wide as a house! [. . .]

But *art* is neither a means for edification in the hands of pedagogues, headmasters, and bearded scholars imposed upon manual workers "starving for education," nor is it a luxury, caviar or opium that makes us forget the ugly details of "dismal daily life."

Art *today* is a floodlight and a weapon! Just as much a weapon as it was two thousand years ago at the time of Aristophanes's comedies, as much a weapon and an instrument of power as five hundred years ago when the Renaissance popes intimidated the people with paintings of Christ's descent into hell by Raphael and Michelangelo, and built St. Peter's to advertise their earthly power! [. . .]

You writers, you who feel the simple, unmythical misery of our time, give us short works that understand a locksmith, an errand girl, a streetcar conductor, or a washer-woman! Art is always only for the few? Humbug! The greatness of Greek, African, Indian art, the greatness of the words of Christ lies in their being understood by every man.

You workers, come in to the Workers' Theater League, to the Proletarian Fighting Troupe, to the Workers' Megaphone, and, above all, to the People's Film Association! *Film* in particular proves how clearly art is a weapon today! It was certainly not because of its artistic value or its beauty that the industrial magnate [Alfred] Hugenberg bought UFA, the largest of all German film companies. It was suffering severe losses at that time. But Hugenberg saw the potential profits! He recognized the tremendous power represented today by film, since millions go to UFA theaters every day. Film as the invisible weapon in the class struggle, as the tasteless and odorless gas that befogs and stupefies the people with kitsch, with smarmy Rheingold films, pale Nibelungs, and Fausts! [. . .]

What a genuine workers' theater, a film production company of the workers' own, could mean for the dissemination, development, and the fighting power of the socialist idea is unimaginable!

A flag, a sword, a power, a weapon!

PHOTOMONTAGE

RAOUL HAUSMANN

First published as "Fotomontage," *a bis z* (May 1931), 61–62.

In the battle of opinions it is often claimed that photomontage is practicable in only two forms, political propaganda and commercial advertising. The first photomonteurs, the dadaists, began from a point of view incontestable for them: that the painting of the war period, post-futurist expressionism, had failed because it was nonrepresentational and it lacked convictions; and that not only painting but all the arts and their techniques required a revolutionary transformation in order to remain relevant to the life of their times. The members of the Club Dada, who all held more or less left-wing political views, were naturally not interested in setting up new aesthetic rules for making art. On the contrary, they at first had almost no interest in art, but were all the more concerned with materially giving new forms of expression to new contents. Dada, which was a kind of cultural criticism, stopped at nothing. It is a fact that many of the early photomontages attacked the political events of the day with biting sarcasm. But just as revolutionary as the content of photomontage was its form—photography and printed texts combined and transformed into a kind of static film. The dadaists, who had "invented" the static, the simultaneous, and the purely phonetic poem, applied these same principles to pictorial expression. They were the first to use the material of photography to combine heterogeneous, often contradictory structures, figurative and spatial, into a new whole that was in effect a mirror image wrenched from the choas of war and revolution, as new to the eye as it was to the mind. And they knew that great propagandistic power inhered in their method, and that contemporary life was not courageous enough to develop and absorb it.

Things have changed a great deal since then. The current exhibition at the Art Library shows the importance of photomontage as a means of propaganda in Russia. And every movie program—be it *The Melody of the World,* Chaplin, Buster Keaton, *Mother Krausen's Journey to Happiness,* or *Africa Speaks*—proves that the business world has largely recognized the value of this propagandistic effect. The advertisements for these films are unimaginable without photomontage, as though it were an unwritten law.

Today, however, some people argue that in our period of New Objectivity, photomontage is already outdated and unlikely to develop further. One could reply that photography is even older, and that nevertheless there are always new men who, through their photographic lenses, find new visual approaches to the world surrounding us. The number of modern photographers is large and growing daily, and no one would think of calling Renger-Patzsch's objective photography outdated because of Sander's exact photography, or of pronouncing the styles of Lerski or Bernatzik more modern or less modern.

The realm of photography, silent film, and photomontage lends itself to as many possibilities as there are changes in the environment, its social structure, and resultant psychological superstructures; and the environment is changing every day. Photomontage has not reached the end of its development any more than silent film has. The formal means of both media need to be disciplined, and their respective realms of expression need sifting and reviewing.

If photomontage in its primitive form was an explosion of viewpoints and a whirling confusion of picture planes more radical in its complexity than futuristic painting, it has since then undergone an evolution one could call constructive. There has been a general recognition of the great versatility of the optical element in pictorial expression. Photomontage in particular, with its opposing structures and dimensions (such as rough versus smooth, aerial view versus close-up, perspective versus flat plane), allows the greatest technical diversity or the clearest working out of the dialectical problems of form. Over time the technique of photomontage has undergone considerable simplification, forced upon it by the opportunities for application that spontaneously presented themselves. As I mentioned previously, these applications are primarily those of political or commercial propaganda. The necessity for clarity in political and commercial slogans will influence photomontage to abandon more and more its initial individualistic playfulness. The ability to weigh and balance the most violent oppositions—in short, the dialectical dynamics of form that are inherent in photomontage—will assure it a long survival and ample opportunities for development.

In the photomontage of the future the exactness of the material, the clear particularity of objects, and the precision of plastic concepts will play the greatest role, despite or because of their mutual juxtaposition. A new form worth mentioning is statistical photomontage— apparently no one has thought of it yet. One might say that like photography and the silent film, photomontage can contribute a great deal to the education of our vision, to our knowledge of optical, psychological, and social structures; it can do so thanks to the clarity of its means, in which content and form, meaning and design, become one.

Photomontage as a Weapon in Class Struggle

Alfred Keményi

First published under the name Durus as "Fotomontage als Waffe im Klassenkampf," *Der Arbeiter-Fotograf* 6, no. 3 (1932), 55–57.

The bourgeois conception of photomontage can be summarized in the following remark made by a well-known bourgeois art critic: "Montage means that the artist and the craftsman are replaced by the engineer. Pieces of photographs are pasted together the way parts of machines are joined together with screws." Is this the actual state of affairs? Has the engineer actually taken the place of the artist? Are pieces of photographs installed like parts of machines? Not at all. The photo "monteur" is an artist—not an engineer. And the photo "montage" is a work of art—not just a machine. A work of art that offers completely new opportunities—with regard to content, not just form—for uncovering relationships, oppositions, transitions, and inter-sections of social reality. Only when the photomonteur makes use of these opportunities does his photomontage become a truly revolutionary weapon in the class struggle.

We must emphasize: In a class society there can be no "classless-revolutionary" photomontage. Like all art forms before the classless society, photomontage is determined by social class. The nonrepresentational stance of formalist photomontage—playing with light effects, superimpositions, overexposures, strange angles "without content"—merely veils the bourgeois contents, the dead-end perspective of rootless bourgeois artists. In this as in any other field, the revolutionary working class does not separate theory from practice—it sets a high value on photomontage as an extraordinarily effective propagandistic and organizational weapon in the class struggle.

It is becoming increasingly obvious that the cognitive value of photomontage is inseparable from its role in the class struggle. Could the development of photomontage take place outside the context of class struggle? Certainly not. Why did formalist photomontage grind to a halt after a few superficially interesting experiments? Because it operated in a vacuum, divorced from the decisive social conflicts of our era; because it could not carry out its essential purpose: to reveal the truth. Why did proletarian-revolutionary photomontage attain such a high level in the Soviet Union and Germany? Because not only did it not oppose the revolutionary development of humanity, but it developed in close conjunction with the revolutionary workers' movement.

And we can see that while in response to the intensified economic crisis the bourgeois advertising industry is dispensing with more and more of its most artistically and technically expert photomonteurs, our publishing houses and our magazines require an ever-greater number of qualified photomonteurs. One need only look at the display windows of our bookstores:

invariably one's eye is caught by interesting, original, and thought-provoking photomontages on the covers of books and brochures.

The very first dadaist works using paste and photographs (by Heartfield, George Grosz, Hausmann, and [Johannes] Baader) set the course for the development of a consciously political proletarian photomontage—despite the anarchist-individualist philosophy of their creators. But the rising line of German proletarian-revolutionary photomontage is most intimately associated with the epoeh-making work of the brilliant monteur John Heartfield.

His works can already be considered classic. He pioneered the use of photomontage for book jackets and in the design of political picture books. He always focused the aesthetically effective elements of photography's "gray-scale structures," of planar division, of combinations of script and photography, on maximizing the political content. All traces of "beautiful, self-contained form" have been ruthlessly swept away. In place of a bourgeois aesthetic we have the sharpest, strongest, most penetrating political militancy of a no longer neutral art. Faced with the powers of inertia and habitual rigidity, Heartfield never took the path of least resistance. After years of stubborn and consistent work, he won the adoption of the line that he considered the most appropriate for the proletarian liberation struggle.

As a creator of satirical photomontages, he is unsurpassed. His satirical contributions to *AIZ*—the "Tiger," the "Cabbage Head," "Solar Eclipse on the 'Liberated' Rhine," "Six Million Nazi Voters: Fodder for a Big Mouth," to mention just a few—are among the most significant satirical creations of our time.

Today the ranks of revolutionary photomonteurs are increasing considerably in Germany. The best photomontages by the members of the League of Revolutionary Artists, who use this art form as a weapon in the daily practice of class struggle, are by no means simple imitations of Heartfield. [. . .] Naturally, as with many other problems awaiting our solution, proletarian photomontage experiences occasional setbacks. Sometimes the work being turned out is politically shallow and the products are frequently slipshod, particularly the designs for magazine covers.

THE THIRD REICH, 1933–45

ENCYCLOPAEDIA BRITANNICA ONLINE

THE NAZI REVOLUTION

When Hitler finally became chancellor, on January 30, 1933, it was not on the crest of a wave of popular support but as the result of backroom political intrigue by Schleicher, Papen, and the president's son, Oskar von Hindenburg. Only Hitler, they believed, could bring together a coalition with Hugenberg's DNVP and possibly the Centre Party that could command a majority in the Reichstag. They assured the reluctant president that Hitler's radical tendencies would be checked by the fact that Papen would hold the vice-chancellorship and that other conservatives would control the crucial ministries, such as those of war, foreign affairs, and economics. The Nazis themselves were restricted to holding the chancellorship and the insignificant federal ministry of the interior. As a sop to the Nazis, Hermann Göring was granted ministerial status but given no portfolio; yet, significantly, he became interior minister in the state of Prussia, which gave him control over the largest police force in Germany.

The Nazis professed an ideology, national socialism, that purported to champion the common man, whom they portrayed as a victim in a world controlled by Jews. Anti-Semitism and notions of German racial superiority were at the core of this ideology, which, in its particulars, was also a catalog of resentments that had accumulated in German society since November 1918. Heading the list were the humiliations associated with Versailles, but not far behind were resentments of big business, big banks, big department stores, and big labour, as well as resentments of the divisiveness and inefficiencies that political parties seemed to foster.

Neither the 25-point party program of 1920 nor Hitler's autobiographical political manifesto, *Mein Kampf* ("My Struggle," 1925), contained clear conceptions of the shape that German politics and society would take under the Nazis, but Hitler and his propagandists had communicated clearly that the changes would be fundamental and come at the expense of Germany's racial enemies. Racially superior Germans were to be gathered into a tightly knit *Volksgemeinschaft,* or racial community, in which divisions of party and class would be transcended in a spirit of racial harmony, a harmony that would necessarily exclude people of inferior blood. This goal logically required a solution to what the Nazis called "the Jewish problem." At the very least it called for a reversal of the trend, more than a century old, of Jewish assimilation into the allegedly superior German nation and into German cultural and economic life. As for Germany's position in international affairs, Hitler had long spoken of Germany's need for additional living space (*Lebensraum*) in the east. First, however, there was the continued need to break the chains of the hated Treaty of Versailles.

Whether the Nazis would ever get a chance to implement their ideological objectives depended, when Hitler became chancellor, upon whether they would be able to tighten their initially tenuous hold on the reins of power. Liberals, socialists, and communists remained bitterly opposed to Hitler; important segments of business, the army, and the churches were to varying degrees suspicious of the measures he might take. It was a combination, finally, of Hitler's daring and brutality, of the weaknesses of his opponents, and of numerous instances of extraordinary good luck that allowed him to establish his totalitarian dictatorship. When the Centre Party refused to join the Nazi-DNVP coalition in January 1933, Hitler demanded elections for a new Reichstag. The elections of March 5, 1933, were preceded by a brutal and violent campaign in which Nazi storm troopers under the command of Ernst Röhm figured prominently. Hitler was also able to take advantage of the Reichstag fire (probably the work of a lone and deranged Dutch communist) of February 27 to suspend civil liberties and arrest communist as well as other opposition leaders. Despite this campaign of terror, the Nazis did not win a majority, gaining only 43.9 percent of the total. The 8 percent acquired by the DNVP, however, was sufficient for the two parties to wield a majority in the Reichstag. At its first meeting on March 23 the new Reichstag—under great pressure from the SA and the SS (Schutzstaffel; "Protective Echelon"), the elite corps of Nazis headed by Heinrich Himmler—voted in favour of the Enabling Act that allowed Hitler to ignore the constitution and to give his decrees the power of law. In this fashion, the Nazis established the regime they called the Third Reich, the presumed successor of the Holy Roman Empire (the First Reich) and of the German Empire ruled by the Hohenzollerns from 1871 to 1918 (the Second Reich).

The decree powers were the pseudolegal base from which Hitler carried out the first steps of the Nazi revolution. Within two weeks of the passing of the Enabling Act, Nazi governors were sent out to bring the federal states into line, and a few months later the states themselves were abolished. On April 7, 1933, Nazis began to purge the civil service, along with the universities, of communists, socialists, democrats, and Jews. On May 2 the trade unions were disbanded and replaced by what the Nazis called a Labour Front. In the meantime Göring had begun refashioning the political arm of the Prussian police into a secret political police, the Gestapo (Geheime Staatspolizei), to serve the Nazi cause, a process that was being duplicated by Himmler with the Bavarian police.

The brutality with which Hitler met any presumed challenge to his authority became dramatically evident when on June 30, 1934, he ordered the murders of the SA leadership. Röhm's storm-trooper street thugs had provided useful muscle during the party's long years of struggle, but their continuing penchant for unruliness, Hitler feared, could invite the army's intervention and therewith his own overthrow. To head off this possibility, Hitler engaged the loyal Himmler, who used his SS during the so-called "Night of the Long Knives" to purge the SA of dozens of its top leaders, including Hitler's longtime friend Röhm. The penultimate step in Hitler's seizure of power came on August 2, 1934, when, upon the death of President Hindenburg, he appropriated the powers of the presidency and combined them with his own as chancellor. The final step came in February 1938 when Hitler took personal command of the three branches of the German armed forces.

The Totalitarian State

The main purpose and goal of the Nazi revolution was to establish a *Volksgemeinschaft*. Its creation required the purification and increase of the German "race" as well as its biological separation from the Jews, whose infusion of evil into the German bloodstream, the Nazis said, served to pollute and undermine Germany's well-being. Nazi efforts to purify the German race gained an air of scientific respectability from the pseudoscience of eugenics, the racial hygiene movement that flourished widely in the early decades of the 20th century. Nazi leaders spoke of their efforts to "reconstruct the German race." The Law for the Protection of Hereditary Health (July 14, 1933) allowed for the eventual sterilization of as many as two million people deemed unworthy of propagating. The Marriage Subsidy Law of July 1933 aimed to stimulate the birth rate by granting loans to newly married couples; these loans would be forgiven incrementally with the birth of each additional child. The Nazi idealization of mothers and the celebration of motherhood as a special service to the Reich had the same objective. Hitler spoke of an eventual doubling of the German population through these measures. The most notorious of the steps taken to purify the German race was also a milestone in the anti-Jewish legislation promulgated by the Nazis: the infamous Nürnberg Laws of September 1935, which forbade marriage or sexual relations between Jews and Germans and assigned to Jews a lower class of citizenship.

Nazi efforts to solve the "Jewish problem" were in fact products of a vicious anti-Semitism that propelled the Nazi regime toward increasingly extreme measures of persecution. SA terrorism, legislation expelling Jews from the civil service and universities, boycotts of Jewish businesses and professionals, and the eventual expropriation of Jewish-owned properties had by 1938 led to the emigration of roughly half of the 1933 Jewish population of 500,000 people. Until the massive campaign of violence against Jews and Jewish property known as Kristallnacht ("Night of Broken Glass"), during the night of November 9–10, 1938, it still seemed possible for some Jews to remain in Germany, albeit in severely circumscribed circumstances. With Kristallnacht the Nazis ushered in a new level of persecution. In its aftermath Hitler put Göring in charge of Jewish policy. Göring coordinated the numerous party and governmental agencies competing for control of—and profit from—the persecutions of the Jews.

For the Nazis, to exclude Jews from the *Volksgemeinschaft* was as important as attracting the German working classes to it, in order to undo the long-standing alienation of the largely socialist-minded German worker from the nationalist consensus. Any success in this effort depended heavily upon the Nazis' ability to provide employment for the millions of jobless whom they inherited in 1933. Public spending on rearmament and on public works projects such as the superhighway, or autobahn, network helped create many of the jobs so desperately needed. By 1937 Germany was beginning to suffer from a labour shortage. It was equally important to inculcate workers with a sense of being an integral part of a racially based national community. For this the Nazis devised an elaborate program of subsidies for leisure-time activities for workers. Called "Strength through Joy," the program subsidized workers' vacations; it made possible excursions to mountain or seaside resorts and offered the possibility of cruises in the Mediterranean or the Baltic Sea. By providing leisure activities for workers until then reserved for their economic and social superiors, the government attempted to integrate them into the *Volksgemeinschaft*. A new, inexpensive automobile, the Volkswagen, was designed to give workers the opportunity to own a car, which had until then in Germany been a symbol of wealth and status largely reserved for the upper classes. Hitler once said that Henry Ford had done more than anyone else to obliterate class differences in America.

FOREIGN POLICY

Hitler kept tight control over foreign affairs, formulating himself both the strategy and the tactics calculated to achieve his goals. The immediate objective was to reestablish Germany's position in world affairs; by this Hitler meant ending the humiliations attending the Treaty of Versailles, such as the demilitarized Rhineland and the limitations on German armaments. The chains of that treaty needed to fall with a loud clang, he said. The larger objective, the one he had spoken about since his entry into politics in the early 1920s, was the conquest for Germany of *Lebensraum*. Hitler believed that this space needed to be acquired in the east, at the expense of the Soviets, so as to secure for Germany the Ukrainian "breadbasket" and open up vast territories for German colonization. Hitler found justification for such conquests in his notions of German racial superiority over the Slavic peoples who inhabited the lands he coveted. Furthermore, he saw the Bolsheviks who now controlled the Soviet Union as the vanguard of the world Jewish conspiracy. Control of this territory was to become the foundation for Germany's economic and military domination of Europe and eventually, perhaps, of the world.

No such domination or expansion was possible without war, of course, and Hitler did not shrink from its implications. His rearming of Germany, begun in secret in 1933, was made public in March 1935 when he announced the creation of an air force and the reintroduction of general military conscription to provide the manpower for 36 new divisions in the army. In June of that same year he signed an agreement with the British that allowed a German naval buildup of up to 35 percent of Britain's surface naval strength and up to 45 percent of its tonnage in submarines. On March 7, 1936, he moved German forces into the demilitarized Rhineland. Versailles was dead. Neither the British nor the French had lifted a finger in its defense, choosing instead to sign agreements expressly negating the terms of Versailles. By 1936 Hitler was spending 10.2 billion marks on rearmament, and Göring was placed in charge of a so-called Four-Year Plan to prepare the German economy for war. On November 5, 1937, Hitler gathered his general staff and admonished them to be prepared for war in the east no later than 1942 or 1943.

As a cover for his true intentions during the first years of power, Hitler spoke long and often of his desire for peace. All he wanted, he said, was a Germany allowed its rightful place in world affairs. As evidence of his pacific intentions, he signed in January 1934 a 10-year nonaggression pact with Poland. A truer picture of his intentions became evident in July 1934, however, when Hitler encouraged the Nazi Party in Austria to attempt an overthrow of the

THINKING, MAKING, DOING

government of Chancellor Engelbert Dollfuss. A Nazi squad shot and killed Dollfuss, but the coup attempt was badly managed. Benito Mussolini's movement of Italian troops to the Austrian border forced Hitler to back away from supporting his Austrian partners.

Propaganda Minister Joseph Goebbels's anti-Bolshevik rhetoric helped Hitler to delude France and Britain, as well as the United States—which was leery of being drawn into another European quarrel—into accepting his claim to be the West's last bulwark against Bolshevik expansion. His agreement with the Japanese in 1936, the Anti-Comintern Pact, was directed against the Third Communist International. A year later Mussolini, after a year of German-Italian cooperation in aiding General Francisco Franco's rebel forces in the Spanish Civil War, added his signature to the pact.

Hitler made two dramatic foreign policy moves in 1938 that helped clarify for the world the extent of his less-than-pacific intentions. In March he annexed Austria to the Reich, justifying the Anschluss ("Annexation") as a fulfillment of the principle of German national self-determination. Britain and France stood by quietly at this additional repudiation of the Versailles treaty. Next Hitler engineered a diplomatic crisis with Czechoslovakia, claiming Czech mistreatment of its German minority in the Sudetenland. Against considerable opposition from his own military, Hitler was determined to go to war with the Czechs. Only through the intervention of Britain's Prime Minister Neville Chamberlain, who offered to come to Germany to appease Hitler and who managed to persuade the Czechs to yield to all of Hitler's demands, was war avoided. Chamberlain's intervention resulted in the Munich agreement in late September 1938, in which the Italians, the French, and the British ceremoniously handed the Sudetenland over to Hitler. Since that time the very word Munich has come to symbolize caving in to the demands of a dictator.

Certain that Britain and France would do nothing to stop him, Hitler decided to move up his timetable for conquests in the east. On March 15, 1939, Hitler seized what remained of Czechoslovakia, reshaping its pieces into a Bohemian and Moravian protectorate and a nominally independent state of Slovakia. Within a week he annexed from Lithuania the city of Memel and the surrounding countryside, territory lost to Germany in the Memel dispute as a consequence of Versailles. When Britain and France countered these moves by guaranteeing armed assistance to Poland—clearly next on Hitler's agenda—in the event of German aggression, a furious Hitler ordered his military to prepare an invasion of that country. Poland was critical to Hitler's long-range strategy for the conquest of *Lebensraum* in the east; any invasion of the Soviet Union required that Polish territory be available as a staging area. Until the British-French guarantee, he had hoped to enlist Poland, mostly through bombast and threat, as an ally in an attack on the Soviet Union, and he believed Poland could be dealt with summarily after the defeat of the Soviet Union. When Poland refused to play the role he had assigned it, Hitler began looking for allies in his resolution of the Polish problem. In late May 1939 he signed his "Pact of Steel" with Mussolini. Then came the most sensational diplomatic rapprochement of the 20th century. Shortly after signing the pact with Italy, Hitler put out feelers to Soviet leader Joseph Stalin about the possibility of dividing eastern Europe, Poland included, into German and Soviet spheres of influence. These negotiations led to the notorious

German-Soviet Nonaggression Pact of August 24, 1939, a pact that secretly sealed Poland's doom and delayed Hitler's unbending determination to conquer *Lebensraum* from the Soviets for almost two years. On September 1, 1939, Hitler launched his invasion of Poland. Two days later Britain and France declared war on Germany.

WORLD WAR II

World War II is appropriately called "Hitler's war." Germany was so extraordinarily successful in the first two years that Hitler came close to realizing his aim of establishing hegemony in Europe. But his triumphs were not part of a strategic conception that secured victory in the long run. Nonetheless, the early successes were spectacular. After the defeat of Poland within a month, Hitler turned his attention westward. He believed that it was necessary to defeat Britain and France before he could again turn eastward to the territories that were to become the "living space" for his new empire. The attack on the Western Front began in the spring of 1940. Hitler took Denmark and Norway during the course of a few days in April, and on May 10 he attacked France, along with Luxembourg, Belgium, and The Netherlands. Once again his armies achieved lightning victories; Luxembourg, Belgium, and The Netherlands were overrun in a few days, and France capitulated on June 21. Only the British, now alone, obstructed Hitler's path to total victory in the west.

Hitler determined that he could take Britain out of the war with air power. German bombers began their attack in August 1940, but the British proved intractable. The vaunted German air force (Luftwaffe) failed to bring Britain to its knees partly because of the strength of the British air force, partly because the German air force was ill-equipped for the task, and partly because the British were able to read German code (*see* Ultra). Yet Hitler had been so confident of a quick victory that, even before the attack began, he had ordered his military planners to draw up plans for an invasion of the Soviet Union. The date he had set for that invasion was May 15, 1941.

Although the defeat of the Soviet Union was central to Hitler's strategic objective, during the early months of 1941 he allowed himself to be sidetracked twice into conflicts that delayed his invasion. In both instances he felt obliged to rescue his ally Mussolini from military difficulties. Mussolini had invaded Greece in October 1940, despite the fact that he was already in difficulty in North Africa, where he was unable to cut off Britain's Mediterranean lifeline in Egypt. In February 1941 Hitler decided to reinforce Mussolini in North Africa by sending an armoured division under the command of General Erwin Rommel. When Mussolini's invasion of Greece also bogged down, Hitler again decided to send reinforcements. To reach Greece, German troops had to be sent through the Balkan countries, all of them officially neutral. Hitler managed to bully these countries into accepting the passage of German troops, but on March 27 a coup in Yugoslavia overthrew the government, and the new rulers reneged on the agreement. In retaliation Hitler launched what he called Operation Punishment against the Yugoslavs. Yugoslav resistance collapsed quickly, but the effect was to delay for another month the planned invasion of the Soviet Union.

When the invasion of the Soviet Union finally came, on June 22, 1941, it did so with both campaigns against the British, across the English Channel and in the Mediterranean, still incomplete. Hitler was prepared to take the risk that fighting on multiple fronts entailed, because he was convinced that the war against the Soviet Union would be over by the onset of the Russian winter. The spectacular German advances during the first weeks of the invasion seemed proof of Hitler's calculation. On July 3 his army chief of staff wrote in his war diary that the war had been won. The German Army Group North was approaching Leningrad; Army Group Centre had broken through the Soviet defenses and was rushing toward Moscow; and Army Group South had already captured vast reaches of Ukraine. The prospect of capturing the summer harvest of Ukraine along with the oil fields of the Caucasus led Hitler to transfer troops driving toward Moscow to reinforce those operating in the south.

Hitler's generals later considered this decision a turning point in the war. The effect was to delay until October the drive toward Moscow. By then an early winter had set in, greatly impeding the German advance and finally bringing it to a halt at the outskirts of Moscow in early December. Then, on December 6, the Soviets, having had time to regroup, launched a massive counteroffensive to relieve their capital city. On the following day the Japanese, nominally Germany's ally, launched their attack on the U.S. naval base at Pearl Harbor in Hawaii. Although they had not bothered to inform Hitler of their intentions, he was jubilant when he heard the news. "Now it is impossible for us to lose the war," he told his aides. On December 11 he declared war on the United States.

Though his plans for a quick defeat of the Soviet Union had not been realized, Hitler's troops at the end of 1941 controlled much of the European territory of the Soviet Union. They stood at the outskirts of Leningrad and Moscow and were in control of all of Ukraine. To prepare for what would now have to be the campaign of 1942, Hitler dismissed a number of generals and assumed himself the strategic and operational command of the armies on the Eastern Front.

At the high point of Hitler's military successes in the Soviet Union, members of the Nazi leadership were, with Hitler's understanding, feverishly planning for the new order they intended to impose on the conquered territories. Its realization called both for the removal of obstacles to German settlements and for a solution to the "Jewish problem." Nazi planners were drafting an elaborate scheme, General Plan East, for the future reorganization of eastern Europe and the western Soviet Union, which called for the elimination of 30 million or more Slavs and the settlement of their territories by German overlords who would control and eventually repopulate the area with Germans. During the fall of 1941 Himmler's SS expanded and refurbished with gas chambers and crematoriums an old Austrian army barracks near the Polish rail junction at Auschwitz. Here was to continue, with greater efficiency, the Holocaust—the mass murder of Jews that had begun with the June invasion, when SS *Einsatzgruppen* ("deployment groups") began rounding up Jews and shooting them by the thousands. The assurance of victory in the east, the heartland of European Jewry, convinced the Nazis that they could implement a "final solution" to the "Jewish problem." Experts estimate that ultimately some six million Jews were murdered in the death factories of eastern Europe. At least an equal number of non-Jews died of murder and starvation in places like Auschwitz, including two and a half million Soviet prisoners of war and countless others from eastern European nationalities.

The success of Nazi armies until the end of 1941 had made it possible to spare German civilians on the home front from the misery and sacrifices demanded of them during World War I. Hitler's imagination, however, was haunted by the memory of the collapse of the home front in 1918, and, to avoid a repetition, the Nazis looted the occupied territories of food and raw materials as well as labour. Food shortages in Germany were not serious until late in the war. Women were allowed to stay at home, and the energies of the German workforce were not stretched to their limits, because eventually some seven million foreign slave labourers were used to keep the war effort going.

Through much of 1942 an ultimate German victory still seemed possible. The renewed offensive in the Soviet Union in the spring at first continued the successes of the previous year. Once again Hitler chose to concentrate on the capture of the Caucasus and its oil at the expense of the Moscow front. The decision entailed a major battle over the industrial centre at Stalingrad (now Volgograd). Elsewhere, by midsummer of 1942, Rommel's Afrika Korps advanced to within 65 miles (105 km) of Alexandria in Egypt. In the naval battle for control of the Atlantic sea lanes, German submarines maintained their ability to intercept Allied shipping into mid-1943.

By early 1943, however, the tide had clearly begun to turn. The great winter battle at Stalingrad brought Hitler his first major defeat. His entire Sixth Army was killed or captured. In North Africa Rommel's long success ended in late 1942 when the British broke through at El Alamein. At the same time, a joint British-American force landed in northwestern Africa, on the coast of Morocco and Algeria. By May 1943 the German and Italian forces in North Africa were ready to surrender. That same summer the Allies broke the back of the German submarine campaign in the Atlantic. On July 10 the Allies landed in Sicily. Two weeks later Mussolini was overthrown, and in early September the Italians withdrew from the war.

The addition of an Italian front made the rollback of German forces on all fronts that much more likely. In the Soviet Union, German forces were stretched across 2,500 miles (4,000 km). They had lost their air superiority when Allied bombing raids on German cities forced the withdrawal of large numbers of fighter planes. British and American bombings reached a high point in midsummer when a raid on Hamburg killed 40,000 of its inhabitants. Similar air raids killed hundreds of thousands of German civilians and leveled large areas of most German cities. Shortages of food, clothing, and housing began to afflict German cities as inevitably as did the Allied bombers.

The rollback of German forces continued inexorably during 1944. On June 6 the Allies in the west launched their invasion of France across the English Channel. In the east the Soviet army was advancing along the entire 2,500-mile front. By the end of the year, it stood poised on the eastern frontiers of prewar Germany. In the west, British and American troops stood ready to attack across the western borders.

On the German home front, 1944 became a year of acute suffering. On July 20, officers carried out a plot, part of a long-simmering opposition to Hitler from within German military and civilian circles, but Hitler managed to escape the dramatic attempt on his life practically unharmed. He attributed his survival of the July Plot to his selection by fate to succeed in his mission of restoring Germany to greatness.

Fate did not again intervene on Hitler's behalf. In mid-January of 1945 he withdrew underground into his bunker in Berlin where he remained until his suicide on April 30. By that time Soviet soldiers were streaming into Berlin. All that remained of the Reich was a narrow wedge of territory running southward from Berlin into Austria.

With the Soviet army in control of Berlin and the Western Allies within striking distance to the west and the south, there was no prospect of dividing them. Nonetheless, when Hitler's successor, Grand Admiral Karl Dönitz, sought to open negotiations for a surrender a few days after Hitler's death, he still hoped that a separate surrender to the British and Americans in the west might allow the Reich to rescue something from the Soviets in the east. The Western Allies, fearful of any move that might feed the suspicions of Stalin, refused to consider the German proposal, insisting that a German surrender be signed with all the Allies at the same time. Early in the morning of May 7, 1945, a German delegation came to U.S. General Dwight D. Eisenhower's headquarters in Rheims, France, and at 2:41 AM signed the surrender documents. Despite the fact that a Soviet major general signed for the Soviet Union, Stalin insisted that a second surrender ceremony take place in Soviet-occupied Berlin. This second surrender was signed in a Berlin suburb the following afternoon.

Karl A. Schleunes

1937: Modern Art and Politics in Prewar Germany

Stephanie Barron

In 1937 the National Socialists staged the most virulent attack ever mounted against modern art with the opening on July 19 in Munich of the *Entartete Kunst* (Degenerate art) exhibition in which were brought together more than 650 important paintings, sculptures, prints, and books that had until a few weeks earlier been in the possession of thirty-two German public museum collections. The works were assembled for the purpose of clarifying for the German public by defamation and derision exactly what type of modern art was unacceptable to the Reich, and thus "un-German." During the four months *Entartete Kunst* was on view in Munich it attracted more than two million visitors; over the next three years it traveled throughout Germany and Austria and was seen by nearly one million more. On most days twenty thousand visitors passed through the exhibition, which was free of charge; records state that on one Sunday—August 2, 1937—thirty-six thousand people saw it.[1] The popularity of *Entartete Kunst* has never been matched by any other exhibition of modern art. According to newspaper accounts, five times as many people visited *Entartete Kunst* as saw the *Grosse Deutsche Kunstausstellung* (Great German art exhibition), an equally large presentation of Nazi-approved art that had opened on the preceding day to inaugurate Munich's Haus der Deutschen Kunst (House of German art), the first official building erected by the National Socialists.

The thoroughness of the National Socialists' politicization of aesthetic issues remains unparalleled in modern history, as does the remarkable set of circumstances that led to the complete revocation of Germany's previous identification of its cultural heroes, not only in the visual arts but also in literature, music, and film. When the National Socialists assumed power in 1933, one of their first acts was an attack on contemporary authors; widespread book-burnings in which thousands of volumes were destroyed in public view announced the new policy toward the arts. The *Entartete Kunst* exhibition was only the tip of the iceberg: in 1937 more than sixteen thousand examples of modern art were confiscated as "degenerate" by a committee empowered by Joseph Goebbels, Adolf Hitler's second-in-command and since March of 1933 Reichsminister für Volksaufklärung und Propaganda (Reich minister for public enlightenment and propaganda). While some of the impounded art was earmarked for *Entartete Kunst* in Munich, hundreds of works were sold for hard currency to foreign buyers. Many of the "dregs," as Goebbels called them, were probably destroyed in a spectacular blaze in front of the central fire department in Berlin in 1939.[2]

The National Socialists rejected and censured virtually everything that had existed on the German modern art scene prior to 1933. Whether abstract or representational, the innocuously beautiful landscapes and portraits by August Macke, the expressionistically colored paintings by the popular Brücke artists Ernst Ludwig Kirchner, Emil Nolde, and Karl Schmidt-Rottluff, the biting social criticism of Max Beckmann, Otto Dix, and George Grosz, or the efforts of the Bauhaus artists to forge a new link between art and industry—all were equally condemned. The Gesetz zur Wiederherstellung des Berufsbeamtentums (Professional civil service restoration act) of April 7, 1933, enabled Nazi officials to dismiss non-Aryan government employees from their jobs. In that year alone more than twenty museum directors and curators, all of whom worked for state institutions, were fired.

Artists were forced to join official groups, and any "undesirables" were dismissed from teaching posts in the academies and artistic organizations. No matter what their political attitudes, artists who worked in abstract, Cubist, Expressionist, Surrealist, or other modern styles came under attack. Nolde, who was actually an early member of the National Socialist party, saw his own work declared "degenerate." Willi Baumeister and Beckmann were dismissed from their positions at the Frankfurt Städelschule (Municipal school), Dix, Paul Klee, and Max Pechstein were fired from the academies in Dresden, Düsseldorf, and Berlin, respectively. The Preussische Akademie (Prussian academy) in Berlin lost many important artists, including Ernst Barlach, Rudolf Belling, Dix, Ludwig Gies, Karl Hofer, Kirchner, Oskar Kokoschka, Käthe Kollwitz, Max Liebermann, Ludwig Mies van der Rohe, Pechstein, and Bruno Taut. Most of the artists who were persecuted were not Jewish, on the contrary, of those mentioned above only Liebermann was Jewish, and of the 112 artists included in *Entartete Kunst* only 6 were Jews. Any artists who were mentioned or whose work was illustrated in any of the well-publicized books on contemporary art by Ludwig Justi or Carl Einstein or in avant-garde periodicals such as *Das Kunstblatt* (The art paper), *Die Aktion* (Action), or *Der Sturm* (The storm) were easy targets for the National Socialists. In 1979 Berthold Hinz produced evidence that Einstein's *Die Kunst des 20. Jahrhunderts* (The art of the twentieth century) was in fact used as a guide by many of the National Socialists in defining who and what was modern, and consequently "un-German" and to be vilified.[3] With the swift imprint of the censor's stamp they outlawed an entire generation of modernism.

While the focus of *"Degenerate Art"*: *The Fate of the Avant-Garde in Nazi Germany* is on events in the visual arts, these can be seen as indicative of prohibitions in the wider spectrum of the cultural arena. It is worthwhile to look at the various areas that came under the jurisdiction of the Reichsministerium für Volksaufklärung und Propaganda. In November 1933 Goebbels established *Reichskammern* (Reich chambers) of film, music, radio broadcasting, press, theater, and writers, in addition to the fine arts (fig. 1). Each of the heads of these chambers had under him (there were no women) seven departments incorporating further subdivisions. The Reichskammer der bildenden Künste (Reich chamber of visual arts), for example, was divided into departments of 1) administration; 2) press and propaganda; 3) architecture, landscape architecture, and interior design; 4) painting, sculpture, and graphic arts; 5) commercial illustration and design; 6) art promotion, artists' associations, and craft associations; and 7) art publishing, sales, and auctioneering.

What becomes apparent is the microscopic attention the Nazi hierarchy accorded the observation and regulation of all aspects of cultural life in the Reich. The government established

Die Reichskulturkammer

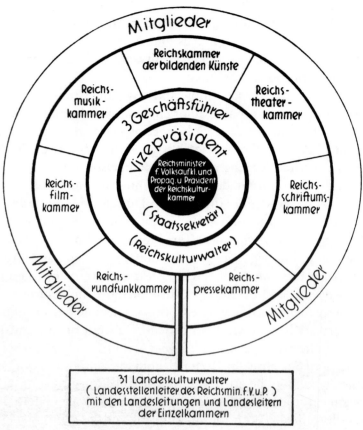

Figure 1

Organizational chart of the Reichskulturkammer (Reich chamber of culture), illustrating its division into chambers of radio broadcasting, film, music, visual arts, theater, literature, and journalism.

procedures whereby it decided what and who was acceptable or undesirable. Exclusion was tantamount to permanent disbarment. One can only wonder at the disproportionate amount of bureaucratic organization, paperwork, rules, and regulations that was aimed at an area of society that was economically, politically, and militaristically unthreatening. Obviously the National Socialists perceived the cultural life of the citizens of the Reich to be extremely important and worthy of such intensive concern. This elevation of art to such a major role in a totalitarian society was without historical precedent, other than in the Soviet Union. Hellmut Lehmann-Haupt wrote in the early 1950s, "Such complete monopolization of the entire creative potential of a people, of every aesthetic instinct, such subjugation of every current of its productivity and its capacity for artistic experience to the purposes of the leaders of collective society does not exist before the present century."[4] Although Hitler had a personal interest and involvement with art, due to his unsuccessful career as a painter in Vienna, Lehmann-Haupt argues convincingly that the preoccupation of the National Socialists with culture far transcended Hitler's own frustrated flirtation with art.[5]

DEGENERACY AND NAZI IDEOLOGY IN THE 1920S AND 1930S

The *Grosse Deutsche Kunstausstellung* and *Entartete Kunst* did not occur as isolated incidents. The issues raised, the fusion of political and aesthetic themes, and the use of the term *entartet* to designate supposedly inferior racial, sexual, and moral types had been in the air for several years. (*Entartet,* which has traditionally been translated as "degenerate" or "decadent," is essentially a biological term, defining a plant or animal that has so changed that it no longer belongs to its species. By extension it refers to art that is unclassifiable or so far beyond the confines of what is accepted that it is in essence "non-art.")

The events leading up to 1937 had their roots in German cultural history long before the National Socialist party was formed. The year 1871 marked both the emergence of the German empire and the publication of Charles Darwin's *The Descent of Man*, a book later used to justify German racism. As a unified country Germany became prone to an intense nationalism that manifested itself quite often as a belief in the natural superiority of the Aryan people. The myth of the blond, blue-eyed Nordic hero as the embodiment of the future of Western civilization was promoted in the writings of several European authors of the early twentieth century, including Count Gobineau, Houston Stewart Chamberlain, Hans Günther, and Alfred Rosenberg. In the decade between 1910 and 1920 the concept of racism had achieved popularity in the middle class. By the 1920s certain authors argued that racial characteristics and art were linked and attempted to "prove" that the style of a work of art was determined by the race of the artist.[6]

This period in German history also saw the efflorescence of modern art, literature, film, and music created by individuals who would be labeled "degenerate" in the 1930s. German art virtually exploded in a series of events in Berlin, Dresden, and Munich. The emergence of the artists' groups Die Brücke (The bridge) and Der Blaue Reiter (The blue rider), the publication of important radical periodicals to which artists contributed, and the intense response by artists and writers to the cataclysmic events of the First World War characterized the first phase of German Expressionism. These artists and writers were also drawn to the exotic: the carvings and wall hangings of African and Oceanic peoples that the Brücke artists saw in the Dresden Völkerkunde-Museum (Ethnographic museum), for example, or the art of the insane that served as inspiration for the poetry and prose of such esteemed authors as Hugo Ball, Alfred Döblin, and Wieland Herzfelde. In the wake of the war avant-garde German art came increasingly into conflict with the nationalistic realism that was more easily understood by the average German. The country had experienced a humiliating defeat and had been assessed for huge war reparations that grievously taxed its already shaky economy. Movements such as

Expressionism, Cubism, and Dada were often viewed as intellectual, elitist, and foreign by the demoralized nation and linked to the economic collapse, which was blamed on a supposed international conspiracy of Communists and Jews. Many avant-garde artists continued their involvement in Socialism during the turbulent Weimar era and made their sentiments known through their art. This identification of the more abstract art movements with internationalism and progressive politics created highly visible targets for the aggressive nationalism that gave birth to the National Socialist party, even as institutions such as the Bauhaus school moved into the cultural mainstream and German museums exhibited more and more avant-garde work.

Concurrent with important artistic developments, pseudoscientific treatises such as Max Nordau's *Entartung* (Degeneration) of 1892 were enjoying renewed popularity.[7] Nordau, himself a Jew, wrote a ponderous text vilifying the Pre-Raphaelites, Symbolism, Henrik Ibsen, and Émile Zola, among others, as he sought to prove the superiority of traditional German culture. In 1895 George Bernard Shaw had written a brilliant and scathing review of Nordau's book,[8] one of several responses provoked internationally. Unfortunately, the criticism had little impact on the architects of Nazi ideology. *Entartung* and other racist works took the widely accepted view that nineteenth-century realistic genre painting represented the culmination of a long tradition of true Aryan art. Even before they obtained a majority in the Reichstag (Parliament), disgruntled theorists and polemicists had written and spoken of how "good German art" was being overrun by "degenerates, Jews, and other insidious influences." The avant-garde artist was equated to the insane, who in turn was synonymous with the Jew: the nineteenth-century founders of German psychiatry felt that the Jew was inherently degenerate and more susceptible than the non-Jew to insanity.[9] As Sander Gilman has pointed out, the classifications of "degenerate" and "healthy" appeared for the first time in the late nineteenth century; by the late 1930s they were fairly standard in discussions about the avant-garde and the traditional.[10]

Opposition to the wave of avant-garde activities in German museums had begun in the 1920s with the founding of the Deutsche Kunstgesellschaft (German art association), which had as its goals a "common action against the corruption of art" and the promotion of an "art that was pure German, with the German soul reflecting art." They attacked exhibitions of the works of Beckmann, Grosz, and other proponents of "Kulturbolschewismus" (art-Bolshevism). In 1927 Rosenberg, the chief architect of Nazi cultural policy, founded the Kampfbund für deutsche Kultur (Combat league for German culture), which had the same goals as the Deutsche Kunstgesellschaft. It was at first an underground organization, but with the rise of National Socialism it worked openly with the party leadership. In 1930 Rosenberg wrote *Der Mythus des 20. Jahrhunderts: Eine Wertung der seelisch-geistigen Gestaltenkämpfe* (The myth of the twentieth century: An evaluation of the spiritual-intellectual confrontations of our age), in which he denounced Expressionism and other modern art forms: "Creativity was broken because it had oriented itself, ideologically and artistically, toward a foreign standard and thus was no longer attuned to the demands of life."[11]

In 1929 the state of Thuringia elected Wilhelm Frick, a member of the Nazi party, as representative to the Reichstag. Frick was named Innenminister (Minister of the interior) for

Thuringia. His actions gave a foretaste of what the Nazi seizure of power would mean: he began by replacing most department heads, issuing new cultural policies, and even encouraging the dismissal of Walter Gropius and the entire twenty-nine-member faculty of the Bauhaus in Weimar, which was located within his jurisdiction.

Frick appointed Paul Schultze-Naumburg, an architect and racial theorist, to replace Gropius. In 1925 Schultze-Naumburg had published an attack on the Bauhaus, *Das ABC des Bauens* (The ABCs of building), and in 1928 he wrote *Kunst und Rasse* (Art and race), which would have a far-reaching influence in the Nazi scheme against modernism. Exploiting the popularity of Nordau's treatise, Schultze-Naumburg attacked modern art as "entartet." He juxtaposed examples of modern art and photographs of deformed or diseased people to suggest that they were the models for the elongated faces of Amedeo Modigliani, the angular physiognomies of Schmidt-Rottluff, and the florid faces of Dix (figs. 2–3). He railed particularly against the Expressionists, who he felt represented the inferior aspect of modern German culture.

Heidelberg had become a center for the study of art produced by schizophrenics as a means of access to the central problems of mental illness. In 1922 psychiatrist Hans Prinzhorn had published his study *Bildnerei der Geisteskranken* (Image-making by the mentally ill), which was based on material he had assembled: he examined more than 5,000 works by 450 patients to demonstrate that the art of the insane exhibited certain specific qualities.[12] The study received serious attention far beyond the medical profession. Although we have no evidence that Hitler, the failed artist, read or even knew of Prinzhorn's book, the attention devoted to it was so widespread that it is more likely than not to have reached him. Thus, it is not surprising that Schultze-Naumburg's methodology of comparing the works of insane artists to avant-garde art was seized upon as a further way to "prove" the "degeneracy" of modern art. The technique of comparison for the purpose of denigration and condemnation thus became a basic tool of the Nazi campaign. In 1933 in Erlangen one of the many precursors of *Entartete Kunst* included thirty-two paintings by contemporary artists shown with works by children and the mentally ill. The same technique was used on several pages in the illustrated brochure published to accompany *Entartete Kunst* as it traveled around Germany.

There emerged in 1934 some confusion about the "official" attitude toward the Expressionists, artists such as Barlach and Nolde in particular. Some factions saw this art as truly German and Nordic, with roots in the Gothic era. Goebbels initially sided with these proponents, in fact, he surrounded himself with examples of Barlach's sculpture and Nolde's painting; he saw the spirit and chaos of Expressionism as analogous to the spirit of Nazi youth. At extreme odds with him was Rosenberg, who sought to promote *völkisch* art (art of and for the German people) over any type of modern aesthetic. Goebbels and Rosenberg took opposing sides in their speeches and writings, neither yet sure of the Führer's opinion.[13] When Hitler appointed Rosenberg early in 1934 to supervise all "intellectual and ideological training," he gave him a rank equal to Goebbels's in his role as president of the Reichskulturkammer (Reich chamber of culture). The ideological tug-of-war continued well into the year, until the controversy required Hitler's intervention. In September, at the party rally in Nuremberg, Hitler spoke of the dangers of artistic sabotage by the Cubists, Futurists, Dadaists, and others

Figure 2–3
Juxtaposition of works of "degenerate" art by Karl Schmidt-Rottluff and Amedeo Modigliani and photographs of facial deformities, from Paul Schultze-Naumburg, *Kunst und Rasse,* 1928.

who were threatening artistic growth, but he also cautioned against excessively retrograde German art. Thus, neither Expressionism nor the conservative *völkisch* art received his blessing. Nazi-approved art would be based exclusively on German racial tradition. Henceforth, all forms of modernism, including art criticism, were outlawed.

The unusual methodology employed by the Nazis in the *Entartete Kunst* exhibition entailed the gathering of works of art for the specific purpose of defamation. Never before had there been such an effort; perhaps only Soviet Russia in the years following the revolution of 1917 offers a parallel for the efflorescence of modernism and its immediate repudiation by the government in power. The late-nineteenth-century French Salons des Réfusés, in which art outside the academic tradition could be seen, were state-sanctioned opportunities for the avant-garde to emerge. By contrast, the Nazis exhibited works contrary to their "approved" art in order to condemn them. There was no chance for an alternative voice to be heard.

As early as 1933 the seeds had been sown for the approach used in the Munich exhibition four years later. In that year the *Deutscher Kunstbericht* (German art report), under Goebbels's jurisdiction, published a five-point manifesto stating "what German artists expect from the new government." Much of the content of the manifesto was generated by artists outside the mainstream avant-garde who felt that the art world had passed them by. They sought revenge on a modern art that was becoming increasingly identified with Germany in the international art world. The manifesto laid the groundwork for the events in 1937:

- All works of a cosmopolitan or Bolshevist nature should be removed from German museums and collections, but first they should be exhibited to the public, who should be informed of the details of their acquisition, and then burned.
- All museum directors who "wasted" public monies by purchasing "un-German" art should be fired immediately.
- No artist with Marxist or Bolshevist connections should be mentioned henceforth.
- No boxlike buildings should be built [an assault on Bauhaus architecture].
- All public sculptures not "approved" by the German public should be immediately removed [this applied especially to Barlach and Wilhelm Lehmbruck].

The Attack on the Museums

Prior to the outbreak of the First World War, museums, art dealers, and periodicals in Germany were greatly attuned to avant-garde activities in Europe and were avid advocates for the most recent developments. Museum curators and directors had responded eagerly to Impressionism and Post-Impressionism. In 1897 the Nationalgalerie in Berlin became the first museum in the world to acquire a painting by Paul Cézanne, and the Museum Folkwang in Essen was among the earliest public supporters of the work of Paul Gauguin and Vincent van Gogh. Herwarth Walden, with his gallery and publication *Der Sturm*, was a staunch supporter of Expressionism, Cubism, Futurism, and the Russian avant-garde.

In 1949 Paul Ortwin Rave, who had become a curator at the Berlin Nationalgalerie in the 1930s, wrote the first book describing the artistic situation under the Nazi regime, *Kunstdiktatur im Dritten Reich* (Art dictatorship in the Third Reich), which contained his eyewitness account of the *Entartete Kunst* exhibition.[14] What emerges from his description of the activities of German museums from 1919 through 1939 is a picture of a country filled with museums actively committed to modern art, to its acquisition and display. Alexander Doerner in Hannover, Gustav Hartlaub and Fritz Wichert in Mannheim, Carl Georg Heise in Lübeck, Ludwig Justi in Berlin, Alfred Lichtwark in Hamburg, Karl Ernst Osthaus in Hagen, Max Sauerlandt in Halle and later in Hamburg, Alois Schardt in Halle, Georg Swarzenski in Frankfurt, and Hugo von Tschudi in Berlin and later in Munich were among the museum directors who proselytized for contemporary art. They were responsible for acquiring, often directly from the artists, major works by Barlach, Beckmann, Lyonel Feininger, Erich Heckel, Kirchner, Lehmbruck, Macke, Franz Marc, Nolde, Pechstein, Christian Rohlfs, and Schmidt-Rottluff, as well as artists of the earlier generation, Lovis Corinth, Liebermann, and Max Slevogt. They were not only committed to contemporary German art but also acquired in significant quantity important works by foreign Impressionists and Post-Impressionists Cézanne, Gauguin, van Gogh, Édouard Manet, Claude Monet, Auguste Renoir, and Paul Signac and the art of contemporary foreigners such as James Ensor, Wassily Kandinsky, El Lissitsky, Henri Matisse, Piet Mondrian, and Pablo Picasso.

The exhibitions they organized, which frequently traveled, helped to define artistic trends and were important signs to foreign museums and dealers of the healthy state of contemporary art in Germany. Important international exhibitions in Cologne in 1912, Dresden in 1919, and Düsseldorf and Hannover in 1928 exposed new German art to a wider public. Contemporary German art was shown in Florence, London, New York, Paris, Pittsburgh, and Stockholm. In 1931 Alfred Barr, Jr., traveled in Germany to prepare his *Modern German Painting and Sculpture* for the fledgling Museum of Modern Art in New York. He was so impressed by what he saw in the museums that he made a point in his catalogue of citing the contemporary collecting policies of German public institutions:

> However much modern German art is admired or misunderstood abroad, it is certainly supported publicly and privately in Germany with extraordinary generosity. Museum directors have the courage, foresight and knowledge to buy works by the most advanced artists long before public opinion forces them to do so. Some fifty German Museums, as the lists in this catalogue suggest, are a most positive factor both in supporting artists and in educating the public to an understanding of their work.[15]

After visiting a New York gallery showing of works of modern German art in 1939 the reviewer for the *New York World-Telegram* wrote: "One's first reaction on seeing them is of amazement that such early examples of work by men who were later to become world famous should have been purchased by museums in Germany so many years ago."[16]

The Nationalgalerie in Berlin housed the most representative collection of contemporary German art. On October 30, 1936, immediately following the close of the Summer Olympics, Goebbels ordered the gallery's contemporary rooms to be closed to the public. From Annegret Janda's essay in this volume we learn how this most visible forum for modern art was a battleground in which a succession of museum directors engaged in a struggle to reorganize and protect the collection, to preserve some aesthetic dignity, and even to continue to acquire contemporary art with dwindling funds. After coming to power the National Socialists began a systematic campaign to confiscate modernist works from public museum collections. Hitler saw an attack on modernism as an opportunity to use the average German's distrust of avant-garde art to further his political objectives against Jews, Communists, and non-Aryans. The charge of "degeneracy" was leveled at avant-garde practitioners of music, literature, film, and visual art, and their works were confiscated to "purify" German culture. In 1933 the earliest exhibitions of "degenerate" art were organized to show the German people the products of the "cultural collapse" of Germany that would be purged from the Third Reich. Confiscated works were assembled into *Schreckenskammern der Kunst* (chambers of horror of art) whose organizers decried the fact that public monies had been wasted on these modern "horrors" and implied that many of the works had been foisted on the museums by a cabal of Jewish art dealers. These precursors to the *Entartete Kunst* exhibition in Munich in 1937 sprang up throughout Germany, often featuring works from the local museums (see Christoph Zuschlag's essay in this catalogue). *Entartete Kunst* was not the only anti-modernist exhibition to occur in 1937. The Institut für Deutsche Kultur- und Wirtschaftspropaganda (Institute for German cultural and economic propaganda), a section of Goebbels's ministry, organized the *Grosse antibolschewistische Ausstellung* (Great anti-Bolshevist exhibition, fig. 4), which ran in Nuremberg from September

Figure 4
Grosse antibolschewistische Ausstellung (Great anti-Bolshevist exhibition), Nuremberg, 1937

5 to September 29 and then traveled to several other venues, and orchestrated the tour of the NSDAP's exhibition *Der ewige Jude* (The eternal Jew, fig. 5) from Munich to Vienna, Berlin, Bremen, Dresden, and Magdeburg from late 1937 to mid-1939.

THE KUNSTHALLE MANNHEIM: AN EXAMPLE

The situation in Mannheim was typical of that of many other German museums out of the spotlight of Berlin; one could just as easily have chosen the Landesmuseum in Hannover, the Kunstsammlungen in Dresden, the Museum Folkwang in Essen, or the Staatliche Galerie Moritzburg in Halle.[17]

Between 1909 and 1923 Fritz Wichert, the director of the Kunsthalle Mannheim, purchased several key examples of French and German Impressionism and German Expressionism, including paintings by Alexander Archipenko, Beckmann, Corinth, Kirchner, and Liebermann.

Figure 5
The exhibition *Der ewige Jude* (The eternal Jew), Munich, 1937; over the title are the words, "very political show"

Sally Falk's donations of works by Lehmbruck and Ernesto de Fiori provided the nucleus for a growing collection of sculpture.[18]

Wichert's successor was Gustav Hartlaub, whose tenure extended from 1923 until 1934, when he was forced to resign. He was responsible for most of the exhibitions and major acquisitions of Expressionist and modern art that made Mannheim a center for those who wanted to see current art in Germany (figs. 6–7). The files of the Kunsthalle yield an interesting picture of the volume and velocity of these purchases and exhibitions and of Hartlaub's voracious interest in contemporary art including the Fauves, Die Brücke, Der Blaue Reiter, Neue Sachlichkeit (New objectivity), and other examples of German and non-German avant-garde art:

1924–25　　Exhibition: *Deutscher Werkbund "Die Form"*
　　　　　　Acquisition: Grosz, *Grosstadt*
1925–26　　Exhibitions: *Edvard Munch; Neue Sachlichkeit*
　　　　　　Acquisitions: Marc Chagall, *Blaues Haus;* Dix, *Die Witwe;*
　　　　　　Grosz, *Max Hermann-Neisse;* Kirchner, *Stilleben*

1927–28	Exhibitions: *James Ensor; Wege und Richtungen der Abstraktion*
	Acquisitions: Baumeister, *Tischgesellschaft*; Robert Delaunay, *St. Severin*;
	Ensor, *Masks and Death*; Oskar Schlemmer, *Frauentreppe*
1928–29	Exhibition: *Max Beckmann*
	Acquisitions: Beckmann, *Pierrette und Clown, Das Liebespaar*; Chagall,
	Rabbiner; André Derain, *Landscape*
1929–30	Acquisition: Heinrich Hoerle, *Melancholie*
1930–31	Exhibitions: *Bauhaus; Neues Von Gestern*
	Acquisition: Jankel Adler, *Zwei Mädchen*
1931–32	Exhibitions: *Oskar Kokoschka; Georg Minne*
1932–33	only graphics
1933–34	nothing major
1934–35	only graphics

As early as the mid-1920s museums had felt the cold wind of censorship. In 1925 Hartlaub's *Neue Sachlichkeit* exhibition traveled to the Chemnitz Kunsthütte, where the director, Dr. Schreiber-Wiegand, asked Hartlaub to make some changes in the catalogue:

> We are most grateful to you for your permission to use your introduction to the catalogue, but with regard to our special art-political conditions, I have one request. Since in the attacks on our collecting activities these [works] are regarded as "Bolshevism in art," might we change a few words in three paragraphs? On page 1 could we simply leave out the word "Katastrophenzeit" [catastrophic time], and maybe on the next page express the sentence a little less controversially? I would like to avoid any problems. . . . [I] ask for your friendly understanding of our local situation. You yourself know how everything now is affected by political conditions and [those who] want to kill everything that does not please them. This includes Expressionism, of course, especially my purchases of pictures by Schmidt-Rottluff, Kirchner, and Heckel.[19]

Hartlaub obliged so that the exhibition and catalogue could proceed as planned. By the early 1930s, however, his own freedom was increasingly hampered. During the last year of his directorship Mannheim was the scene of public protests against some of his acquisitions, including Chagall's *Rabbiner* (Rabbi, fig. 118), which was the subject of a window display in the town incorporating the sign, "Taxpayer, you should know how your money was spent." In 1934 Hartlaub became the first museum director to be fired by the National Socialists. Other directors who soon joined the ranks of those dismissed by the Nazis included Heise in Lübeck; Justi in Berlin; Sauerlandt, then director of the Hamburg Museum für Kunst und Gewerbe; Schreiber-Wiegand in Chemnitz; and Swarzenski in Frankfurt.

On two separate occasions, July 8 and August 28, 1937, the Kunsthalle Mannheim was visited by the special committee empowered by Goebbels to confiscate examples of "degenerate" art from German museums. Mannheim was one of their most successful stops: they seized over six hundred works by artists such as non-Germans Chagall, Delaunay, Derain, Ensor, and Edvard Munch and Germans Beckmann, Corinth, Grosz, Lehmbruck, Nolde, and

Figure 6
Gallery in the Kunsthalle Mannheim during the defamatory exhibition *Kulturbolschewistische Bilder* (Images of cultural Bolshevism), 1933; work later in *Entartete kunst*: 1. Schlemmer, *Frauentreppe*, 2. Beckmann, *Christus und die Ehebrecherin*, 3. Hoerle, *Melancholie*, 4. Adler, *Mutter and Tochter*, 5. Baumeister, *Tischgesellschaft*.

Figure 7
Poster for an exhibition of paintings and graphic works by Max Beckmann, Kunsthalle Mannheim, 1928.

THINKING, MAKING, DOING

Schlemmer. Most of these masterworks are lost; a few fortunately, have been reacquired by the Kunsthalle, and others are dispersed in public and private collections.

The "Grosse Deutsche Kunstausstellung," 1937

On October 15, 1933, at the ground-breaking ceremony for the Haus der Deutschen Kunst, Hitler said he was laying the "foundations for this new temple in honor of the goddess of art." The architect, Paul Troost, insisted from the beginning that the building was to be a representative structure for the new German art. Due to the expensive materials used and the monumental scale of the rooms the building attracted enormous attention. Hitler announced that it was the first new building worthy to take its place among the immortal achievements of the German artistic heritage.[20] (It was also in this speech that he delivered the ultimatum that the National Socialists would give the people four years time to adjust to the cultural policies of the new government.)

The year 1937 represents both a nadir and zenith for the National Socialists in terms of their campaign against modern art. Hitler evidently concurred with Troost that the Haus der Deutschen Kunst should display contemporary art; in fact, he planned to use an exhibition of approved German art as a chance to further shape cultural policy.[21] To find the art to fill the spacious new halls the National Socialists staged an open competition chaired by Adolf Ziegler, president of the Reichskammer der bildenden Künste. The competition was open to all German artists, and approximately fifteen thousand works were submitted. Much to the frustration of the organizers they were provided with no clear guidelines for the selection of works to be included in the exhibition. Goebbels and Hitler himself participated in the selection (figs. 8–9), and Goebbels noted in his diary, "The sculpture is going well, but the painting is a real catastrophe at the moment. They have hung works that make us shudder. . . . The Führer is in a rage."[22] Hitler added some artists who had previously been rejected and threw out the work of several who had been judged acceptable. He abhorred "unfinished work," which subsequently became a criterion in the selection process. Eventually, nine hundred works were chosen from which the final selection would be made.

On July 18 in Munich, Hitler presided over the opening, held with great pomp and ceremony, of the Haus der Deutschen Kunst and its inaugural exhibition of approved art. The *Grosse Deutsche Kunstausstellung* (fig. 10) brought together over six hundred paintings and sculptures that were intended to demonstrate the triumph of German art in the Third Reich. Hitler announced:

> *From now on we are going to wage a merciless war of destruction against the last remaining elements of cultural disintegration. . . . Should there be someone among [the artists] who still believes in his higher destiny—well now, he has had four years' time to prove himself. These four years are sufficient for us, too, to reach a definite judgment. From now on—of that you can be certain—all those mutually supporting and thereby sustaining cliques of chatterers, dilettantes, and art forgers*

will be picked up and liquidated. For all we care, those prehistoric Stone-Age culture-barbarians and art-stutterers can return to the caves of their ancestors and there can apply their primitive international scratchings.[23]

Figure 8–9
Heinrich Hoffmann's candid photographs of Adolf Hitler and Adolf Ziegler choosing sculpture for inclusion in the *Grosse Deutsche Kunstausstellung* (Great German art exhibition), Munich, 1937.

Figure 10
Hoffmann's photograph of a gallery in the *Grosse Deutsche Kunstausstellung*; Josef Thorak's sculpture *Kameradschaft* can be seen against the far wall.

The *Grosse Deutsche Kunstausstellung* was the first of eight annual exhibitions, from 1937 to 1944, mounted in the Haus der Deutschen Kunst in the Nazis' attempt to present the best of German artistic creation, a continuation of the exhibitions that had formerly taken place in the Munich Glaspalast (Glass palace), which had burned to the ground in 1931. There was a tradition in several German cities of staging annual open competitive exhibitions for local artists in which all the works of art were for sale; they were characterized by the display of distinctly conservative and traditional art, which entertained a consistently loyal public. In this respect the *Grosse Deutsche Kunstausstellungen* were no different, except that they were larger, less parochial, and actively sponsored by the government. Installation photos and film footage indicate that the art was arranged by category—landscapes, portraits, nudes, military subjects—in the way commodities would be sold in separate areas in a market. The sales opportunities were fairly promising, and this alone may have convinced some artists to embrace National Socialist policies, since without their approval it was virtually impossible to sell contemporary art in Germany. Many of the purchases were used to decorate public buildings and offices. Several of the buyers were among the Nazi elite, who purchased the works for their official residences.[24]

At the time of each opening there occurred an elaborate pageant on the "Tag der Deutschen Kunst" (German art day). Participants wore historical costumes and created floats featuring models of well-known works of art that were driven through the streets of Munich. The opening ceremonies attracted anywhere from 400,000 to 800,000 visitors. In his inaugural speech in 1937 Hitler announced that, "When we celebrated the laying of the cornerstone for this building four years ago, we were all aware that we had to lay not only the cornerstone for a new home but also the foundations for a new and genuine German art. We had to bring about a turning point in the evolution of all our German cultural activities." The 1937 pageant was centered around the theme, "Zweitausend Jahre Deutsche Kultur" (Two thousand years of German culture). Hundreds of thousands of spectators watched the spectacle of a parade of more than three thousand costumed participants and four hundred animals. Immediately following this overblown performance thousands of uniformed soldiers marched through the streets, as if to provide the ultimate marvel. The official National Socialist newspaper, the *Völkischer Beobachter,* described the events in glowing words: "Today we sat as spectators in the theater of our own time and saw greatness" (July 19, 1937).

In the *Grosse Deutsche Kunstausstellung* the Nazis sought to promote mediocre genre painting as mainstream art, the most recent achievement in a continuum of centuries of German art. It was meant to wipe out any hint of the modernism, Expressionism, Dada, New Objectivity, Futurism, and Cubism that had permeated the museums, galleries, journals, and press since 1910. The National Socialists sought to rewrite art history, to omit what we know as the avant-garde from the history of modern art.

The situation was slightly different for sculpture. Guidelines were more difficult to observe, artists' motives more difficult to judge. Sculptors were apt to discover that some examples of their work were championed by the National Socialists and others lumped with "degenerate" art. One artist's work was inadvertently included in both the *Grosse Deutsche Kunstausstellung* and *Entartete Kunst*: Belling's *Boxer Max Schmeling* was on view in the Haus der Deutschen Kunst, while his *Dreiklang* (Triad) and *Kopf* (Head) were branded "degenerate" next door. Georg Kolbe and Gerhard Marcks had some of their earlier Expressionist works confiscated from German museums, yet their contemporary images found favor with the Nazi elite, and they continued to work openly (although two of Marcks's works were in *Entartete Kunst*). Even Arno Breker, the Nazis' sculptor of choice, saw one of his early sculptures confiscated. More conservative sculpture in the tradition of Aristide Maillol and Auguste Rodin had a significant following before the Nazis came to power and continued to be appreciated under Hitler's regime.

The Campaign Against Modern Art in Museums

Goebbels issued a decree on June 30, 1937, giving Ziegler and a five-man commission the authority to visit all major German museums and select works for an exhibition of "degenerate" that was to open in Munich at the same time as the *Grosse Deutsche Kunstausstellung*:

> On the express authority of the Führer I hereby empower the president of the Reichskammer der bildenden Künste, Professor Ziegler of Munich, to select and secure for an exhibition works of German degenerate art since 1910, both painting and sculpture, which are now in collections owned by the German Reich, individual regions, or local communities. You are requested to give Prof. Ziegler your full support during his examination and selection of these works.[25]

The directive went on to define works of "degenerate" art as those that either "insult German feeling, or destroy or confuse natural form, or simply reveal an absence of adequate manual and artistic skill." To have the *Grosse Deutsche Kunstausstellung* and *Entartete Kunst* on view simultaneously would underscore the triumph of official art over "degenerate" art. This was to be a far more ambitious action than any of the small exhibitions mounted since 1933.

Ziegler's commission was made up of individuals who, as critics of modernism, were well suited to their task; among them were Count Klaus von Baudissin, an SS officer who during his brief tenure as director of the Museum Folkwang in Essen had already cleared the museum of "offensive" examples of modern art, and Wolfgang Willrich, author of *Säuberung des Kunsttempels* (Cleansing of the temple of art), a racist pamphlet whose methods of excoriation of modern art (figs. 11–12) played an important role in the concept and content of the *Entartete Kunst* exhibition. The other members were commissioner for artistic design Hans Schweitzer, art theoretician Robert Scholz, and art teacher and polemicist Walter Hansen.

According to Rave, in the first two weeks of July about seven hundred works were shipped to Munich from thirty-two museums in twenty-eight cities. Museums in Berlin, Bielefeld, Bremen, Breslau, Chemnitz, Cologne, Dresden, Düsseldorf, Erfurt, Essen, Frankfurt, Hamburg, Hannover, Jena, Karlsruhe, Kiel, Königsberg, Leipzig, Lübeck, Mannheim, Munich, Saarbrücken, Stettin, Stuttgart, Ulm, Weimar, Wiesbaden, and Wuppertal were purged of their holdings of Expressionism, Futurism, Constructivism, Dada, and New Objectivity. At the Kunsthalle Mannheim, for example, the commission selected eighteen paintings, five sculptures, and thirty-five graphic works, which were shipped immediately to Munich.

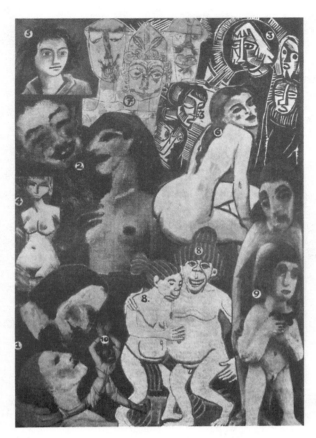

Figure 11
Collage of "Expressionist art of the [Communist] school," from Wolfgang Willrich, *Säuberung des Kunsttempels*, 1937; work later in *Entartete Kunst*: 1. Nolde, *Christus und die Sünderin*; other work: 2. Nolde; 3. Schmidt-Rottluff; 4. Mueller; 5. Hofer; 6. Pechstein; 7. Klee; 8. Rohlfs; 9. Kirchner; 10. Beckmann.

The commission revisited most of the museums later in the summer and selected additional works, so that a total of approximately sixteen thousand paintings, sculptures, drawings, and prints by fourteen hundred artists were confiscated and shipped to Berlin to await final disposal. The commission overstepped its authority and seized works created prior to 1910, as well as those by non-German artists. The plundering continued until 1938 and was finally "legalized" retroactively under a law of May 31, 1938, that stated that "products of degenerate art that have been secured in museums or in collections open to the public before this law went in to effect . . . may be appropriated by the Reich without compensation."

The works not included in *Entartete Kunst* and those from the second round of confiscations were sent to Berlin and stored in a warehouse on Köpenicker Strasse where they were inventoried. Those of "international value" that could be sold outside Germany for substantial sums were later weeded out and sent to another storage facility at Schloss Niederschönhausen. Goebbels created another commission, for the "disposal of confiscated works of

Figure 12
Collage of "degenerate" art from the Stadtmuseum Dresden, from Willrich, *Säuberung des Kunsttempels*; work later in *Entartete Kunst*: 1. Dix, *Kriegskrüppel*; 3. Voll, *Schwangere Frau*; 4. Segall, *Die ewigen Wanderer*; 5. Schwitters, *Merzbild* (sideways), 6. Kokoschka, *Die Heiden;* other work: 2. Eugen Hoffmann.

degenerate art," which was to decide which works were to be sold for foreign currency and at what prices. This group included Ziegler, Schweitzer, and Scholz, with the addition of Franz Hofmann, Carl Meder, Karl Haberstock, and Max Taeuber.

"Entartete Kunst"

On July 19, 1937, Ziegler opened the *Entartete Kunst* exhibition across the park from the *Grosse Deutsche Kunstausstellung,* in a building formerly occupied by the Institute of Archeology. The exhibition rooms had been cleared, and temporary partitions were erected on which the objects were crowded together in a chaotic arrangement (figs. 13–15), which is not surprising when one considers that the art was confiscated, shipped to Munich, and installed in less than two weeks. The paintings, some of which had had their frames removed, were vaguely organized into thematic groupings, the first time Expressionist works were presented in this way. While the first rooms were tightly grouped according to themes—religion, Jewish artists, the vilification of women—the rest of the exhibition was a composite of subjects and styles that were anathema to the National Socialists, including abstraction, antimilitarism, and art that seemed

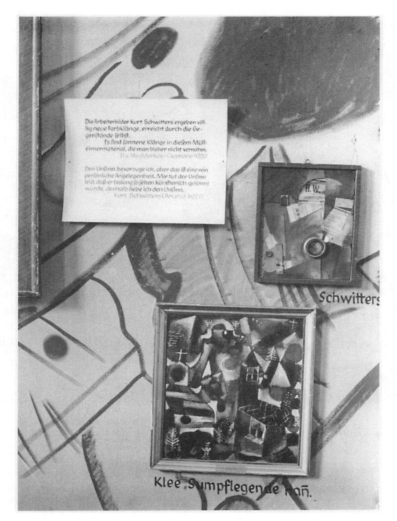

Figure 13
Detail of the Dada wall in Room 3 of *Entartete Kunst,* Munich, 1937, work by Klee and Schwitters.

to be (or at least to be related to) the work of the mentally ill. Directly on the wall under many of the works were hand-lettered labels indicating how much money had been spent by each museum to acquire this "art." The fact that the radical postwar inflation of the 1920s had led to grossly exaggerated figures—in November 1920 a dollar was worth 4.2 billion marks!—was conveniently not mentioned. Quotations and slogans by proscribed critics and museum directors and condemnatory statements by Hitler and other party members were scrawled across the walls. Since every work of art included in *Entartete Kunst* had been taken from a public collection, the event was meant not only to denigrate the artists but also to condemn the actions of the institutions, directors, curators, and dealers involved with the acquisition of modern art.

Figure 14
View of a portion of the south wall in Room 5; work by Beckmann, Fuhr, Kirchner, Mueller, Nolde, Rohlfs, and Schmidt-Rottluff.

Entartete Kunst was to have been on view through the end of September, but the astonishing attendance prompted the organizers to extend the run until the end of November. Plans were also made to circulate the exhibition to other German cities, with Berlin as the first stop. The leaders of the various *Gaus* (regions into which Germany had been divided by the National Socialists for administrative reasons) vied for the opportunity to present the exhibition, but only the most important were accorded the chance. *Entartete Kunst* in varying configurations ultimately traveled to thirteen German and Austrian cities through April of 1941. Shortly before the show closed in Munich, Ziegler's office appointed Hartmut Pistauer as the exhibition coordinator. It was his job to make the arrangements for each venue, supervise the installation, and greet any important party visitors at the opening (fig. 16) on behalf of the Propagandaministerium (Ministry of propaganda).[26]

When *Entartete Kunst* opened in Munich, no catalogue was available. Shortly before the exhibition closed in November, a thirty-two page booklet was published to accompany the touring presentation. This *Ausstellungsführer* (exhibition guide) stated the aims of the exhibition and reproduced excerpts from Hitler's speeches condemning the art and the artists that

Figure 15
View of a portion of the south wall of Room 3; work by Baum, Belling, Campendonk, Dexel, Felixmüller, Eugen Hoffmann, Klee, and Nolde.

produced it. Some of the same quotations that were used on the walls in Munich found their way into the booklet, and Schultze-Naumburg's technique of juxtaposition was prominently featured: images of art by the mentally ill from the Prinzhorn Collection were placed next to photographs of works by Rudolf Haizmann, Eugen Hoffmann, Klee, and Kokoschka, with captions such as, "Which of these three drawings is the work of . . . an inmate of a lunatic asylum?" Although not all the works illustrated in the booklet were included in *Entartete Kunst,* all were by artists who were represented in the exhibition. The cover featured *Der neue Mensch* (The new man), a famous sculpture (later destroyed) by the Jewish artist Otto Freundlich, with the words *Entartete "Kunst"* partly obscuring the image. By printing *Kunst* to look as if it had been rudely scrawled in red crayon and by enclosing it in quotation marks, the National Socialists clearly made the point that although they considered this material degenerate, they certainly did not consider it art.

One of the inevitable questions about the *Entartete Kunst* exhibition concerns its purpose. Why did the National Socialists go to such an effort to mount, publicize, and circulate it? What did they hope to gain? One explanation at least offers itself. If the Nazis had merely confiscated and destroyed the art, it would have been the cultural equivalent of creating a martyr. By staging *Entartete Kunst* they were able to appeal to the majority of the German people who must have considered most modern art incomprehensible and elitist. To all modernists, not

Figure 16
Hartmut Pistauer (in dark suit, center) leads Nazi party officials through the Düsseldorf venue of *Entartete Kunst,* 1938; work by Gies and Nolde can be seen in the background.

just those represented in *Entartete Kunst,* the Nazis sent the message that such art would no longer be tolerated in Germany, an official position that, thanks to the cleverly manipulated complicity of the German people, had the force of a popular mandate.

One thing that emerges from any examination of the cultural activities in Germany under the National Socialists is that, despite every attempt to provide rigorous definitions of "healthy" and "degenerate" art and to remove all traces of the latter from public view, the actions against modern visual arts (as well as those against literature, music, and film) were enormously problematic and contradictory. Ultimately, however, the brilliant flowering of modernism in Germany that had begun in the early years of the century came to a halt in 1937 with the opening of *Entartete Kunst* and the *Grosse Deutsche Kunstausstellung*. Artists, writers, filmmakers, poets, musicians, critics, and intellectuals of all disciplines were forced to take drastic action, either to emigrate or to resort to a deadening "inner immigration." Much of the confiscated art was destroyed or has vanished, and many of the most powerfully creative artists of Germany's golden era were broken in spirit, forced to flee, or killed. But the art, the documents, and the memories that have survived enable us to reconstruct the era and ensure that, in the end, the National Socialists failed—the modern art of Germany was not and will never be eradicated. Collectively, the works of art and the pieced-together fragments of history remind us that art may be enjoyed or abhorred but it is a force whose potency should never be underestimated.

It is ironic that some of the issues raised by an examination of these events should have such resonance today in America. Newspaper articles on public support for the arts and the situation facing the National Endowment for the Arts emphasize an uncomfortable parallel between these issues and those raised by the 1937 exhibition, between the enemies of artistic freedom today and those responsible for organizing the *Entartete Kunst* exhibition. Perhaps after a serious look at events that unfolded over half a century ago in Germany, we may apply what we learn to our own predicament, in which for the first time in the postwar era the arts and freedom of artistic expression in America are facing a serious challenge.

Notes

1. Hildegard Brenner, *Die Kunstpolitic des Nationalsozialismus* (Reinbek: Rowohlt, 1963), 109

2. While all accounts from the immediate postwar era confirm this event, first reported by Paul Ortwin Rave in 1949 (*Kunstdiktatur im Dritten Reich* [Hamburg: Gebrüder Mann]), more recent works by authors including Georg Bussmann and Eckhardt Klessman have questioned whether there was in fact such a wholesale destruction of works of art; see Bussmann, "'Degenerate Art': A Look at a Useful Myth," in *German Art in the 20th Century: Painting and Sculpture 1905–1985* (exh cat., London: Royal Academy of Arts, 1985), 113–24, and Klessmann, "Barlach in der Barbarei," *Frankfurter Allgemeine Zeitung*, December 13, 1983, literary supplement. In Sofie Fohn's recently published account of her and her husband's art exchanges with Berlin in the late 1930s she challenged the Nazis' contention that approximately five thousand works were burned on March 20, 1939, and suggested that only the frames may have been destroyed in the fire; see Carla Schultz-Hoffmann, ed., *Die Sammlung Sofie und Emanuel Fohn: Eine Dokumentation* (Munich: Hirmer, 1990), 27.

3. Carl Einstein, *Die Kunst des 20. Jahrhunderts* (Berlin. Propyläen, 1926, 2d ed. 1928, 3d ed. 1931, Leipzig: Reclam, 1988); Berthold Hinz, *Art in the Third Reich* (New York: Random House, 1979), 24.

4. Hellmut Lehmann-Haupt, *Art under a Dictatorship* (New York: Oxford University Press, 1954), 3.

5 Ibid., 45–46.

6. In 1909 Julius Langbehn published *Rembrandt als Erzieher* (Rembrandt as teacher) and in 1928 his *Dürer als Führer* (Dürer as leader), completed by Momme Nissen, was issued posthumously; these two immensely popular books made strong appeals to German nationalism in art.

7. For a particularly helpful analysis of Nordau's book see George L. Mosse's introduction to the 1968 English edition (Max Nordau, *Degeneration* {New York: Howard Fertig, 1968}.

8. George Bernard Shaw, "The Sanity of Art: An Exposure of the Current Nonsense about Artists Being Degenerate," in *Major Citical Essays* (London: Constable and Company, 1932, St. Clair Shores, Mich.: Scholarly Press, 1976), 281–332.

9. See Theodor Kirchhoff, *Handbook of Insanity for Practitioners and Students* (New York: William Wood, 1893), and Richard M. Goodman, *Genetic Disorders among the Jewish People* (Baltimore: Johns Hopkins University Press, 1979), 421–31. The term *corruzione* (corruption) had been used by the seventeenth-century Italian critic Giovanni Pietro Bellori in an attack on Vasari and Michelangelo.

10. Sander Gilman, "Madness and Representation: Hans Prinzhorn's Study of Madness and Art in Its Historical Context," in *The Prinzborn Collection* (exh. cat., Champaigne Ill.: Krannert Art Museum, 1984), 7–14; idem, "The Mad Man as Artist: Medicine, History, and Degenerate Art," *Journal of Contemporary History* 20 (1985): 575–97.

11. Alfred Rosenberg. *"Race and Race History" and Other Essays,* ed. Robert Pois (New York: Harper and Row, 1970), 154.

12. Hans Prinzhorn, *Bildnerei der Geisteskranken: Ein Beitrag zur Psychologie and Psychopathologie der Gestaltung* (Berlin: Julius Springer, 1922), published in English as *Aritistry of the Mentally Ill: A Contribution to the Psychology and Psychopathology of Configuration,* trans. Eric von Brockdorff (New York Springer, 1972).

13. Hildegard Brenner, Barbara Miller Lane, and George L. Mosse have described the conflict and power struggle between Rosenberg and Goebbels over modern art, particularly German Expressionism and Italian Futurism; see Lane, *Architecture and Politics in Germany 1918–45* (Cambridge: Harvard University Press, 1968); Brenner, "Art in the Political Struggle of 1933–34," in Hajo Holborn, ed., *From Republic to Reich: The Making of the Nazi Revolution* (New York: Pantheon, 1972), 395–434; and Mosse, *Nazi Culture: Intellectual, Cultural, and Social Life in the Third Reich* (New York: Schocken Books, 1981).

14. Paul Ortwin Rave, *Kunstdiktatur in Dritten Reich,* rev. ed, ed. Uwe M. Schneede (Berlin: Argon, 1987), 103–4

15. Alfred Bart, Jr., *Modern German Painting and Sculpture* (exh. cat., New York Musuem of Modern Art, 1933), 7–8. Barr also indicated which German museums collected examples by each artist.

16. "European Works at Buchholz," *New York World-Telegram,* September 30, 1939.

17. Hans-Jürgen Buderer, *"Entartete Kunst." Beschlagnahme in der Städtische Kunsthalle Mannheim* 1937, Kunst + Documentation, no. 10 (exh. cat., Mannheim. Städtische Kunsthalle Mannheim, 1987). I am grateful to Dr. Manfred Fath, director of the Kunsthalle Mannheim, for permission to examine museum files related to the "degenerate" art action.

For recent publication on the special situation in other museums mentioned see the following. Essen: Paul Vogt, ed., *Dokumente zur Geschichte des Museum Folkwang 1942–1945* (Essen: Museum Folkwang, 1983); Halle: Andreas Hüneke, *Die faschistische Aktion "Entartete Kunst" 1937* in *Halle,* (Halle: Staatliche Galerie Moritzburg, 1987); Hannover: *Beschlagnahme-Aktion im Landesmuseum Hannover 1937* (exh. cat., Hannover: Landesmuseum Hannover, 1983).

In addition to the acknowledgments I have made elsewhere in these notes, I would like to thank Markus Kersting of the Städtische Galerie in Frankfurt for providing data on the purchases of Georg Swarzenski and to Hans Göpfert of the Staatliche Kunst-sammlung Dresden for details on the collecting and exhibitions there in the 1920s and 1930s. Contemporary articles in the journals *Museum der Gegenwart* and *Die Kunst für Alle* also provided much background information.

18. Buderer, *"Entartete Kunst,"* 8.

19. Ibid, 11.

20. Hinz, *Art of the Third Reich,* 163.

21. Rave, *Kunstdikatur,* 54.

22. *Die Tagebücher von Joseph Goebbels: Sämtliche Fragment,* ed. Elke Fröhlich (Munich: G.K. Saur, 1987), pt 1, vol. 3, 166.

23. Adolf Hitler, speech at the opening of the Haus der Deutschen Kunst, Munich, July 18, 1937; cited and translated in Lehmann-Haupt, *Art under a Dictatorship.* 76–77.

24. Jonathan Petropoulos, "Art as Politics: The Nazi Elite's Quest for the Political and Material Control of Art" (Ph.D. diss., Harvard University, 1990).

25. Joseph Goebbels, decree sent to all major museums, June 30, 1937; a copy is preserved in the archives of the Bayerische Staatsgemäldesammlungen, Munich, Akt 712a. 12.7.1937, Nr. 1983; cited in Mario-Andreas von Lüttichau, " 'Deutsche Kunst' und 'Entartete Kunst': Die Münchner Ausstellungen 1937," in Peter-Klaus Schuster, ed., *Die "Kunststadt" München 1937: Nationalsozialismus und "Entartete Kunst"* (Munich: Prestel, 1987), 92.

26. I am indebted to Christoph Zuschlag who first brought Pistauer and his role in *Entartete Kunst* to my attention.

Beauty without Sensuality: The Exhibition *Entartete Kunst*

George L. Mosse

The National Socialist standards for art were based upon the idealized figures and sentimental landscapes that had informed nineteenth-century popular taste and upon the neoclassical themes that were Adolf Hitler's favorites. National Socialism annexed neoromantic and neoclassical art, defining it as racially pure, an art that could easily be understood and whose depictions of men and women exemplified the Germanic race. This was the official art that dominated the annual *Grosse Deutsche Kunstausstellung* (Great German art exhibition) in Munich, beginning in 1937, for which the paintings and sculptures were often selected by Hitler himself.

There was deeper purpose to the acceptance of such art: it symbolized a certain standard of beauty that might serve to cement the unity of the nation by projecting a moral standard to which everyone should aspire. Respectability was to inform personal and public morality, which true art must support. The men and women in Nazi painting and sculpture thus embodied the proper morality and sexual behavior. Beauty without sensuality was demanded of artists and sculptors, a beauty that had to reflect the generally accepted moral standards that the Nazis championed as their own. For it was the strength and appeal of National Socialism that it did not invent anything new in its effort at self-representation but simply appropriated long-standing popular tradition and taste.

The *Entartete Kunst* exhibition was staged in 1937 as a foil to the *Grosse Deutsche Kunstausstellung*. Painting and sculpture that supposedly reflected life in the Weimar Republic (1919–33) were displayed as concrete evidence that the Nazis had saved German society from Weimar's onslaught upon all the moral values people held dear: marriage, the family, chastity, and a steady, harmonious life. Weimar culture was "Bolshevist" culture, manipulated by the Jews, as the guide to the exhibition and the inscriptions on the gallery walls stated repeatedly. The destruction of respectability and the destruction of society and the nation were linked.

The exhibition must not be seen simply as Nazi propaganda, for it played upon basic moral attitudes that inform all modern societies. The concept of respectability has lasted, after all; even today art is condemned if it transgresses the normative morality in too shocking a fashion. That *Entartete Kunst* exists in a continuum is demonstrated by the controversy in 1980 over Robert Mapplethorpe's homoerotic photographs, which were thought to offend against public decency. Beauty with sensuality presented a danger to society because of what it symbolized, namely, a revolt against respectability as a principle of unity and order—thus, the destruction of the immutable values upon which society supposedly rested. If we are to understand the true significance of the *Entartete Kunst* exhibition, we must examine the relevant history in order to see how the forces of respectability coped with their "enemies" and what was at stake, for the exhibition itself was like the tip of an iceberg, and that iceberg has not yet melted.

Hitler pointed out at the 1934 Nazi party rally in Nuremberg that "anyone who seeks the new for its own sake strays all too easily into the realm of folly," a remark that was printed in the *Entartete Kunst* exhibition guide. What was at issue was art as the expression of supposedly unchanging values in a society in search of such values. The modern age seemed to threaten the coherence of life itself. The accelerated pace of industrial and technological change in the nineteenth and twentieth centuries produced a certain disorientation, a "simultaneity of experience" with which people had to cope. By the mid-nineteenth century there were already complaints that railroad travel had destroyed nature, as the landscape performed a wild dance before the trains' windows. Just so, the invention of the telephone, the motorcar, and the cinema introduced a new velocity of time that menaced the unhurried pace of life in an earlier age. Such concerns were reflected in a heightened quest for order in the face of instability.

Respectability ensured security, order, and the maintenance of values, taming the chaos that seemed always to threaten society; it reflected people's attitudes toward themselves and toward all that was "different." The enemies of respectability, it was said, could not control themselves: they were creatures of instinct, with unbridled passions. Such accusations were scarcely to be found before the age of the French Revolution, but from then on they became common: whether it was Englishmen at the time of the Napoleonic wars claiming that the French were sending dancers to England to undermine the islanders' morality or whether it was First World War propaganda seeking by means of words and pictures to impute to the enemy every kind of so-called sexual perversion, respectability was made a political issue from the very beginning.

During the course of the nineteenth century an increasingly clear distinction was drawn between "normal" and "immoral" behavior, "normal" and "abnormal" sexuality. It was doctors, above all, using categories of health and sickness, who threw their weight behind society's constantly threatened moral norms, lending them legitimacy and thus defining the stereotypes of abnormality.

Those whom society treated as outsiders were now credited with all those characteristics that ran counter to society's image of itself. The mentally ill, Jews, homosexuals, and habitual criminals were all said to be physically unbalanced. Nervousness had been designated a serious illness—one that unleashed the passions—by the famous French neurologist Jean-Martin Charcot in the 1880s. It was now seen as the chief threat to mainstream bourgeois morality, which emphasized steadiness and restraint. Sharing the iconography of illness in general—exhaustion, contortions, and grimaces—nervousness was thought to symbolize the opposite of normative standards of beauty. The *Entartete Kunst* exhibition was built upon such views of the outsider, using modern art to construct a "chamber of horrors."

Looked at closely, nervousness itself was seen as a product of modernity. The outsiders were always city-dwellers (fig. 1), further proof that they scorned the tranquillity of eternal values: for them, time never stood still. One of the most despicable Nazi propagandists, Johann von Leers, expressed it in this way, no doubt speaking for many others in doing so: the city was the refuge of immorality and crime, and it was here that the "Jewish conspiracy" tried to gain control over German hearts and minds in order to drive them insane with frenzy and

Figure 1
Urban scene from the film *Der Tunnel* (The tunnel), 1933.

lust. For all its exaggeration and racial hatred, this view was still indebted to the nineteenth-century notion of respectability with its emphasis on controlling the passions and on the consequences of losing that control. There is a continuity here that we constantly encounter: the National Socialists' attitude toward sexuality cannot be separated from the general history of respectability.

Degeneration was, in its modern sense, a medical term used during the second half of the nineteenth century to identify the condition of those who had departed from the "normal" because of shattered nerves, inherited abnormalities, or behavioral or sexual excess. Degenerates could be identified by their bodily deformities, red eyes, feebleness, and exhaustion. Such conditions signaled the start of a process that would inevitably lead to destruction. What haunted society from the *fin de siècle* onward was the fear that not only humans but nations as well could degenerate, a process thought to have begun already because of the falling birth rates in France and other countries. Those who refused to conform to the moral dictates of society were labeled "degenerate," and as they themselves were doomed to destruction they might destroy society as well.

The physician Max Nordau in his book *Entartung* (Degeneration) of 1892 did much to popularize the term in its application to modern literature and art, modern artists, whether Impressionists or Expressionists, were incapable of reproducing nature because they had lost the faculty of accurate observation and painted instead distorted and irregular forms mirroring their own nervous deformities and stunted growth. In Hitler's view the artists in the 1937 exhibition symbolized degeneracy: "And what do you create?" the exhibition guide quotes Hitler as asking "Misshapen cripples and cretins, women who can arouse only revulsion . . . as the expression of all that molds and sets its stamp on the present age." Against a background of attempts to define the boundaries of bourgeois morality, Hitler's pronouncement resurrects the nineteenth- and early twentieth-century iconography of the outsider as described by physicians such as Nordau. Moreover, it had the effect of advancing a certain concept of beauty as a readily understood symbol of society's values.

The ideal of beauty played a dominant role as a symbol of morality, extending far beyond the realm of art: beauty helped to maintain control over the passions. Friedrich Schiller, for example, in his series of letters *Über die aesthetische Erziehung des Menschen* (On the aesthetic education of mankind) of 1795 wrote that beauty ennobled the otherwise merely instinctive sexual act, transcending it by virtue of its external values. But what is "beauty"? This question penetrated to the very heart of society's morals. In neoromantic or neoclassical art beauty became the self-portrait of society, the view it liked to have of itself.

How deeply respectability and its concept of beauty were embedded in society can be inferred from the ways in which the concept was presented long before National Socialism. At the beginning of the nineteenth century it was religion, especially Protestantism, that took upon itself the task of promoting respectability, whereas by the end of the century that role had been assigned to the people themselves. The stricter attitude toward sodomy, which was made a criminal offense in many countries in *fin de siècle* Europe, appealed no longer to religious but to supposed popular sentiment. The clear and unambiguous distinction between the socially normal and the so-called deviant—a distinction that was now supported medically and icono-graphically as well as by religion and education—had been internalized. (Propagandaminister Joseph Goebbels knew he was risking very little when, in 1936, he banned art criticism on the grounds that the general public should make up its own mind; that year more paintings offered at the annual exhibition of German art were sold than at almost all earlier exhibitions.)

The achievement of beauty without sensuality presented a special challenge in the repre-sentation of the ideal male, who, inspired by Greek models, was often represented in the nude (fig. 2). The evolution of bourgeois morality was contemporaneous with the rediscovery of clas-sical sculpture. J. J. Winckelmann, describing Greek male statuary as the paradigm of beauty for all time in his *Geschichte der Kunst des Alterthums* (History of the art of antiquity) of 1774, made this art acceptable to the middle classes by raising nudity to an abstract plane and turn-ing it into a stylistic principle. Such beauty was perceived as somehow sexless, a conviction shared by others at a later date, aided by the belief that the almost transparent whiteness of these figures raised them above the personal and sensual. At roughly the same time Winckel-mann wrote his famous book, Johann Wolfgang von Goethe wrote, "Apollo Belvedere, why do you show yourself to us in all your nudity, making us ashamed of our own nakedness?" Male symbolism could not be stripped of all physicality; the beauty of the Greek youths—lithe and supple, muscular and harmonious bodies—lay in their nakedness. It was precisely the corpo-reality of the sculpture that expressed strength and harmony, order and dynamism, in other words, the ideal qualities of both burgher and nation (fig. 3). For the Nazis such men symbolized the true German upon whose commitment the Third Reich depended.

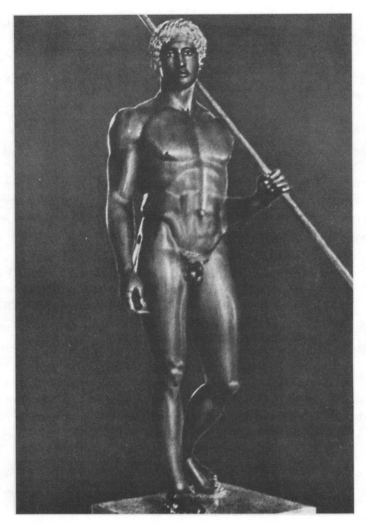

Figure 2
Speerträger (Spear-bearer), copy of the *Doryphobus* by Polyclitus (c. 450–420 B.C.), monument to the fallen of the First World War, bronze, formerly at the University of Munich.

From the moment when bourgeois morality was first established, the ideals of male and female beauty differed radically, a circumstance that largely determined the political role of women as a national symbol. The male was regarded as dynamic, promising to bring about a timeless order and cure an ailing world; Friedrich Theodor Vischer, the nineteenth century's foremost German writer on aesthetics, assigned to beauty and manliness the task of preventing chaos. Women, by contrast, were turned into passive figures such as Germania or Queen Luise of Prussia (1776–1810), who was stylized as the "Prussian Madonna." While the male was often depicted nude, the woman was almost always fully clothed, at least to the extent that she functioned as a national symbol. And yet, for all their differences, public representations of men and women had one important point in common: they transcended sensuality.

THINKING, MAKING, DOING

Figure 3
Richard Scheibe, figure from an unidentified war memorial, bronze, location unknown.

The nakedness of the male stereotype displayed on so many Nazi buildings and monuments, however, never lost its unsettling and latently threatening effect. In this context it is not without significance that nudism was banned immediately after the Nazis came to power (it was said to deaden women's natural shame). On much the same level was a warning issued by the Reichsministerium des Innern (Reich ministry of the interior) in 1935 to the effect that nude bathing by people of the same sex could be seen as the first step toward the violation of Paragraph 175, which punished homosexual acts.

In its attempt to strip nakedness of its sensuality the Third Reich drew a sharp distinction between private life and public representation. Arno Breker's nude male sculptures (fig. 18) continued to be in official demand, and statues of seminude men and women still decorated public spaces. But it was an abstract, smooth, almost transparent nakedness and a frozen posture achieved by recourse to Winckelmann's purified concept of beauty.

The Nazis encouraged physical training, and here the problem of nudity arose once more. Hans Surén in his *Gymnastik der Deutschen* (German gymnastics) of 1938, a book that went through several editions during the Third Reich, exemplified the effort to divest the nude body of its sensuous appeal in this particular setting. He advocated nearly complete nudity in the pursuit of sport or while roaming though the countryside, but the male body had to be carefully prepared before it could be offered to public scrutiny: the skin had to be hairless, smooth, and bronzed. The body had become an abstract symbol of Aryan beauty, as it was in Lent Riefenstahl's film of the 1936 Olympic Games. Sensuality was transcended by an alignment with Greek form figures that could be worshipped but neither desired nor loved.

And the Nazi view of women? Goebbels insisted that girls should be strong, healthy and good to look at, which meant that, as he put it, in contrast to the male, the muscles of their arms and legs should not be visible. (The importance of iconography can be judged by the extent to which the Nazis described physical detail.) But how could this ideal of womankind be reconciled with the naked sports-woman, for the latter did indeed exist. The simple answer was that the female athlete's body was often approximated to that of the male. Without emphasizing the obvious feminine contours, it was thus, in principle, identical to that of the male youth in nakedness without sensuality.

While, on the one hand, Goebbels launched his attacks on "sports girls," on the other, the Bund Deutscher Mädel (League of German girls) was liberating the mass of young girls for the first time in their history from some home and family restraints, an act of emancipation achieved through sports and country walks. The National Socialist view of women was clearly not free of incongruity. Perhaps the reason for this is that National Socialism was based on a consciously male society that often behaved in a contradictory way toward women. Male homosexuality, for example, was ruthlessly persecuted, but the same was not true of lesbianism, which was ignored as a punishable crime.

In the depiction of women the main concern was, once again, to separate private from public representation. In the private sphere women could be completely naked and sensual, for how else can we interpret the paintings by Hitler's favorite artist, Adolf Ziegler (fig. 4)— paintings that hung not only in the Führer's private apartments but also in the *Grosse Deutsche*

THINKING, MAKING, DOING

Kunslausstellung? Ziegler's fleshy and often full-bosomed nudes, who left nothing to the imagination, hung side by side with typical chaste German maidens with blonde plaits. Public representation was political representation, however, and here the aim was to integrate the masses into the Third Reich with the aid of stereotypes that would treat the beautiful as a reflection of the eternal and immutable, revealing it as something pure and removed from all materialism and sensuality.

The ideal of manly beauty must be seen in contrast to the weak, exhausted, unmuscular figure of the outsider. The youthfulness of the male stereotype symbolized the dynamic of bourgeois society and of the nation as well, outsider figures, by contrast, were generally old. We find very few young Jews represented in nineteenth-century German drama, for example: they were almost without exception old and lonely.

Figure 4
Adolf Ziegler, *Akt* (Nude), 1939; oil on canvas, 86 × 145 cm (33 7/8 × 57 1/8 in); Bayerische Staatsgemäldesammlungen, Munich (on deposit).

Society expressed its morality in terms of generally accepted ideals of beauty while projecting its fears and ideas of ugliness onto the very groups the National Socialists were eventually determined to exterminate: Jews, homosexuals, habitual criminals, and the mentally disturbed. Even before the Nazis' electoral victory in 1930, Alfred Rosenberg, the Nazi ideologist, had written in his book about the Weimar Republic, *Der Sumpf* (The swamp): "Democracy has apparently been stabilized. Yet with its pederasty, lesbianism, and procuration it has been defeated all along the line."

The open homosexuality of Ernst Röhm, the powerful chief of the SA (Sturmabteilung, storm troops), and other SA leaders was indicative of the ambivalent attitude toward bourgeois respectability on the part of some members of the early National Socialist movement. This is true of Hitler himself, who defended Röhm against attack by declaring that the latter's private life was his own affair as long as he used some discretion. When, in 1934, Hitler ordered the murder of Röhm and other leaders of the SA who were known homosexuals, it had in fact little to do with their sexual inclinations: the SA was by then threatening Hitler's own power and destroying his relationship with the regular army. Be that as it may, the opportunity was seized to underline the role of the party and the regime as the defenders of respectability. Mock trials were held in which Catholic priests were accused of homosexuality, and the family was given a central role in National Socialist propaganda.

The foundations for such developments had been laid immediately after Hitler took power on January 30, 1933. As early as February 23 all so-called pornographic literature had been banned and prostitution drastically curbed. It is no wonder that organizations such as the Deutsch-Evangelische Sittlichkeitsbewegung (German evangelical morality league) welcomed Hitler's seizure of power, since it apparently brought an end to the moral chaos of the postwar period, and this was by no means the only organization of its kind that supported the Nazis in their self-styled role as the saviors of bourgeois morality. (Was it only Albert Speer's mother who voted for the Nazis because their youngsters marching though the streets of Berlin looked so neat?) Hitler himself boasted that with his advent the "nervous nineteenth century" had finally come to an end. But a threat to respectability remained.

The Nazi party sought to build upon wartime experiences by first presenting itself as a continuation of the male camaraderie that had existed in the trenches. Even when it broadened its base of appeal, it never lost the character of a *Männerbund,* a league of men, an institution that had a long tradition in Germany. Important subgroups of the party such as the SA or the SS (Schutzstaffel, elite guard) were proud of being male organizations that excluded "unmanly" men. But such conscious male bonding seemed to raise the danger of homoeroticism or even homosexuality, a possibility that frightened some of the leadership.

The driving force behind the purge of all that might pose a threat to respectability was Heinrich Himmler, the leader of the SS, who more clearly than anyone else articulated the sexual policies of the Third Reich and thus revealed its underlying fears. (These same fears were also behind the organization of *Entartete Kunst,* which was an attempt to demonstrate the consequences of the rejection of social and sexual norms.) Himmler's obsessional regard for respectability and his fear of all sensuality encouraged him to magnify the homoerotic and homosexual potentialities of the *Männerbund*, including his own SS, which often represented itself symbolically as an idealized seminude male. If he emphasized the contrast between homosexuality and manliness, it was because of his fear that the one could easily turn into the other. At the same time he affirmed that the Third Reich was a state based upon the comradeship of men and that indeed "for centuries, yea, millennia, the Germans have been ruled as a *Männerstaat*" [state of men].

But that state was now threatened with self-destruction as a result of homosexuality, as Himmler made clear in November 1937 in a speech delivered to the SS leadership in Bad Tölz. He regarded homosexuality as a sickness that poisoned both body and mind (he even suggested prostitution—otherwise strictly prohibited—as a remedy), but he now went a stage further and drew on the imagery of the "natural" and "unnatural." In the good old days of the Teutonic tribes, Himmler told his Bad Tölz audience, homosexuals were drowned in the swamps: "This was no punishment, but simply the extinction of abnormal life." Nature rectified her own mistake, and Himmler lamented that this kind of extinction was no longer possible. For him, deviants from the sexual norm were not only outsiders, they were also racial enemies. The desire for their deaths, presented here as the goal of the struggle for purity and respectability, points the way to the Holocaust.

It must be stressed that doctors such as Charcot who described Jews as particularly subject to nervous diseases had never for a moment thought of killing them; for Charcot, anyone who was ill could be cured. It was racism that determined Himmler's offensive against outsiders, but it was also the wish to protect respectability, no matter what the price.

All this is the indispensable background to the *Entartete Kunst* exhibition. It was designed to be out of the ordinary, a survey of all that was indecent and ugly, all that represented an assault on bourgeois morality through the latter's concept of beauty. Works by modern artists were treated not as evidence of individual creativity but as representative of something undesirable; they were accorded no individual value, only a symbolic status. This, of course, made a mockery of those artists who vaunted their individuality above all else. It was the reaction of a society that felt itself to be under a constant threat, a society, moreover, that was bonded together by respectability and the security that it radiated. Morality and its symbols, of which beauty was the positive and nervousness the negative, were an issue of the first order in an age when society believed itself on the very brink of chaos as a result of the pace of change and the Great War. In this context the concept of "degenerate art" merely added to the general sense of anxiety.

And yet foreign newspapers reported in 1937 that far more people had visited *Entartete Kunst* than the parallel exhibition devoted to officially approved German art. According to the *Manchester Guardian* there were five times as many visitors to *Entartete Kunst* each day, while the *New York Times* reported that there had been 396,000 visitors, as opposed to 120,000 at the *Grosse Deutsche Kunstausstellung*, within the space of a week. What was the explanation? It is a question that is difficult to answer, but it is unlikely that an interest in modern art played any part. The Nazis themselves encouraged people to visit the exhibition. Had the latent temptation to act unconventionally—a temptation almost encouraged by the Reich's anti-bourgeois rhetoric—become acute once more?

Respectability and all that it implied remained an essential part of the regime, and in the exhibition guide all those outsiders who had threatened society's conformist principles since the beginning of the last century were blamed for the degeneration of art. The paintings on display were presented as the work of madmen disfigured by sexual excesses, they represented Marxist and Jewish attacks on all that was German. The texts of the guide summed up a tradition that drew an increasingly sharp distinction between respectability—that is, normality—and abnormality, between the healthy and the sick, and between the natural and the unnatural. By embracing the respectable, people could resist the chaos of the age embodied by "degenerate" art and accept a "slice of eternity" into their lives. What was sacrificed in the process was sensuality, passion, and, to a great extent, individuality itself.

The analysis of "beauty without sensuality" undertaken here can be seen as a critique of bourgeois morality and, finally, of the never-ending attempt to distinguish between this morality, viewed as the norm, and what was seen as "abnormal." But we must never forget that for most people respectability was and is much more than merely a form of behavior or an ideal of beauty; for many, perhaps even for the vast majority, it offers cogent proof of the cohesiveness of society, a cohesiveness necessary for all systems of government, not just for National Socialism. Hence, the favorable response encountered by the premise of the *Entartete Kunst* exhibition, even in places where we would least expect it: the London *New Statesman*, for example, a left-wing journal, wrote that the exhibition was the best thing Mr. Hitler had done so far.

The smooth functioning of a generally accepted morality was just as important for the cohesion of society as the more often cited economic and social factors. At the same time it was something that people understood, something that impinged on their daily lives in a wholly concrete and comprehensive way. The ideal of beauty as the exemplification of society's norms was influenced not only by sentimentalism and romanticism, it had a social function as well. The aesthetics of politics, of daily life, had involved a degree of social control ever since bourgeois morality first came into being. Not only the works of art but much of the popular literature was filled with passion and love that were supposedly devoid of sensuality. For example, Agnes Günther's novel *Die Heilige and ihr Narr* (The saint and her fool, 1913), a runaway best-seller during the Weimar Republic, was a sentimental love story in which sensuality was equated with sickness. The representational art and the literature of the time fell readily into a tradition that the National Socialists merely took to its extreme.

And today? If my analysis is correct, I can only say that the same social needs still exist, that our modern tolerance toward the individual and sensuality is more an extension of what is permissible than an actual breach in the principle of respectability. There may be additional proof of this in the fact that after periods of sexual tolerance the limits are always reimposed. We are seeing this rhythm repeated today in episodes like that of the Mapplethorpe exhibition and in the continued effort in the United States to control the erotic content of publicly funded art.

Marcel Proust gave perhaps the finest expression to that reciprocal relationship between conformism and tolerance that we can see all around us: Swann, the Jewish hero of *À la recherche du temps perdu,* is welcomed among the aristocratic and snobbish Guermantes as an exotic plant until he becomes a Dreyfusard, defending the captain against his reactionary accusers, at which point they see him as a threat to their political and social position. This seems to me to symbolize the reality of a situation in which we continue to find ourselves: bourgeois morality, once a newcomer in our midst, now appears so much a part of the way we see ourselves, so essential to our society, that we can scarcely imagine a different kind of morality, with the result that we have forgotten that, like everything else in this world, it is the result of historical evolution.

NOTE

This is a revised version of the author's article "Schönheit ohne Sinnlichkeit: Nationalsozialismus und Sexualität," *Zeitmitschrift,* special ed., 1987, 96–109. See also his *Nationalism and Sexuality: Respectability and Abnormal Sexuality in Modern Europe* (Madison: University of Wisconsin Press, 1988).

Figure 5
The vilification of jazz in the exhibition *Entartete Musik,* Kunstpalast Ehrenhof, Düsseldorf, 1938.

Speech of 19 July 1937

Adolf Hitler

What then were the criteria used by the Nazis to define what was or what was not artistically desirable? As an artist manqué, Hitler had strong views about art and, although he rarely intervened directly, it was his views, to which he gave vent in a number of speeches, which provided the basis of Nazi cultural policy. In his speech of 19 July 1937, opening the House of German Art in Munich, which was intended to house the officially approved art, he contrasted his own view of the artistic ideal with that expressed by the modern artists whose works were being displayed simultaneously in another building in an exhibition of 'Degenerate Art' organized by Adolf Ziegler, President of the Reich Chamber of Art:

. . . But the House is not enough: it must house an exhibition, and if now I venture to speak of art I can claim a title to do so from the contribution which I myself have made to the restoration of German art. For our modern German State, which I with my associates have created, has alone brought into existence the conditions for a new and vigorous flowering of art. It is not Bolshevist art collectors or their henchmen who have laid the foundations, for we have provided vast sums for the encouragement of art and have set before art itself great, new tasks. As in politics, so in German art-life, we are determined to make a clean sweep of empty phrases. Ability is the necessary qualification if an artist wishes his work to be exhibited here. People have attempted to recommend modern art by saying that it is the expression of a new age; but art does not create a new age, it is the general life of peoples which fashions itself anew and often looks for a new expression. . . . A new epoch is not created by *littérateurs* but by the fighters, those who really fashion and lead people, and thus make history. . . . It is either impudent effrontery or an almost inconceivable stupidity to exhibit to people of today works which perhaps ten or twenty thousand years ago might have been made by a man of the Stone Age. They talk of primitive art, but they forget that is is not the function of art to retreat backwards from the development of a people: its sole function must be to symbolize that living development.

The new age of today is at work on a new human type. Men and women are to be healthier and stronger. There is a new feeling of life, a new joy in life. Never was humanity in its external appearance and in its frame of mind nearer to the ancient world than it is today. . . . This, my good prehistoric art stutterers, is the type of the new age, but what do you manufacture? Misformed cripples and cretins, women who inspire only disgust, men who are more like wild beasts, children who, were they alive, must be regarded as under God's curse. And let no one tell me that that is how these artists see things. From the pictures sent in for exhibition it is clear that the eye of some men portrays things otherwise than as they are, that there really are men who on principle feel meadows to be blue, the heaven green, clouds sulphur-yellow, or, as perhaps they prefer to say, 'experience' them thus. I need not ask whether they really do see or feel things in this way, but in the name of the German people I have only to prevent these miserable unfortunates, who clearly suffer from defects of vision, attempting with violence to persuade contemporaries by their chatter that these faults of observation are indeed realities or from presenting them as 'art.' There are only two possibilities here. Either these 'artists' do really see things in this way and believe in what they represent. Then one has only to ask how the defect in vision arose, and if it is hereditary the Minister for the Interior will have to see to it that so ghastly a defect of vision shall not be allowed to perpetuate itself. Or if they do *not* believe in the reality of such impressions but seek on other grounds to burden the nation with this humbug, then it is a matter for a criminal court. There is no place for such works in this building. The industry of architects and workmen has not been employed to house canvases daubed over in five hours, the patients being assured that the boldness of the pricing could not fail to produce its effect, that the canvas would be hailed as the most brilliant lightning creation of a genius. No, they can be left to cackle over each other's eggs!

The artist does not create for the artist. He creates for the people, and we will see to it that the people in future will be called in to judge his art. No one must say that the people has no understanding for a really valuable enrichment of its cultural life. Before the critics did justice to the genius of a Richard Wagner, he had the people on his side, whereas the people has had nothing to do with so-called 'modern art.' The people has regarded this art as the outcome of an impudent and shameless arrogance or of a simply deplorable lack of skill. It has felt that this art stammer, these achievements which might have been produced by untalented children of eight to ten years old, could never be considered an expression of our own times or of the German future. When we know today that the development of millions of years, compressed into a few decades, repeats itself in every individual, then this art, we realize, is not 'modern.' It is on the contrary to the highest degree 'archaic,' far older probably than the Stone Age. The people in passing through these galleries will recognize in me its own spokesman and counsellor. It will draw a sigh of relief and gladly express its agreement with this purification of art. And that is decisive: an art which cannot count on the readiest and most intimate agreement of the great mass of the people, an art which must rely upon the support of small cliques, is intolerable. Such an art only tries to confuse, instead of gladly reinforcing, the sure and healthy instinct of a people. The artist cannot stand aloof from his people. This exhibition is only a beginning, but the end of Germany's artistic stultification has begun. Now is the opportunity for youth to start its industrious apprenticeship, and when a sacred conscientiousness has at last come into its own, then I have no doubt that the Almighty from the mass of these decent creators of art will once more raise up individuals to the eternal starry heaven of the imperishable God-favoured artists of the great periods. We believe that especially today, when in so many spheres the highest individual achievements are being manifested, in art also the highest value of personality will once again assert itself.

Soviet Literature

Maxim Gorky 1934

. . . There is every ground for hoping that when the history of culture will have been written by the Marxists, we shall see that the role of the bourgeoisie in the process of cultural creation has been greatly exaggerated, especially in literature, and still more so in painting, where the bourgeoisie has always been the employer, and, consequently, the law-giver. The bourgeoisie has never had any proclivity towards the creation of culture—if this term be understood in a broader sense than as a mere steady development of the exterior material amenities of life and the growth of luxury. The culture of capitalism is nothing but a system of methods aimed at the physical and moral expansion and consolidation of the power of the bourgeoisie over the world, over men, over the treasures of the earth and the powers of nature. The meaning of the process of cultural development was never understood by the bourgeoisie as the need for the development of the whole mass of humanity. It is a well known fact that, by virtue of bourgeois economic policy, every nation organized as a state became hostile to its neighbours, while the less well organized races, especially the coloured peoples, served the bourgeoisie as slaves, disfranchised to an even greater extent than the bourgeoisie's own white-skinned slaves.

The peasants and the workers were deprived of the right to education—the right to develop the mind and will towards comprehension of life, towards altering the conditions of life, towards rendering their working surroundings more tolerable. The schools trained and are still training no one but obedient servants of capitalism, who believe in its inviolability and legitimacy. The need for "educating the people" was talked of and written about, and the progress of literacy was even boasted of, but in actual fact the working people were only being split up, imbued with the idea of incompatible distinctions between races, nations and religions. This doctrine is used to justify an inhuman colonial policy, which gives an ever wider scope to the insane lust for profit, to the idiotic greed of shopkeepers. This doctrine has been upheld by bourgeois science, which has even sunk so low as to assert that a negative attitude on the part of people of the Aryan race towards all others "has grown organically out of the metaphysical activity of the whole nation"—although it is quite obvious that if "the whole nation" has become infected with an infamous animal hostility towards the coloured races or the Semites, this infection has been engrafted on it in an actual, physical sense by the foul work of the bourgeoisie, wielding fire and sword. If we remember that the Christian church has turned this work into a symbol of the suffering of the loving son of god, the grim humour of it is exposed with disgusting transparency. We may note in passing that Christ, "the son of god," is the only "positive type" created by ecclesiastical literature, and this type of one who vainly seeks to reconcile all life's contradictions is an especially striking proof of this literature's creative feebleness . . .

Social and cultural progress develop normally only when the hands teach the head, after which the head, now grown more wise, teaches the hands, and the wise hands once again, this time even more effectually, promote the growth of the mind. This normal process of cultural growth in men of labour was in ancient times interrupted by causes of which you are aware. The head became severed from the hands, and thought from the earth. Speculative dreamers made their appearance among the mass of active men; they sought to explain the world and the growth of ideas in the abstract, independent of the labour processes, which change the world in conformity with the aims and interests of man. Their function at first was, probably, that of organizing labour experience; they were just such "illustrious men," heroes of labour, as we see now in our own day, in our country. And then, among these people, the source of all social ills was born—the temptation of one to wield power over many, the desire to lead an easy life at the expense of other men's labour, and a depraved, exaggerated notion of one's own individual strength, a notion that was originally fostered by the acknowledgment of exceptional abilities, although these abilities were but a concentration and reflection of the labour achievements of the working collective—the tribe or clan. The severance of labour from thought is attributed by historians of culture to the whole mass of primitive mankind, while the breeding of individualists is even credited to them as a positive achievement. The history of the development of individualism is given with splendid fullness and lucidity in the history of literature. I again call your attention, comrades, to the fact that folklore, i.e., the unwritten compositions of tolling man, has created the most profound, vivid and artistically perfect types of heroes. . . .

What has brought the literature of Europe to the state of creative impotence which it has revealed in the twentieth century? The liberty of art, the freedom of creative thought have been upheld with passionate redundance; all sorts of arguments have been produced to show that literature can exist and develop without reference to classes, that it is not dependent on social politics. This was bad policy, for it imperceptibly impelled many men of letters to constrict their observations of real life, within narrow bounds, to abstain from a broad and many-sided study of life, to shut themselves up "in the solitude of their soul," to confine themselves to a fruitless form of "self-cognition" by way of introspection and arbitrary thought, altogether detached from life. It has turned out, however, that people cannot be grasped apart from real life, which is steeped in politics through and through. It has turned out that man, no matter what crotchety ideas he may fabricate in regard to himself, still remains a social unit, and not a cosmic one, like the planets. And moreover it has turned out that individualism, which turns into egocentrism, breeds "superfluous people." . . .

Once, in ancient times, the unwritten artistic compositions of the working people represented the sole organizer of their experience, the embodiment of ideas in imagery and the spur to the working energy of the collective body. We should try to understand this. The object our country has set itself is to ensure the equal cultural education of all units, the equal acquaintance of all its members with the victories and achievements of labour, aspiring to convert the work of men into the art of controlling the forces of nature. We are more or less familiar with the process of the economic—and therefore political—stratification of people with the process by which the labouring people's right to the free development of their minds is usurped by others. When the task of interpreting the world became the affair of priests, the latter could arrogate it to themselves only by giving a metaphysical explanation of phenomena and of the resistance offered by the elemental forces of nature to the aims and energies of men of labour. This criminal process of excluding, debarring millions of people from the work of understanding the world, initiated in antiquity and continuing down to our own day, has resulted in hundreds of millions of people, divided by ideas of race, nationality and religion, remaining in a state of the most profound ignorance, of appalling mental blindness, in the darkness of superstition and prejudices of every kind; The Communist-Leninist Party, the workers and peasants government of the Union of Socialist Soviets, which have destroyed capitalism throughout the length and breadth of tsarist Russia, which have handed over political power to the workers and the peasants, and which are organizing a free classless society, have made it the object of their daring, sage and indefatigable activity to free the working masses from the age-old yoke of an old and outworn history, of the capitalist development of culture, which today has glaringly exposed all its vices and its creative decrepitude. And it is from the height of this great aim that we honest writers of the Union of Soviets must examine, appraise and organize our work.

We must grasp the fact that it is the toll of the masses which forms the fundamental organizer of culture and the creator of all ideas, both those which in the course of centuries have minimized the decisive significance of labour—the source of our knowledge and those ideas of Marx, Lenin and Stalin which in our time are fostering a revolutionary sense of justice among the proletarians of all countries, and in our country are lifting labour to the level of a power which serves as the foundation for the creative activity of science and art. To be successful in our work, we must grasp and fully realize the fact that in our country the socially organized labour of semi-literate workers and a primitive peasantry has in the short space of ten years created stupendous values and armed itself superbly for defence against an enemy attack. Proper appreciation of this fact will reveal to us the cultural and revolutionary power of a doctrine which unites the whole proletariat of the world.

All of us—writers, factory workers, collective farmers still work badly and cannot even fully master everything that has been made by us and for us. Our working masses do not yet quite grasp the fact that they are working only for themselves. This feeling is smouldering everywhere, but it has not yet blazed up into a mighty and joyous flame. But nothing can kindle until it has reached a certain temperature, and nobody ever was so splendidly capable of raising the temperature of labour energy as is the Party organized by the genius of Vladimir Lenin, and the present-day leader of this Party.

As the principal hero of our books we should choose labour, i.e., a person, organized by the processes of labour, who in our country is armed with the full might of modern technique, a person who, in his turn, so organizes labour that it becomes easier and more productive, raising it to the level of an art. We must learn to understand labour as creation. Creation is a concept which we writers use all too freely, though we hardly possess the right to do so.

In our Union of Socialist Soviets, there should not, there cannot be superfluous people. Every citizen enjoys wide freedom for the development of his abilities, talents and faculties. One thing only is demanded of personality: Be honest in your attitude to the heroic work of creating a classless society.

In the Union of Socialist Soviets the workers and peasants government has called upon the whole mass of the population to help build a new culture—and it follows from this that the responsibility for mistakes, for hitches, for spoilage, for every display of middle-class meanness, for perfidy, duplicity and unscrupulousness lies on each and all of us. That means our criticism must really be self-criticism; it means that we must devise a system of socialist morality as a regulating factor in our work and our relationships . . .

The growth of the new man [for Gorky, the new *Soviet* man, RGM] can be seen with especial clarity among children, yet children remain quite outside literature's sphere of observation. Our writers seem to consider it beneath their dignity to write about children and for children.

I believe I will not be mistaken in saying that fathers are beginning to show more care and tenderness for their children, which, in my view, is quite natural, as children for the first time in the whole life of mankind are now the inheritors not of their parents money, houses and furniture, but of a real and mighty fortune—a socialist state created by the labour of their fathers and mothers. Never before have children been such intelligent and stern judges of the past, and I quite believe the fact that was related to me of an eleven year-old tubercular little girl who said to the doctor in the presence of her father; pointing her finger at him: "It is his fault that I am ill. Till he was forty years old, he wasted his health on all sorts of bad women, and then married mama. She is only twenty-seven, she is healthy, and he—you can see how miserable he is, and I have taken after him."

There is every reason to expect that such reasoning among children will be no uncommon thing.

Reality is giving us ever more "raw material" for artistic generalizations. But neither the drama nor the novel has yet given an adequately vivid portrayal of the Soviet woman, who is distinguishing herself as a free agent in all spheres where the new socialist life is being built. It is even noticeable that playwrights are endeavoring to write as few women's parts as possible. It is hard to understand why. Though woman in our country is the social equal of man, and though she is successfully proving the diversity of her endowments and the breadth of her capacities, this equality is all too frequently and in many ways external and formal. The man has not yet forgotten, or else he has prematurely forgotten, that for centuries woman has been brought up to be a sensual plaything and a domestic animal, fitted to pay the part of "housewife." This old and odious debt of history to half the earth's inhabitants ought to be paid off by the men of our country first and foremost, as an example to all other men. And here literature should try to depict the work and mentality of woman in such a manner as to raise the attitude towards her above the general level of accepted middle-class behaviour, which is borrowed from the poultry yard . . .

Socialist individuality, as exemplified by our heroes of labour, who represent the flower of the working class, can develop only under conditions of collective labour, which has set itself the supreme and wise aim of liberating the workers of the whole world from the man-deforming power of capitalism.

Life, as asserted by socialist realism, is deeds, creativeness, the aim of which is the uninterrupted development of the priceless individual faculties of man, with a view to his victory over the forces of nature, for the sake of his health and longevity, for the supreme joy of living on an earth which, in conformity with the steady growth of his requirements, he wishes to mould throughout into a beautiful dwelling place for mankind, united into a single family . . .

The proletarian state must educate thousands of first class "craftsmen of culture," "engineers of the soul." This is necessary in order to restore to the whole mass of the working people the right to develop their intelligence, talents and faculties—a right of which they have been deprived everywhere else in the world. This aim, which is a fully practicable one, imposes on us writers the need of strict responsibility for our work and our social behaviour. This places us not only in the position, traditional to realist literature, of "judges of the world and men," "critics of life," but gives us the right to participate directly in the construction of a new life, in the process of "changing the world." The possession of this right should impress every writer with a sense of his duty and responsibility for all literature, for all the aspects in it which should, not be there.

Program Notes: *Lady Macbeth of Mtsensk*

Lisa Y. Christensen

This summary is reposted from the website of the LA Opera: http://laopera.com/learn_more/article _detail.asp? productionid5149&articleid576

Russian composer Dmitri Shostakovich composed his four act opera *Lady Macbeth of Mtsensk* from 1930–1932. The work's complex libretto (which draws from Nicolai Leskov's short story by the same name) presents a sea of conflicted motives which ultimately culminates in disaster as the characters unleash both their emotional and physical passions. The intensity of the plot is readily evident in Shostakovich's score. The harmonic language is accessible, but what strikes the listener is the oscillation between varying musical styles and moods—the composer moves almost seamlessly between the absurd and the grotesque to the touching and the traditional.

Aside from the opera's stunning musical and dramatic content, *Lady Macbeth of Mtsensk* is remarkable in its cultural, historical and even political significance. Many cultural aspects of the work deserve lengthy discussion—among them the topic of Shostakovich's "feminist" retelling of the drama. Both the short story and the opera recount the tale of Katerina, a young and bored housewife who keenly feels the burden of both her marriage and her social position. But the similarity ends here; in Leksov's version, Katerina is portrayed as a woman utterly lacking in ethics and remorse. In contrast, Shostakovich's female protagonist is complex, and moments such as her pre-bedtime soliloquy at the end of Act One convince the listener that her desperate loneliness is far from superficial.

The opera was composed at a significant moment in Russia's history; Joseph Stalin had secured his position as leader of the nation—a role he would retain until his death in 1953. Today, the question of Shostakovich's stance with regard to the Soviet regime continues to be a matter of considerable debate. Nonetheless, *Lady Macbeth of Mtsensk*, dubbed a "tragedy-satire" by the composer, seems somehow unrelenting in its quest to expose the darker side of Russian existence.

Lady Macbeth of Mtsensk received its premiere at Leningrad's Malïy Theatre on January 22, 1934. While the work enjoyed resounding success during its first two years, its popularity came to a halt on January 26, 1936 when Stalin himself attended a performance of the Bolshoi production. Stalin left before the end of the performance, and two days later the newspaper *Pravda* published "Muddle Instead of Music"—an open attack against the opera's music and subject matter. The opera was quickly withdrawn and did not re-emerge in Russia until the 1960's.

Today, *Lady Macbeth of Mtsensk* is recognized as a twentieth-century masterpiece. The opera was revised in 1935 and reworked yet again from 1956 to 1963—an endeavor which resulted in a substantially different work with a new title: *Katerina Ismailova*. With this Company Premiere, Los Angeles Opera presents the original 1932 version and pays homage to Russia's rich musical legacy.

SYNOPSIS: *Lady Macbeth of Mtsensk*

Act One

Katerina Ismailova is bored with her life and loveless marriage ("Akh, nye spitsa bolshe"). Boris, her father-in-law, complains that she has not yet given his son an heir—no doubt she would like to take a lover, but he'll keep his eyes open ("Vsyo ot babi zavisi"). Leaving the room, Boris tells Katerina to prepare rat poison. Nothing would please her more than to feed it to him. He returns in a moment with his son, Zinovy. When a messenger arrives with news that a dam on their property needs immediate repair ("Plotinuto na myelnitse prorvalo"), Zinovy says he will oversee the work himself. Before leaving, Zinovy introduces to his father a new laborer named Sergei. Boris insists his son make Katerina swear on oath to be faithful while he is away and, in spite of Zinovy's protests, forces her to kneel. The men leave. The cook, Aksinya, gossips that the handsome Sergei was dismissed from his last job because the mistress fell for him.

In the yard, workmen molest Aksinya. Katerina appears and berates the men, declaring the bravery of women ("Mnogo vy, muzhiki"). Sergei, insisting on shaking Katerina's hand, squeezes it until she cries out in pain and pushes him away. Sergei and Katerina wrestle. He throws her just as Boris comes out of the house. Boris threatens to tell Zinovy about his wife's behavior, then sends them all back to work. Katerina goes to her bedroom. Her father-in-law comes in to scold her for wasting a candle. She undresses, singing of her sexual frustration ("Ya vakoshka adnazhdy u vibyeda"). On the pretext of wanting to borrow a book, Sergei knocks at her door and reminds her how agreeable their wrestling match was ("Skuka odolyevayet"). An embrace leads to passionate lovemaking, interrupted momentarily when Boris asks if she is in bed.

Act Two

In the courtyard, Boris is considering giving Katerina what he knows she needs when he sees Sergei at the window kissing Katerina good-bye. When the young man leaves, Boris grabs him by the collar and, shouting for help, has Sergei stripped and tied up. After summoning Katerina to the window to watch, Boris flogs Sergei ("Smotri, Katerina, zanyatoye zrelishche"). Katerina screams to be let out of her room, but no one moves; in the end she escapes and hurls herself at her father-in-law. Sergei is locked in the storeroom, and Boris demands something to eat, meanwhile sending his son a message that there is trouble at home. Katerina serves him mushrooms she has laced with rat poison. As Boris cries out for a priest to hear his final confession ("Zhzhot . . . tochna pozhor"), Katerina coldly takes the keys from his pocket and goes to release Sergei. Laborers arriving for work cannot understand the old man's babblings, but a priest gets there in time to hear him accuse his daughter-in-law of murder. Katerina mourns so eloquently, however ("Akh, Boris Timofeyevich"), that the priest ponders the mysteries of dying.

In Katerina's room, Sergei fans her passion by telling her that Zinovy's return will bring an end to their love. After declaring he wishes he were her husband, Sergei falls asleep. Katerina's thoughts are interrupted by the appearance of Boris's ghost. Unable at first to frighten her, the ghost eventually causes the girl to scream in terror, waking Sergei, who sees nothing. Katerina hears someone coming. Realizing it is Zinovy, Sergei hides. Entering, Zinovy begins to question her on how she spent her time while he was away ("Kak zhivyotye, mozhetye?"). When he asks why the bed is made up for two, she replies that she was anticipating his return. Noticing a man's belt on the bed, Zinovy seizes it and begins to beat Katerina, shouting that he knows all about her scandalous behavior. Sergei rushes forward to defend her. Zinovy tries to escape, but Katerina pulls him back, and Sergei helps her to strangle him. The lovers hide the body.

Act Three

On their wedding day, Katerina and Sergei think about the hidden corpse. As they leave for their wedding, a drunken Shabby Peasant, searching for liquor ("U menya byla kuma"), finds the body.

At the local jail, the Police Sergeant and his men sit idle. A nihilist teacher is brought in and questioned, but even this sport cannot compensate for the fact that none of them has been invited to Katerina's wedding feast. When the Shabby Peasant bursts in with the news that he has found a corpse at the Ismailovs', the chief and his men, glad for an excuse to crash the celebration, hurry off to investigate.

The wedding feast is in progress. Realizing they have been discovered, Katerina tells Sergei that they must leave immediately ("Sergei, nado bezhat"). The Police Sergeant and his men enter. Sergei becomes nervous and confused, but Katerina, realizing there is no point in pretense, holds out her wrists to be handcuffed. Sergei tries to escape but is captured.

Act Four

Shackled convicts stop for the night, men and women in separate groups. An Old Convict sings of the long, hard road to Siberia. Bribing a guard to let her go to the men, Katerina finds Sergei, who rebuffs her, blaming her for his predicament. Returning to the women, she laments that, difficult as her trial and subsequent flogging were, it is harder still to bear Sergei's hatred ("Nye lekhko posle pochota"). Meanwhile, Sergei flirts with another convict, Sonyetka, whose stockings are torn; she promises Sergei she will be his if he can get her another pair—from his rich wife. He goes to Katerina, pretending he will soon be taken to a doctor because the fetters have rubbed his legs raw and saying her stockings would help. Katerina gives him her stockings, and he immediately gives them to Sonyetka. The two find a corner together, leaving Katerina in despair as the rest of the women taunt her. An Officer, finally wakened by the noise, orders everyone to get ready to continue the march. The Old Convict rouses Katerina, who slowly goes over to Sonyetka, standing near the bridge. Katerina drags Sonyetka with her to death in the swiftly flowing river.

© copyright *OPERA NEWS 2002*. Reprinted with permission.

CHAOS INSTEAD OF MUSIC. JANUARY 28, 1936

Original Source: Sumbur vmeste muzyki, Pravda, January 28, 1936.

With the general cultural development of our country there grew also the necessity for good music. At no time and in no other place has the composer had a more appreciative audience. The people expect good songs, but also good instrumental works, and good operas.

Certain theatres are presenting to the new culturally mature Soviet public Shostakovich's opera Lady Macbeth as an innovation and achievement. Musical criticism, always ready to serve, has praised the opera to the skies, and given it resounding glory. The young composer, instead of hearing serious criticism, which could have helped him in his future work, hears only enthusiastic compliments.

From the first minute, the listener is shocked by deliberate dissonance, by a confused stream of sound. Snatches of melody, the beginnings of a musical phrase, are drowned, emerge again, and disappear in a grinding and squealing roar. To follow this "music" is most difficult; to remember it, impossible.

Thus it goes, practically throughout the entire opera. The singing on the stage is replaced by shrieks. If the composer chances to come upon the path of a clear and simple melody, he throws himself back into a wilderness of musical chaos—in places becoming cacophony. The expression which the listener expects is supplanted by wild rhythm. Passion is here supposed to be expressed by noise. All this is not due to lack of talent, or lack of ability to depict strong and simple emotions in music. Here is music turned deliberately inside out in order that nothing will be reminiscent of classical opera, or have anything in common with symphonic music or with simple and popular musical language accessible to all. This music is built on the basis of rejecting opera—the same basis on which "Leftist" Art rejects in the theatre simplicity, realism, clarity of image, and the unaffected spoken word—which carries into the theatre and into music the most negative features of "Meyerholdism" infinitely multiplied. Here we have "leftist" confusion instead of natural human music. The power of good music to infect the masses has been sacrificed to a petty-bourgeois, "formalist" attempt to create originality through cheap clowning. It is a game of clever ingenuity that may end very badly.

The danger of this trend to Soviet music is clear. Leftist distortion in opera stems from the same source as Leftist distortion in painting, poetry, teaching, and science. Petty-bourgeois "innovations" lead to a break with real art, real science and real literature.

The composer of Lady Macbeth was forced to borrow from jazz its nervous, convulsive, and spasmodic music in order to lend "passion" to his characters. While our critics, including music critics, swear by the name of socialist realism, the stage serves us, in Shostakovich's creation, the coarsest kind of naturalism. He reveals the merchants and the people monotonously and bestially. The predatory merchant woman who scrambles into the possession of wealth through murder is pictured as some kind of "victim" of bourgeois society. Leskov's story has been given a significance which it does not possess.

And all this is coarse, primitive and vulgar. The music quacks, grunts, and growls, and suffocates itself in order to express the love scenes as naturalistically as possible. And "love" is smeared all over the opera in the most vulgar manner. The merchant's double bed occupies the central position on the stage. On this bed all "problems" are solved. In the same coarse, naturalistic style is shown the death from poisoning and the flogging—both practically on stage.

The composer apparently never considered the problem of what the Soviet audience looks for and expects in music. As though deliberately, he scribbles down his music, confusing all the sounds in such a way that his music would reach only the effete "formalists" who had lost all their wholesome taste. He ignored the demand of Soviet culture that all coarseness and savagery be abolished from every corner of Soviet life. Some critics call the glorification of the merchants' lust a satire. But there is no question of satire here. The composer has tried, with all the musical and dramatic means at his command, to arouse the sympathy of the spectators for the coarse and vulgar inclinations and behavior of the merchant woman Katerina Izmailova.

Lady Macbeth is having great success with bourgeois audiences abroad. Is it not because the opera is non-political and confusing that they praise it? Is it not explained by the fact that it tickles the perverted taste of the bourgeois with its fidgety, neurotic music?

Our theatres have expended a great deal of energy on giving Shostakovich's opera a thorough presentation. The actors have shown exceptional talent in dominating the noise, the screaming, and the roar of the orchestra. With their dramatic action, they have tried to reinforce the weakness of the melodic content. Unfortunately, this has served only to bring out the opera's vulgar features more vividly. The talented acting deserves gratitude, the wasted efforts—regret.

Source: Composer Biographies. 1996

THE CITY OF QUARTZ: EXCAVATING THE FUTURE IN LOS ANGELES (EXCERPT)

MIKE DAVIS

Mike Davis published *The City of Quartz* in 1990, before the riots associated with Rodney King, and long before 9/11. In the following pages, Davis puts forward his thesis that architecture in Los Angeles has been dominated by an interest in security. How, if at all, would you modify his thesis in 2009?

The carefully manicured lawns of Los Angeles's Westside sprout forests of ominous little signs warning: 'Armed Response!' Even richer neighborhoods in the canyons and hillsides isolate themselves behind walls guarded by gun-toting private police and state-of-the-art electronic surveillance. Downtown, a publicly-subsidized 'urban renaissance' has raised the nation's largest corporate citadel, segregated from the poor neighborhoods around it by a monumental architectural glacis. In Hollywood, celebrity architect Frank Gehry, renowned for his 'humanism', apotheosizes the siege look in a library designed to resemble a foreign-legion fort. In the Westlake district and the San Fernando Valley the Los Angeles Police barricade streets and seal off poor neighborhoods as part of their 'war on drugs'. In Watts, developer Alexander Haagen demonstrates his strategy for recolonizing inner-city retail markets: a panoptican shopping mall surrounded by staked metal fences and a substation of the LAPD in a central surveillance tower. Finally on the horizon of the next millennium, an ex-chief of police crusades for an anti-crime 'giant eye'—a geo-synchronous law enforcement satellite—while other crops discreetly tend versions of 'Garden Plot', a hoary but still viable 1960s plan for a law-and-order armageddon.

Welcome to post-liberal Los Angeles, where the defense of luxury lifestyles is translated into a proliferation of new repressions in space and movement, undergirded by the ubiquitous 'armed response'. This obsession with physical security systems, and, collaterally, with the architectural policing of social boundaries, has become a zeitgeist of urban restructuring, a master narrative in the emerging built environment of the 1990s. Yet contemporary urban theory, whether debating the role of electronic technologies in precipitating 'postmodern space', or discussing the dispersion of urban functions across poly-centered metropolitan 'galaxies', has been strangely silent about the militarization of city life so grimly visible at the street level. Hollywood's pop apocalypses and pulp science fiction have been more realistic, and politically perceptive, in representing the programmed hardening of the urban surface in the wake of the social polarizations of the Reagan era. Images of carceral inner cities (*Escape from New York, Running Man*), high-tech police death squads (*Blade Runner*), sentient buildings (*Die Hard*), urban bantustans (*They Live!*), Vietnam-like street wars (*Colors*), and so on, only extrapolate from actually existing trends.

Such dystopian visions grasp the extent to which today's pharaonic scales of residential and commercial security supplant residual hopes for urban reform and social integration. The dire predictions of Richard Nixon's 1969 National Commission on the Causes and Prevention of Violence have been tragically fulfilled: we live in 'fortress cities' brutally divided between 'fortified cells' of affluent society and 'places of terror' where the police battle the criminalized poor. The 'Second Civil War' that began in the long hot summers of the 1960s has been institutionalized into the very structure of urban space. The old liberal paradigm of social control, attempting to balance repression with reform, has long been superseded by a rhetoric of social warfare that calculates the interests of the urban poor and the middle classes as a zero-sum game. In cities like Los Angeles, on the bad edge of postmodernity, one observes an unprecedented tendency to merge urban design, architecture and the police apparatus into a single, comprehensive security effort.

This epochal coalescence has far-reaching consequences for the social relations of the built environment. In the first place, the market provision of 'security' generates its own paranoid demand. 'Security' becomes a positional good defined by income access to private 'protective services' and membership in some hardened residential enclave or restricted suburb. As a prestige symbol—and sometimes as the decisive borderline between the merely well-off and the 'truly rich'—'security' has less to do with personal safety than with the degree of personal insulation, in residential, work, consumption and travel environments, from 'unsavory' groups and individuals, even crowds in general.

Secondly, as William Whyte has observed of social intercourse in New York, 'fear proves itself'. The social perception of threat becomes a function of the security mobilization itself, not crime rates. Where there is an actual rising arc of street violence, as in Southcentral Los Angeles or Downtown Washington D.C., most of the carnage is self-contained within ethnic or class boundaries. Yet white middle-class imagination, absent from any firsthand knowledge of inner-city conditions, magnifies the perceived threat through a demonological lens. Surveys show that Milwaukee suburbanites are just as worried about violent crime as inner-city Washingtonians, despite a twenty-fold difference in relative levels of mayhem. The media, whose function in this arena is to bury and obscure the daily economic violence of the city, ceaselessly throw up spectres of criminal underclasses and psychotic stalkers. Sensationalized accounts of killer youth gangs high on crack and shrilly racist evocations of marauding Willie Hortons foment the moral panics that reinforce and justify urban apartheid.

Moreover, the neo-military syntax of contemporary architecture insinuates violence and conjures imaginary dangers. In many instances the semiotics of so-called 'defensible space' are just about as subtle as a swaggering white cop. Today's upscale, pseudo-public spaces—sumptuary malls, office centers, culture acropolises, and so on—are full of invisible signs warning off the underclass 'Other'. Although architectural critics are usually oblivious to how the built environment contributes to segregation, pariah groups—whether poor Latino families, young Black men, or elderly homeless white females—read the meaning immediately.

THE DESTRUCTION OF PUBLIC SPACE

The universal and ineluctable consequence of this crusade to secure the city is the destruction of accessible public space. The contemporary opprobrium attached to the term 'street person' is in itself a harrowing index of the devaluation of public spaces. To reduce contact with untouchables, urban redevelopment has converted once vital pedestrian streets into traffic sewers and transformed public parks into temporary receptacles for the homeless and wretched. The American city, as many critics have recognized, is being systematically turned inside out—or, rather, outside in. The valorized spaces of the new megastructures and super-malls are concentrated in the center, street frontage is denuded, public activity is sorted into strictly functional compartments, and circulation is internalized in corridors under the gaze of private police.

The privatization of the architectural public realm, moreover, is shadowed by parallel restructurings of electronic space, as heavily policed, pay-access 'information orders', elite data-bases and subscription cable services appropriate parts of the invisible agora. Both processes, of course, mirror the deregulation of the economy and the recession of non-market entitlements. The decline of urban liberalism has been accompanied by the death of what might be called the 'Olmstedian vision' of public space. Frederick Law Olmsted, it will be recalled, was North America's Haussmann, as well as the Father of Central Park. In the wake of Manhattan's 'Commune' of 1863, the great Draft Riot, he conceived public landscapes and parks as social safety-valves, *mixing* classes and ethnicities in common (bourgeois) recreations and enjoyments. As Manfredo Tafuri has shown in his well-known study of Rockefeller Center, the same principle animated the construction of the canonical urban spaces of the La Guardia–Roosevelt era.

This reformist vision of public space—as the emollient of class struggle, if not the bedrock of the American *polis*—is now as obsolete as Keynesian nostrums of full employment. In regard to the 'mixing' of classes, contemporary urban America is more like Victorian England than Walt Whitman's or La Guardia's New York. In Los Angeles, once-upon-a-time a demi-paradise of free beaches, luxurious parks, and 'cruising strips', genuinely democratic space is all but extinct. The Oz-like archipelago of Westside pleasure domes—a continuum of tony malls, arts centers and gourmet strips—is reciprocally dependent upon the social imprisonment of the third-world service proletariat who live in increasingly repressive ghettoes and barrios. In a city of several million yearning immigrants, public amenities are radically shrinking, parks are becoming derelict and beaches more segregated, libraries and playgrounds are closing, youth congregations of ordinary kinds are banned, and the streets are becoming more desolate and dangerous.

Unsurprisingly, as in other American cities, municipal policy has taken its lead from the security offensive and the middle-class demand for increased spatial and social insulation. De facto disinvestment in traditional public space and recreation has supported the shift of fiscal resources to corporate-defined redevelopment priorities. A pliant city government—in this case ironically professing to represent a bi-racial coalition of liberal whites and Blacks—has collaborated in the massive privatization of public space and the subsidization of new, racist enclaves (benignly described as 'urban villages'). Yet most current, giddy discussions of the 'postmodern' scene in Los Angeles neglect entirely these overbearing aspects of counter-urbanization and

counter-insurgency. A triumphal gloss—'urban renaissance', 'city of the future', and so on—is laid over the brutalization of inner-city neighborhoods and the increasing South Africanization of its spatial relations. Even as the walls have come down in Eastern Europe, they are being erected all over Los Angeles.

The observations that follow take as their thesis the existence of this new class war (sometimes a continuation of the race war of the 1960s) at the level of the built environment. Although this is not a comprehensive account, which would require a thorough analysis of economic and political dynamics, these images and instances are meant to convince the reader that urban form is indeed following a repressive function in the political furrows of the Reagan–Bush era. Los Angeles, in its usual prefigurative mode, offers an especially disquieting catalogue of the emergent liaisons between architecture and the American police state.

THE ARCHITECTURE OF HAPPINESS (EXCERPT)

ALAIN DE BOTTON

Alain de Botton is not an architect. He is a novelist and literary journalist. In *The Architecture of Happiness*, de Botton reads a great many examples of built environments with an eye to the stories they tell or the arguments they make about human happiness.

9.

Taking architecture seriously therefore makes some singular and strenuous demands upon us. It requires that we open ourselves to the idea that we are affected by our surroundings even when they are made of vinyl and would be expensive and time-consuming to ameliorate. It means conceding that we are inconveniently vulnerable to the colour of our wallpaper and that our sense of purpose may be derailed by an unfortunate bedspread. At the same time, it means acknowledging that buildings are able to solve no more than a fraction of our dissatisfactions or prevent evil from unfolding under their watch. Architecture, even at its most accomplished, will only ever constitute a small, and imperfect (expensive, prone to destruction and morally unreliable), protest against the state of things. More awkwardly still, architecture asks us to imagine that happiness might often have an unostentatious, unheroic character to it, that it might be found in a run of old floorboards or in a wash of morning light over a plaster wall—in undramatic, frangible scenes of beauty that move us because we are aware of the darker backdrop against which they are set.

18.

Buildings are not simply visual objects without any connection to concepts which we can analyse and then evaluate. Buildings *speak*—and on topics which can readily be discerned. They speak of democracy or aristocracy, openness or arrogance, welcome or threat, a sympathy for the future or a hankering for the past.

Any object of design will give off an impression of the psychological and moral attitudes it supports. We can, for example, feel two distinct conceptions of fulfillment emanating from a plain Scandinavian crockery set on the one hand and an ornate Sèvres one on the other—an invitation to a democratic graceful sensibility in the former case, to a ceremonial and class-bound disposition in the latter.

In essence, what works of design and architecture talk to us about is the kind of life that would most appropriately unfold within and around them. They tell us of certain moods that they seek to encourage and sustain in their inhabitants. While keeping us warm and helping us in mechanical ways, they simultaneously hold out an invitation for us to be specific sorts of people. They speak of visions of happiness.

To describe a building as beautiful therefore suggests more than a mere aesthetic fondness; it implies an attraction to the particular way of life this structure is promoting through its roof, door handles, window frames, staircase and furnishings. A feeling of beauty is a sign that we have come upon a material articulation of certain of our ideas of a good life.

Left: Tias Eckhoff, Regent Service, Porsgrund, 1961
Right: Blue Cameo Service, Sèvres, 1778

Similarly, buildings will strike us as offensive not because they violate a private and mysterious visual preference but because they conflict with our understanding of the rightful sense of existence—which helps to explain the seriousness and viciousness with which disputes about fitting architecture tend to unfold.

19.

The advantage of shifting the focus of discussion away from the strictly visual towards the values promoted by buildings is that we become able to handle talk about the appearance of works of architecture rather as we do wider debates about people, ideas and political agendas.

Arguments about what is beautiful emerge as no easier to resolve, but then again no harder, than disputes about what is wise or right. We can learn to defend or attack a concept of beauty in the same way we might defend or attack a legal position or an ethical stance. We can understand, and publically explain, why we believe a building to be desirable or offensive on the basis of the things it talks to us about.

The notion of buildings that speak helps us to place at the very centre of our architectural conundrums the question of the values we want to live by—rather than merely of how we want things to look.

5.

Once we start to look, we will find no shortage of suggestions of living forms in the furniture and houses around us. There are penguins in our water jugs and stout and self-important personages in our kettles, graceful deer in our desks and oxen in our dining-room tables.

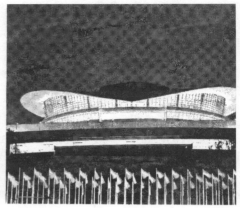

Hedgehogs, beetles, eyes and legs:
Clockwise from top left: Foster and Partners, Sage Arts Centre, Gateshead, 2005
Hijjas Kasturi, Convention Centre, Putrajaya, 2003
Alfred Messel, Wertheim Department Store, Berlin, 1904
Hector Guimard, Castel, Paris, 1896

THINKING, MAKING, DOING

A weary, sceptical eye gazes out at us from the roof of Alfred Messel's Wertheim Department Store in Berlin, while upturned insect legs guard the Castel Béranger in Paris. An aggressive beetle lurks in Malaysia's Putrajaya Convention Centre and a warmer, hedgehog-related creature in the Sage Arts Centre in Gateshead.

Even in something as diminutive as the letters of a typeface, we may detect well-developed personalities, about whose lives and daydreams we could without great difficulty write a short story. The straight back and alert upright bearing of a Helvetican 'f' hint at a punctual, clean and optimistic protagonist, whereas his Poliphilus cousin, with a droopy head and soft features, strikes a sleepier, more sheepish and more pensive note. The story may not end well for him.

Helvetica   Poliphilus

In a kitchenware shop may be found an equally vivid assortment of types. Stemmed glasses seem generically feminine, though this category nonetheless encompasses warm-hearted matrons, nymphets and nervy blue-stockings, while the more masculine tumblers count among their number lumberjacks and stern civil servants.

The tradition of equating furniture and buildings with living beings can be traced back to the Roman author Vitruvius, who paired each of the three principal classical orders with a human or divine archetype from Greek mythology. The Doric column, with its plain capital and squat profile, had its equivalent in the muscular, martial hero Hercules; the Ionic column, with its decorated scrolls and base, corresponded with the stolid, middle-aged goddess Hera; and the Corinthian column, the most intricately embellished of the three and the one with the tallest, slenderest profile, found its model in the beautiful adolescent deity Aphrodite.

In homage to Vitruvius, we might pass the time on car journeys aligning the pillars of motorways bridges to appropriate bipedal counterparts. A drive might reveal a sedentary and cheerful woman holding up one bridge, a punctilious, nervous accountant with an authoritarian air supporting another.

To feel that a building is unappealing may simply be to dislike the temperament of the creature or human we dimly recognise in its elevation—just as to call another edifice beautiful is to sense the presence of a character we would like if it took on a living form. What we search for in a work of architecture is not in the end so far from what we search for in a friend. The objects we describe as beautiful are versions of the people we love.

6.

Even when objects don't look anything like people, we can find it easy to imagine what kinds of human characters they might have.

So refined is our skill at detecting parallels to human beings in forms, textures and colours that we can interpret a character from the humblest shape. A line is eloquent enough. A straight example will signal someone stable and dull, a wavy one will appear foppish and calm, and a jagged one angry and confused.

Consider the struts on the backs of two chairs. Both seem to express a mood. The curved struts speak of ease and playfulness, the straight ones of seriousness and logic. And yet neither set approximates a human shape. Rather, the struts abstractly represent two different temperaments. A straight piece of wood behaves in its own medium as a stable, unimaginative person will act in his or her life, while the meanders of a curved piece correspond, however obliquely, with the casual elegance of an unruffled and dandyish soul.

The ease with which we can connect the psychological world with the outer, visual and sensory one seeds our language with metaphors. We can speak of someone being twisted or dark, smooth or hard. We can develop a steely heart or fall into a blue mood. We can compare a person to a material like concrete or a colour like burgundy and be sure thereby to convey something of his or her personality.

The German psychologist Rudolf Arnheim once asked his students to describe a good and a bad marriage using only line drawings. Although we might be hard pressed, working backwards, to divine Arnheim's brief from the ensuing squiggles, we could come close, for they are strikingly successful at capturing something of the qualities of two different kinds of relationship. In one example, smooth curves mirror the peaceable and flowing course of a loving union, while violently gyrating spikes serve as a visual shorthand for sarcastic putdowns and slammed doors.

Two stories about married life from Rudolf Arnheim, *Visual Thinking*, 1969

If even crude scratches on a piece of paper can speak accurately and fluently of our psychic states, when whole buildings are at stake, expressive potential is exponentially increased. The pointed arches of Bayeux Cathedral convey ardour and intensity, while their rounded counterparts in the courtyard of the Ducal Palace in Urbino embody serenity and poise. Like a person weathering life's challenges, the palace's arches equitably resist pressure from all sides, avoiding the spiritual crises and emotional effusions to which the cathedral's appear ineluctably drawn.

Contrasting temperaments:
Left: Ducal Palace, Urbino, 1479; right: Bayeux Cathedral, 1077

If, to take Arnheim's exercise several steps further, we were tasked with producing metaphoric images of Germany in two periods of her history, as a fascist state and a democratic republic, and if we were allowed to work with stone, steel and glass rather than with just a pencil, it is likely we could not better the iconic designs of Albert Speer and Egon Eiermann, who created national pavilions for World's Fairs on either side of the Second World War. Speer's offering, for the Paris Fair of 1937, makes use of the quintessential visual metaphors of power: height, mass and shadow. Without even laying eyes on the insignia of the government which sponsored it, we would almost certainly sense something ominous, aggressive and defiant emanating from this 500-foot Neoclassical colossus. Twenty-one years and a world war later, in his German Pavilion for the 1958 World Exposition in Brussels, Egon Eiermann would resort to a trio of very different metaphors: horizontality to suggest calm, lightness to imply gentleness and transparency to evoke democracy.

So eloquent are materials and colours, then, that a façade can be made to speak of how a country should be ruled and which principles ought to govern its foreign policy. Political and ethical ideas can be written into window frames and door handles. An abstract glass box on a stone plinth can deliver a paean to tranquility and civilisation.

POISON IVY

WILLIAM J. MITCHELL

William J. Mitchell is Professor of Architecture and Media Arts and Sciences at MIT. His book, *Placing Words: Symbols, Space, and the City*, writes about architecture with an eye to understanding its public uses and meanings. He is addressing general readers with an interest in the public life of design, rather than professional architects. In this essay, he discusses some recent building projects on college campuses.

At Washington University in St. Louis, they recently constructed a huge parking structure in the style known on American campuses as "Collegiate Gothic." It's not easy, of course, to combine a stubbornly horizontal building type with famously vertical motifs. The trick is to avoid the really pointy stuff (which costs too much anyway), and to clad the exterior with rows of flat, vaguely Tudor arches. This produces a stack of cloistered quadrangles stuffed with rusting cars. Comparing it with an unloved law school from the in-your-face concrete era, local wags like to point out that Washington University once built law schools like parking structures, but now does parking structures like law schools.

For much the same reason, the President and Fellows of Harvard annually instruct the grounds staff, in the spring, to plant Harvard Yard with new grass beneath the elms. When sentimental old alumni return for class reunions, with checkbooks at the ready, it is as sweetly green as they picture it in their memories. American colleges and universities are in the nostalgia theme park business. Trustees call it tradition. The student recruitment and fundraising people know that it's about enlisting architecture to brand a product. If you're selling entry to the ivied establishment (or reassurance of continued membership), you want the customers to know it.

At Princeton, they are as careful about theming as the Disney Corporation. The incomparable Ralph Adams Cram got them into the game, around 1900, by introducing elegantly detailed Tudor Gothic quadrangles. The students loved them, and Woodrow Wilson, Princeton's president at the time, approvingly commented that they "added a thousand years to the history of Princeton." As the twentieth century unfolded, the suburban New Jersey campus frequently wobbled into modernism—some of it distinguished—but the trustees have now mandated a return to the Cramesque for the twenty-first. Volkswagen is building Beetles again, and BMW is building Minis (with a successful move upmarket in both cases), so why can't Princeton build Gothic?

Of course, you cannot just replicate Cram these days. As with retro cars, there are new standards and requirements to accommodate. For one thing, you have to provide elevator access for those with disabilities, so you end up stringing the student rooms along double-loaded corridors instead of clustering them around stairways—a spatial organization that is more Motel 6 than medieval. Compared to a thousand, or even a hundred years ago, there will be a lot more plumbing and shower stalls to jam in somewhere. Fireplaces are out of the question (too dangerous), and as for operable windows, they pose a suicide risk—not to mention an opportunity to toss out the furniture, like Russell Crowe in *A Beautiful Mind*: better just go for standard HVAC. Desks? Don't imagine that the freshmen, sophomores, and seniors will be silently poring over texts like the Venerable Bede: they will be surfing the Web on their wireless laptops, listening through headphones to MPG files downloaded from KaZaA, and pinging SMS flirtation to one another—simultaneously.

The truth is that the branding is all in the wrapper. Inside, a different logic takes over. As parents who trundle their kids off on the college application tour quickly discover, today's dorm rooms hardly vary from sea to shining sea. It's not surprising: they mostly respond to the same surveys and focus-groups, use the same technologies, and get held to the same cost-per-bed numbers plugged into the same spreadsheet business models. The product is as generic as bottled water, so as the marketing gurus will tell you—you get into a game of distinctive labeling, associating yourself with the images and lifestyles that appeal to your target demographics, and differentiating yourself from your competitors.

But there are, in the end, some crucial differences between Classic Coke and Gothic Princeton. Historic fancy dress can be fun for a while, and can provide welcome opportunities for irony, contradiction, and witty transgression. But if you strut around garbed like Henry VII all the time, you quickly become a tiresome bore. Similarly, fancy-dress architecture flirts with the sin of pretentious affectation. Do the world's most privileged undergraduates really need that?

Then, there's the treacherous messiness of metonymy. Evoke the virtues of some particular point in the past, and others may recall its vices. (Just ask Senator Trent Lott.) Exactly what *were* the social attitudes of Ivy League gentlemen circa 1900? Weren't their faces uniformly white (in contrast to the kitchen help)? Where were the women? What if you were gay? What about the endemic anti-Semitism? Creditably, great institutions like Princeton have moved on. So isn't it just a bit unseemly, today, to identify with that moment? It's like flying the Confederate flag over Southern statehouses.

Most importantly, institutions of higher learning have a responsibility to be more than lifestyle marketing organizations. Their business, they would claim, is the rigorous, critical, adventurous investigation of ideas—so why not in architecture, just as in scholarship and science? If they believe their own rhetoric, they should take major campus construction projects as exciting opportunities to probe and rethink the nature of their communities, to reflect upon their relationships to larger society, to respond in some articulate way to a cultural moment, and to add layers to the complex, multigenerational discourses that campuses represent. They would not give tenure to a professor who merely recycled the same old stuff between covers calibrated for maximum marketability, and they should not give campus space to buildings that do no better.

Steven Holl's new Simmons Hall, on the MIT campus in Cambridge, Massachusetts, brilliantly demonstrates that the more intellectually ambitious path remains possible—as it was when Thomas Jefferson planned the University of Virginia, when Alvar Aalto designed MIT's Baker House, and when Charles Moore and his colleagues did Kresge College for the University of California at Santa Cruz in the 1960s. It is not a perfect building: the cost escalated to a troublesome extent, the structure is not particularly rational, and there are some details that don't really work. But it is a brave and passionate one (for which we must credit both the vision of the architect and the determined idealism of MIT's President Charles Vest), and it is bursting with ideas.

Unlike the house of Harvard Yard, it is not in the bricks-and-ivy, four hundred years of history part of Cambridge. It is squarely on the other side of the tracks—built on a flat expanse of fill, right beside a railway line, in a decayed and obsolete industrial area that is currently being reborn as a biotech hotspot. It is not about the comfortable continuity of tradition (specially for those who have been privileged by it), but about transformation and social mobility—not about fitting in, but breaking out. It wants to attract the first-generation migrant kids whose parents have worked long hours to get them into college and on course for a better life, the children of blue-collar families who start with little but make it on sheer merit, the high school misfits who will thrive when they reach the company of others as smart as they are. Appropriately then, it avoids culture-specific motifs and class-bound imagery (except, maybe, for a hint of Corb), and employs an exterior vocabulary of rigorously abstract forms that doesn't even give you much clue, from a distance, about the true scale. It is what you choose to make of it, and it takes some work.

At first glance, the plan is just a straightforward rendition of the ubiquitous double-loaded corridor. But it turns out, on closer inspection, to be splattered with free-form blobs. And, in section, these reveal themselves as sinuous wormholes snaking up through the floors, creating a marvelous system of unexpected interconnections and informal social spaces.

The real jaw-dropper, though, is in the endlessly inventive animation through light and color. The deeply revealed, gridded façade provides shifts from apparent solidity to airy openness, from neutral to vividly hued, and from reflective to sharply shadow-lined as you move on by. Hundreds of tiny operable windows end up at varied horizontal angles to morning and evening sun, providing changing patterns of glitter and dazzle for passing joggers. The aluminum cladding responds subtly to the shifting balance of cloudy sky and the snowy ground. At night, the square openings with their individual curtains read like pixels. Inside, there are pretty moves with meshed metal screens and colored lights diffused by perforated plywood. And, in the individual rooms, you encounter the surprising warmth of curved, polished plywood furniture—homage to Aalto across the athletic fields.

And what's the lesson for all those crusty old trustees? Forget about mandating historic styles—which is as silly and stultifying as requiring email to be written in Shakespearean English! Leave the logo-led marketing to the T-shirt and coffee mug vendors! Architecture can do more for you than that.

DESIGNS FOR WORKING (EXCERPT)

MALCOLM GLADWELL

Malcolm Gladwell is a literary journalist. He writes for *The New Yorker* and has also published several books. In this essay, he applies Jane Jacobs' idea of the city to contemporary office design.

The miracle of Hudson Street, according to [Jane] Jacobs, was created by the particular configuration of the streets and buildings of the neighborhood. Jacobs argued that when a neighborhood is oriented toward the street, when sidewalks are used for socializing and play and commerce, the users of that street are transformed by the resulting stimulation: they form relationships and casual contacts they would never have otherwise. The West Village, she pointed out, was blessed with a mixture of houses and apartments and shops and offices and industry, which meant that there were always people "outdoors on different schedules and . . . in the place for different purposes." It had short blocks, and short blocks create the greatest variety in foot traffic. It had lots of old buildings, and old buildings have the low rents that permit individualized and creative uses. And, most of all, it had people, cheek by jowl, from every conceivable walk of life. Sparsely populated suburbs may look appealing, she said, but without an active sidewalk life, without the frequent, serendipitous interactions of many different people, "there is no public acquaintanceship, no foundation of public trust, no cross-connections with the necessary people—and no practice or ease in applying the most ordinary techniques of city public life at lowly levels."

Jane Jacobs did not win the battle she set out to fight. The West Village remains an anomaly. Most developers did not want to build the kind of community Jacobs talked about, and most Americans didn't want to live in one. To reread *Death and Life* today, however, is to be struck by how the intervening years have given her arguments a new and unexpected relevance. Who, after all, has a direct interest in creating diverse, vital spaces that foster creativity and serendipity? Employers do. On the fortieth anniversary of its publication, *Death and Life* has been reborn as a primer on workplace design.

The parallels between neighborhoods and offices are striking. There was a time, for instance, when companies put their most valued employees in palatial offices, with potted plants in the corner, and secretaries out front, guarding access. Those offices were suburbs-gated communities, in fact—and many companies came to realize that if their best employees were isolated in suburbs they would be deprived of public acquaintanceship, the foundations of public trust, and cross-connections with the necessary people. In the eighties and early nineties, the fashion in corporate America was to follow what designers called "universal planning"—rows of identical cubicles, which resembled nothing so much as a Levittown. Today, universal planning has fallen out of favor, for the same reason that the postwar suburbs like Levittown did: to thrive, an office space must have a diversity of uses—it must have the workplace equivalent of houses and apartments and shops and industry.

If you visit the technology companies of Silicon Valley, or the media companies of Manhattan, or any of the firms that self-consciously identify themselves with the New Economy, you'll find that secluded private offices have been replaced by busy public spaces, open-plan areas without walls, executives next to the newest hires. The hush of the traditional office has been supplanted by something much closer to the noisy, bustling ballet of Hudson Street. Forty years ago, people lived in neighborhoods like the West Village and went to work in the equivalent of suburbs. Now, in one of the odd reversals that mark the current economy, they live in suburbs and, increasingly, go to work in the equivalent of the West Village.

THE COOLHUNT

MALCOLM GLADWELL

MARCH 17, 1997
ANNALS OF STYLE

In this piece, published in *The New Yorker*, literary journalist Malcolm Gladwell wrote the first major description of "cool hunting" to appear in mainstream media. Since then, cool hunting has appeared in a novel by William Gibson (*Pattern Recognition*) and is the name or express purpose of many web sites. How has cool hunting changed since the rise of social media, and why?

Who decides what's cool? Certain kids in certain places—and only the coolhunters know who they are.

I.

Baysie Wightman met DeeDee Gordon, appropriately enough, on a coolhunt. It was 1992. Baysie was a big shot for Converse, and DeeDee, who was barely twenty-one, was running a very cool boutique called Placid Planet, on Newbury Street in Boston. Baysie came in with a camera crew—one she often used when she was coolhunting—and said, "I've been watching your store, I've seen you, I've heard you know what's up," because it was Baysie's job at Converse to find people who knew what was up and she thought DeeDee was one of those people. DeeDee says that she responded with reserve—that "I was like, 'Whatever'"—but Baysie said that if DeeDee ever wanted to come and work at Coverse she should just call, and nine months later DeeDee called. This was about the time the cool kids had decided they didn't want the hundred-and-twenty-five-dollar basketball sneaker with seventeen different kinds of high-technology materials and colors and air-cushioned heels anymore. They wanted simplicity and authenticity, and Baysie picked up on that. She brought back the Converse One Star, which was a vulcanized, suède, low-top classic old-school sneaker from the nineteen-seventies, and, sure enough, the One Star quickly became the signature shoe of the retro era. Remember what Kurt Cobain was wearing in the famous picture of him lying dead on the ground after committing suicide? Black Converse One Stars. DeeDee's big score was calling the sandal craze. She had been out in Los Angeles and had kept seeing the white teen-age girls dressing up like cholos, Mexican gangsters, in tight white tank tops known as "wife beaters," with a bra strap hanging out, and long shorts and tube socks and shower sandals. DeeDee recalls, "I'm like, 'I'm telling you, Baysie, this is going to hit. There are just too many people wearing it. We have to make a shower sandal.'" So Baysie, DeeDee, and a designer came up with the idea of making a retro sneaker-sandal, cutting the back off the One Star and putting a thick outsole on it. It was huge, and, amazingly, it's still huge.

Today, Baysie works for Reebok as general-merchandise manager—part of the team trying to return Reebok to the position it enjoyed in the mid-nineteen-eighties as the country's hottest sneaker company. DeeDee works for an advertising agency in Del Mar called Lambesis, where she puts out a quarterly tip sheet called the L Report on what the cool kids in major American cities are thinking and doing and buying. Baysie and DeeDee are best friends. They talk on the phone all the time. They get together whenever Baysie is in L.A. (DeeDee: "It's, like, how many times can you drive past O. J. Simpson's house?"), and between them they can talk for hours about the art of the coolhunt. They're the Lewis and Clark of cool.

What they have is what everybody seems to want these days, which is a window on the world of the street. Once, when fashion trends were set by the big couture houses—when cool was trickle-down—that wasn't important. But sometime in the past few decades things got turned over, and fashion became trickle-up. It's now about chase and flight—designers and retailers and the mass consumer giving chase to the elusive prey of street cool—and the rise of coolhunting as a profession shows how serious the chase has become. The sneakers of Nike and Reebok used to come out yearly. Now a new style comes out every season. Apparel designers used to have an eighteen-month lead time between concept and sale. Now they're reducing that to a year, or even six months, in order to react faster to new ideas from the street. The paradox, of course, is that the better coolhunters become at bringing the mainstream close to the cutting edge, the more elusive the cutting edge becomes. This is the first rule of the cool: The quicker the chase, the quicker the flight. The act of discovering what's cool is what causes cool to move on, which explains the triumphant circularity of coolhunting: because we have coolhunters like DeeDee and Baysie, cool changes more quickly, and because cool changes more quickly, we need coolhunters like DeeDee and Baysie.

DeeDee is tall and glamorous, with short hair she has dyed so often that she claims to have forgotten her real color. She drives a yellow 1977 Trans Am with a burgundy stripe down the center and a 1973 Mercedes 450 SL, and lives in a spare, Japanese-style cabin in Laurel Canyon. She uses words like "rad" and "totally," and offers non-stop, deadpan pronouncements on pop culture, as in "It's all about Pee-wee Herman." She sounds at first like a teen, like the same teens who, at Lambesis, it is her job to follow. But teen speech—particularly girl-teen speech, with its fixation on reported speech ("so she goes," "and I'm like," "and he goes") and its stock vocabulary of accompanying grimaces and gestures—is about using language less to communicate than to fit in. DeeDee uses teen speech to set herself apart, and the result is, for lack of a better word, really cool. She doesn't do the teen thing of climbing half an octave at the end of every sentence. Instead, she drags out her vowels for emphasis, so that if she mildly disagreed with something I'd said she would say "Maalcolm" and if she strongly disagreed with what I'd said she would say "Maaalcolm."

Baysie is older, just past forty (although you would never guess that), and went to Exeter and Middlebury and had two grandfathers who went to Harvard (although you wouldn't guess that, either). She has curly brown hair and big green eyes and long legs and so much energy that it is hard to imagine her asleep, or resting, or even standing still for longer than thirty seconds. The hunt for cool is an obsession with her, and DeeDee is the same way. DeeDee used to sit on the corner of West Broadway and Prince in SoHo—back when SoHo was cool—and take pictures of everyone who walked by for an entire hour. Baysie can tell you precisely where she goes on her Reebok coolhunts to find the really cool alternative white kids ("I'd maybe go to Portland and hang out where the skateboarders hang out near that bridge") or which snowboarding mountain has cooler kids—Stratton, in Vermont, or Summit County, in Colorado. (Summit, definitely.) DeeDee can tell you on the basis of the L Report's research exactly how far Dallas is behind New York in coolness (from six to eight months). Baysie is convinced that Los Angeles is not happening right now: "In the early nineteen-nineties a lot more was coming from L.A. They had a big trend with the whole Melrose Avenue look—the stupid goatees, the shorter hair. It was cleaned-up aftergrunge. There were a lot of places you could go to buy vinyl records. It was a strong place to go for looks. Then it went back to being horrible." DeeDee is convinced that Japan is happening: "I linked onto this future-technology thing two years ago. Now look at it, it's huge. It's the whole resurgence of Nike—Nike being larger than life. I went to Japan and saw the kids just bailing the most technologically advanced Nikes with their little dresses and little outfits and I'm like, 'Whoa, this is trippy!' It's performance mixed with fashion. It's really superheavy." Baysie has a theory that Liverpool is cool right now because it's the birthplace of the whole "lad" look, which involves soccer blokes in the pubs going superdressy and wearing Dolce & Gabbana and Polo Sport and Reebok Classics on their feet. But when I asked DeeDee about that, she just rolled her eyes: "Sometimes Baysie goes off on these tangents. Man, I love that woman!"

I used to think that if I talked to Baysie and DeeDee long enough I could write a coolhunting manual, an encyclopedia of cool. But then I realized that the manual would have so many footnotes and caveats that it would be unreadable. Coolhunting is not about the articulation of a coherent philosophy of cool. It's just a collection of spontaneous observations and predictions that differ from one moment to the next and from one coolhunter to the next. Ask a coolhunter where the baggy-jeans look came from, for example, and you might get any number of answers: urban black kids mimicking the jailhouse look, skateboarders looking for room to move, snowboarders trying not to look like skiers, or, alternatively, all three at once, in some grand concordance.

Or take the question of exactly how Tommy Hilfiger—a forty-five-year-old white guy from Greenwich, Connecticut, doing all-American preppy clothes—came to be the designer of choice for urban black America. Some say it was all about the early and visible endorsement given Hilfiger by the hip-hop auteur Grand Puba, who wore a dark-green-and-blue Tommy jacket over a white Tommy T-shirt as he leaned on his black Lamborghini on the cover of the hugely influential "Grand Puba 2000" CD, and whose love for Hilfiger soon spread to other rappers. (Who could forget the rhymes of Mobb Deep? "Tommy was my nigga/And couldn't figure/How me and Hilfiger/used to move through with vigor.") Then I had lunch with one of Hilfiger's designers, a twenty-six-year-old named Ulrich (Ubi) Simpson, who has a Puerto Rican mother and a Dutch-Venezuelan father, plays lacrosse, snowboards, surfs the long board, goes to hip-hop concerts, listens to Jungle, Edith Piaf, opera, rap, and Metallica, and has working with him on his design team a twenty-seven-year-old black guy from Montclair with dreadlocks, a twenty-two-year-old Asian-American who lives on the Lower East Side, a twenty-five-year-old South Asian guy from Fiji, and twenty-one-year-old white graffiti artist from Queens. That's when it occurred to me that maybe the reason Tommy Hilfiger can make white culture cool to black culture is that he has people working for him who are cool in both cultures simultaneously. Then again, maybe it was all Grand Puba. Who knows?

One day last month, Baysie took me on a coolhunt to the Bronx and Harlem, lugging a big black canvas bag with twenty-four different shoes that Reebok is about to bring out, and as we drove down Fordham Road, she had her head out the window like a little kid, checking out what everyone on the street was wearing. We went to Dr. Jay's, which is the cool place to buy sneakers in the Bronx, and Baysie crouched down on the floor and started pulling the shoes out of her bag one by one, soliciting opinions from customers who gathered around and asking one question after another, in rapid sequence. One guy she listened closely to was maybe eighteen or nineteen, with a diamond stud in his ear and a thin beard. He was wearing a Polo baseball cap, a brown leather jacket, and the big, oversized leather boots that are everywhere uptown right now. Baysie would hand him a shoe and he would hold it, look at the top, and move it up and down and flip it over. The first one he didn't like: "Oh-kay." The second one he hated: he made a growling sound in his throat even before Baysie could give it to him, as if to say, "Put it back in the bag—now!" But when she handed him a new DMX RXT—a low-cut run/walk shoe in white and blue and mesh with a translucent "ice" sole, which retails for a hundred and ten dollars—he looked at it long and hard and shook his head in pure admiration and just said two words, dragging each of them out: "No doubt."

Baysie was interested in what he was saying, because the DMX RXT she had was a girls' shoe that actually hadn't been doing all that well. Later, she explained to me that the fact that the boys loved the shoe was critical news, because it suggested that Reebok had a potential hit if it just switched the shoe to the men's section. How she managed to distill this piece of information from the crowd of teenagers around her, how she made any sense of the two dozen shoes in her bag, most of which (to my eyes, anyway) looked pretty much the same, and how she knew which of the teens to really focus on was mystery. Baysie is a Wasp from New England, and she crouched on the floor in Dr. Jay's for almost an hour, talking and joking with the homeboys without a trace of condescension or self-consciousness.

Near the end of her visit, a young boy walked up and sat down on the bench next to her. He was wearing a black woollen cap with white stripes pulled low, a blue North Face pleated down jacket, a pair of baggy Guess jeans, and, on his feet, Nike Air Jordans. He couldn't have been more than thirteen. But when he started talking you could see Baysie's eyes light up, because somehow she knew the kid was the real thing.

"How many pairs of shoes do you buy a month?" Baysie asked.

"Two," the kid answered. "And if at the end I find one more I like I get to buy that, too."

Baysie was onto him. "Does your mother spoil you?"

The kid blushed, but a friend next to him was laughing. "Whatever he wants, he gets."

Baysie laughed, too. She had the DMX RXT in his size. He tried them on. He rocked back and forth, testing them. He looked back at Baysie. He was dead serious now: "Make sure these come out."

Baysie handed him the new "Rush" Emmitt Smith shoe due out in the fall. One of the boys had already pronounced it "phat," and another had looked through the marbleized-foam cradle in the heel and cried out in delight, "This is bug!" But this kid was the acid test, because this kid knew cool. He paused. He looked at it hard. "Reebok," he said, soberly and carefully, "is trying to get butter."

In the car on the way back to Manhattan, Baysie repeated it twice. "Not better. Butter! That kid could totally tell you what he thinks." Baysie had spent an hour coolhunting in a shoe store and found out that Reebok's efforts were winning the highest of hip-hop praise. "He was so fucking smart."

2.

If you want to understand how trends work, and why coolhunters like Baysie and DeeDee have become so important, a good place to start is with what's known as diffusion research, which is the study of how ideas and innovations spread. Diffusion researchers do things like spending five years studying the adoption of irrigation techniques in a Colombian mountain village, or developing complex matrices to map the spread of new math in the Pittsburgh school system. What they do may seem like a far cry from, say, how the Tommy Hilfiger thing spread from Harlem to every suburban mall in the country, but it really isn't: both are about how new ideas spread from one person to the next.

One of the most famous diffusion studies is Bruce Ryan and Neal Gross's analysis of the spread of hybrid seed corn in Greene County, Iowa, in the nineteen-thirties. The new seed corn was introduced there in about 1928, and it was superior in every respect to the seed that had been used by farmers for decades. But it wasn't adopted all at once. Of two hundred and fifty-nine farmers studied by Ryan and Gross, only a handful had started planting the new seed by 1933. In 1934, sixteen took the plunge. In 1935, twenty-one more followed; the next year, there were thirty-six, and the year after that a whopping sixty-one. The succeeding figures were then forty-six, thirty-six, fourteen, and three, until, by 1941, all but two of the two hundred and fifty-nine farmers studied were using the new seed. In the language of diffusion research, the handful of farmers who started trying hybrid seed corn at the very beginning of the thirties were the "innovators," the adventurous ones. The slightly larger group that followed them was the "early adopters." They were the opinion leaders in the community, the respected, thoughtful people who watched and analyzed what those wild innovators were doing and then did it themselves. Then came the big bulge of farmers in 1936, 1937, and 1938—the "early majority" and the "late majority," which is to say the deliberate and the skeptical masses, who would never try anything until the most respected farmers had tried it. Only after they had been converted did the "laggards," the most traditional of all, follow suit. The critical thing about this sequence is that it is almost entirely interpersonal. According to Ryan and Gross, only the innovators relied to any great extent on radio advertising and farm journals and seed salesmen in making their decision to switch to the hybrid. Everyone else made his decision overwhelmingly because of the example and the opinions of his neighbors and peers.

Isn't this just how fashion works? A few years ago, the classic brushed-suède Hush Puppies with the lightweight crêpe sole—the moc-toe oxford known as the Duke and the slip-on with the golden buckle known as the Columbia—were selling barely sixty-five thousand pairs a year. The company was trying to walk away from the whole suède casual look entirely. It wanted to do "aspirational" shoes: "active casuals" in smooth leather, like the Mall Walker, with a Comfort Curve technology outsole and a heel stabilizer—the kind of shoes you see in Kinney's for $39.95. But then something strange started happening. Two Hush Puppies executives—Owen Baxter and Jeff Lewis—were doing a fashion shoot for their Mall Walkers and ran into a creative consultant from Manhattan named Jeffrey Miller, who informed them that the Dukes and the Columbias weren't dead, they were dead chic. "We were being told," Baxter recalls, "that there were areas in the Village, in SoHo, where the shoes were selling in resale shops and that people were wearing the old Hush Puppies. They were going to the ma-and-pa stores, the little stores that still carried them, and there was this authenticity of being able to say, 'I am wearing an original pair of Hush Puppies.'"

Baxter and Lewis—tall, solid, fair-haired Midwestern guys with thick, shiny wedding bands—are show men, first and foremost. Baxter was working the cash register at his father's shoe store in Mount Prospect, Illinois, at the age of thirteen. Lewis was doing inventory in his father's shoe store in Pontiac, Michigan, at the age of seven. Baxter was in the National Guard during the 1968 Democratic Convention, in Chicago, and was stationed across the street from the Conrad Hilton downtown, right in the middle of things. Today, the two men work out of Rockford, Michigan (population thirty-eight hundred), where Hush Puppies has been making the Dukes and the Columbias in an old factory down by the Rogue River for almost forty years. They took me to the plant when I was in Rockford. In a crowded, noisy, low-slung building, factory workers stand in long rows, gluing, stapling, and sewing together shoes in dozens of bright colors, and the two executives stopped at each production station and described it in detail. Lewis and Baxter know shoes. But they would be the first to admit that they don't know cool. "Miller was saying that there is something going on with the shoes—that Isaac Mizrahi was wearing the shoes for his personal use," Lewis told me. We were seated around the conference table in the Hush Puppies headquarters in Rockford, with the snow and the trees outside and a big water tower behind us. "I think it's fair to say that at the time we had no idea who Isaac Mizrahi was."

By late 1994, things had begun to happen in a rush. First, the designer John Bartlett called. He wanted to use Hush Puppies as accessories in his spring collection. Then Anna Sui called. Miller, the man from Manhattan flew out to Michigan to give advice on a new line ("Of course, packing my own food and thinking about 'Fargo' in the corner of my mind"). A few months later, in Los Angeles, the designer Joel Fitzpatrick put a twenty-five-foot inflatable basset hound on the roof of his store on La Brea Avenue and gutted his adjoining art gallery to turn it into a Hush Puppies department, and even before he opened—while he was still painting and putting up shelves—Pee-wee Herman walked in and asked for a couple of pairs. Pee-wee Herman! "It was total word of mouth. I didn't even have a sign back then," Fitzpatrick recalls. In 1995, the company sold four hundred and thirty thousand pairs of the classic Hush Puppies. In 1996, it sold a million six hundred thousand, and that was only scratching the surface, because in Europe and the rest of the world, where Hush Puppies have a huge following—where they might outsell the American market four to one—the revival was just beginning.

The cool kids who started wearing old Dukes and Columbias from thrift shops were the innovators. Pee-wee Herman, wandering in off the street, was an early adopter. The million six hundred thousand people who bought Hush Puppies last year are the early majority, jumping in because the really cool people have already blazed the trail. Hush Puppies are moving through the country just the way hybrid seed corn moved through Greene County—all of which illustrates what coolhunters can and cannot do. If Jeffrey Miller had been wrong—if cool people hadn't been digging through the thrift shops for Hush Puppies—and he had arbitrarily decided that Baxter and Lewis should try to convince non-cool people that the shoes were cool, it wouldn't have worked. You can't convince the late majority that Hush Puppies are cool, because the late majority makes its coolness decisions on the basis of what the early majority is doing, and you can't convince the early majority, because the early majority is looking at the early adopters, and you can't convince the early adopters, because they take their cues from the innovators. The innovators do get their cool ideas from people other than their peers, but the fact is that they are the last people who can be convinced by a marketing campaign that a pair of suède shoes is cool. These are, after all, the people who spent hours sifting through thrift-store bins. And why did they do that? Because their definition of cool is doing something that nobody else is doing. A company can intervene in the cool cycle. It can put its shoes on really cool celebrities and on fashion runways and on MTV. It can accelerate the transition from the innovator to the early adopter and on to the early majority. But it can't just manufacture cool out of thin air, and that's the second rule of cool.

At the peak of the Hush Puppies craziness last year, Hush Puppies won the prizes for best accessory at the Council of Fashion Designers' awards dinner, at Lincoln Center. The award was accepted by the Hush Puppies president, Louis Dubrow, who came out wearing a pair of custom-made black patent-leather Hush Puppies and stood there blinking and looking at the assembled crowd as if it were the last scene of "Close Encounters of the Third Kind." It was a strange moment. There was the president of the Hush Puppies company, of Rockford, Michigan, population thirty-eight hundred, sharing a stage with Calvin Klein and Donna Karan and Isaac Mizrahi—and all because some kids in the East Village began combing through thrift shops for old Dukes. Fashion was at the mercy of those kids, whoever they were, and it was a wonderful thing if the kids picked you, but a scary thing, too, because it meant that cool was something you could not control. You needed someone to find cool and tell you what it was.

3.

When Baysie Wightman went to Dr. Jay's, she was looking for customer response to the new shoes Reebok had planned for the fourth quarter of 1997 and the first quarter of 1998. This kind of customer testing is critical at Reebok, because the last decade has not been kind to the company. In 1987, it had a third of the American athletic-shoe market, well ahead of Nike. Last year, it had sixteen per cent. "The kid in the store would say, 'I'd like this shoe if your logo wasn't on it,'" E. Scott Morris, who's a senior designer for Reebok, told me. "That's kind of a punch in the mouth. But we've all seen it. You go into a shoe store. The kid picks up the shoe and says, 'Ah, man, this is nice.' He turns the shoe around and around. He looks at it underneath. He looks at the side and he goes, 'Ah, this is Reebok,' and says, 'I ain't buying this,' and puts the shoe down and walks out. And you go, 'You was just digging it a minute ago. What happened?'" Somewhere along the way, the company lost its cool, and Reebok now faces the task not only of rebuilding its image but of making the shoes so cool that the kids in the store can't put them down.

Every few months, then, the company's coolhunters go out into the field with prototypes of the upcoming shoes to find out what kids really like, and come back to recommend the necessary changes. The prototype of one recent Emmitt Smith shoe, for example, had a piece of molded rubber on the end of the tongue as a design element; it was supposed to give the shoe a certain "richness," but the kids said they thought it looked overbuilt. Then Reebok gave the shoes to the Boston College football team for wear-testing, and when they got the shoes back they found out that all the football players had cut out the rubber component with scissors. As messages go, this was hard to miss. The tongue piece wasn't cool, and on the final version of the shoe it was gone. The rule of thumb at Reebok is that if the kids in Chicago, New York, and Detroit all like a shoe, it's a guaranteed hit. More than likely, though, the coolhunt is going to turn up subtle differences from city to city, so that once the cool-hunters come back the designers have to find out some way to synthesize what was heard, and pick out just those things that all the kids seemed to agree on. In New York, for example, kids in Harlem are more sophisticated and fashion-forward than kids in the Bronx, who like things a little more colorful and glitzy. Brooklyn, meanwhile, is conservative and preppy, more like Washigton, D.C. For reasons no one really knows, Reeboks are coolest in Philadelphia. In Philly, in fact, the Reebok Classics are so huge they are known simply as National Anthems, as in "I'll have a pair of blue Anthems in nine and a half." Philadelphia is Reebok's innovator town. From there trends move along the East Coast, trickling all the way to Charlotte, North Carolina.

Reebok has its headquarters in Stoughton, Massachusetts, outside Boston—in a modern corporate park right off Route 24. There are basketball and tennis courts next to the building, and a health club on the ground floor that you can look directly into from the parking lot. The front lobby is adorned with shrines for all of Reebok's most prominent athletes—shrines complete with dramatic action photographs, their sports jerseys, and a pair of their signature shoes—and the halls are filled with so many young, determinedly athletic people that when I visited Reebok headquarters I suddenly wished I'd packed my gym clothes in case someone challenged me to wind sprints. At Stoughton, I met with a handful of the company's top designers and marketing executives in a long conference room on the third floor. In the course of two hours, they put one pair of shoes after another on the table in front of me, talking excitedly about each sneaker's prospects, because the feeling at Reebok is that things are finally turning around. The basketball shoe that Reebok brought out last winter for Allen Iverson, the star rookie guard for the Philadelphia 76ers, for example, is one of the hottest shoes in the country. Dr. Jay's sold out of Iversons in two days, compared with the week it took the store to sell out of Nike's new Air Jordans. Iverson himself is brash and charismatic and faster from foul line to foul line than anyone else in the league. He's the equivalent of those kids in the East Village who began wearing Hush Puppies way back when. He's an innovator, and the hope at Reebok is that if he gets big enough the whole company can ride back to coolness on his coattails, the way Nike rode to coolness on the coattails of Michael Jordan. That's why Baysie was so excited when the kid said Reebok was trying to get butter when he looked at the Rush and the DMX RXT: it was a sign, albeit a small one, that the indefinable, abstract thing called cool was coming back.

When Baysie comes back from a coolhunt, she sits down with marketing experts and sales representatives and designers, and reconnects them to the street, making sure they have the right shoes going to the right places at the right price. When she got back from the Bronx, for example, the first thing she did was tell all these people they had to get a new men's DMX RXT out, fast because the kids on the street loved the women's version. "It's hotter than we realized," she told them. The coolhunter's job in this instance is very specific. What DeeDee does, on the other hand, is a little more ambitious. With the L Report, she tries to construct a kind of grand matrix of cool, comprising not just shoes but everything kids like, and not just kids of certain East Coast urban markets but kids all over. DeeDee and her staff put it out four times a year, in six different versions—for New York, Los Angeles, San Francisco, Austin-Dallas, Seattle, and Chicago—and then sell it to manufacturers, retailers, and ad agencies (among others) for twenty thousand dollars a year. They go to each city and find the coolest bars and clubs, and ask the coolest kids to fill out questionnaires. The information is then divided into six categories—You Saw It Here First, Entertainment and Leisure, Clothing and Accessories, Personal and Individual, Aspirations, and Food and Beverages—which are, in turn, broken up into dozens of subcategories, so that Personal and Individual, for example, included Cool Date, Cool Evening, Free Time, Favorite Possession, and on and on. The information in those subcategories is subdivided again by sex and by age bracket (14–18, 19–24, 25–30), and then, as a control, the L Report gives you the corresponding set of preferences for "mainstream" kids.

Few coolhunters bother to analyze trends with this degree of specificity. DeeDee's biggest competitor, for example, is something called the Hot Sheet, out of Manhattan. It uses a panel of three thousand kids a year from across the country and divides up their answers by sex and age, but it doesn't distinguish between regions, or between trendsetting and mainstream respondents. So what you're really getting is what all kids think is cool—not what cool kids think is cool, which is a considerably different piece of information. Janine Misdom and Joanne DeLuca, who run the Sputnik coolhunting group out of the garment district in Manhattan, meanwhile, favor an entirely impressionistic approach, sending out coolhunters with video cameras to talk to kids on the ground that it's too difficult to get cool kids to fill out questionnaires. Once, when I was visiting the Sputnik girls—as Misdom and DeLuca are known on the street, because they look alike and their first names are so similar and both have the same awesome New York accents—they showed me a video of the girl they believe was the patient zero of the whole eighties revival going on right now. It was back in September of 1993. Joanne and Janine were on Seventh Avenue, outside the Fashion Institute of Technology, doing random street interviews for a major jeans company, and, quite by accident, they ran into this nineteen-year-old raver. She had close-cropped hair, which was green at the top, and at the temples was shaved even closer and dyed pink. She had rings and studs all over her face, and a thick collection of silver tribal jewelry around her neck, and vintage jeans. She looked into the camera and said, "The sixties came in and then the seventies came in and I think it's ready to come back to the eighties. It's totally eighties: the eye makeup, the clothes. It's totally going back to that." Immediately, Joanne and Janine started asking around. "We talked to a few kids on the Lower East Side who said they were feeling the need to start breaking out their old Michael Jackson jackets," Joanne said. "They were joking about it. They weren't doing it yet. But they were going to, you know? They were saying, 'We're getting the urge to break out our Members Only jackets.'" That was right when Joanne and Janine were just starting up; calling the eighties revival was their first big break, and now they put out a full-blown videotaped report twice a year which is a collection of clips of interviews with extremely progressive people.

What DeeDee argues, though, is that cool is too subtle and too variegated to be captured with these kind of broad strokes. Cool is a set of dialects, not a language. The L Report can tell you, for example, that nineteen- to twenty-four-year-old male trendsetters in Seattle would most like to meet, among others, King Solomon and Dr. Seuss, and that nineteen- to twenty-four-year-old female trendsetters in San Francisco have turned their backs on Calvin Klein, Nintendo Gameboy, and sex. What's cool right now? Among male New York trendsetters: North Face jackets, rubber and latex, khakis, and the rock band Kiss. Among female trendsetters: ska music, old-lady clothing, and cyber tech. In Chicago, snowboarding is huge among trendsetters of both sexes and all ages. Women over nineteen are into short hair, while those in their teens have embraced mod culture, rock climbing, tag watches, and bootleg pants. In Austin-Dalls, meanwhile, twenty-five to thirty-year-old women trendsetters are into hats, heroin, computers, cigars, Adidas, and velvet, while men in their twenties are into video games and hemp. In all, the typical L Report runs over one hundred pages. But with that flood of data comes an obsolescence disclaimer: "The fluctuating nature of the trendsetting market makes keeping up with trends a difficult task." By the spring, in other words, everything may have changed.

The key to coolhunting, then, is to look for cool people first and cool things later, and not the other way around. Since cool things are always changing, you can't look for them, because the very fact they are cool means you have no idea what to look for. What you would be doing is thinking back on what was cool before and extrapolating, which is about as useful as presuming that because the Dow rose ten points yesterday it will rise another ten points today. Cool people, on the other hand, are a constant.

When I was in California, I met Salvador Barbier, who had been described to me by a coolhunter as "the Michael Jordan of skateboarding." He was tall and lean and languid, with a cowboy's insouciance, and we drove through the streets of Long Beach at fifteen miles an hour in a white late-model Ford Mustang, a car he had bought as a kind of ironic status gesture ("It would look good if I had a Polo jacket or maybe Nautica," he said) to go with his '62 Econoline van and his '64 T-bird. Sal told me that he and his friends, who are all in their mid-twenties, recently took to dressing up as if they were in eighth grade again and gathering together—having a "rally" on old BMX bicycles in front of their local 7-Eleven. "I'd wear muscle shirts, like Def Leppard or Foghat or some old heavy-metal band, and tight, tight tapered Levi's, and Vans on my feet—big, like, checkered Vans or striped Vans or camouflage Vans—and then wristbands and gloves with the fingers cut off. It was total eighties fashion. You had to look like that to participate in the rally. We had those denim jackets with patches on the back and combs that hung out the back pocket. We went without I.D.s, because we'd have to have someone else buy us beers." At this point, Sal laughed. He was driving really slowly and staring straight ahead and talking in a low drawl—the coolhunter's dream. "We'd ride to this bar and I'd have to carry my bike inside, because we have really expensive bikes, and when we got inside people would freak out. They'd say, 'Omigod,' and I was asking them if they wanted to go for a ride on the handlebars. They were like, 'What is wrong with you. My boyfriend used to dress like that in the eighth grade!' And I was like, 'He was probably a lot cooler then, too.'"

This is just the kind of person DeeDee wants. "I'm looking for somebody who is an individual, who has definitely set himself apart from everybody else, who doesn't look like his peers. I've run into trendsetters who look completely Joe Regular Guy. I can see Joe Regular Guy at a club listening to some totally hardcore band playing, and I say to myself 'Omigod, what's that guy doing here?' and that totally intrigues me, and I have to walk up to him and say, 'Hey, you're really into this band. What's up?' You know what I mean? I look at everything. If I see Joe Regular Guy sitting in a coffee shop and everyone around him has blue hair, I'm going to gravitate toward him, because, hey, what's Joe Regular Guy doing in a coffee shop with people with blue hair?"

We were sitting outside the Fred Segal store in West Hollywood. I was wearing a very conservative white Brooks Brothers button-down and a pair of Levi's, and DeeDee looked first at my shirt and then my pants and dissolved into laughter: "I mean, I might even go up to you in a cool place."

Picking the right person is harder than it sounds, though. Piney Kahn, who works for DeeDee, says, "There are a lot of people in the gray area. You've got these kids who dress ultra funky and have their own style. Then you realize they're just running after their friends." The trick is not just to be able to tell who is different but to be able to tell when that difference represents something truly cool. It's a gut thing. You have to somehow just know. DeeDee hired Piney because Piney clearly knows: she is twenty-four and used to work with the Beastie Boys and has the formidable self-possession of someone who is not only cool herself but whose parents were cool. "I mean," she says, "they named me after a tree."

Piney and DeeDee said that they once tried to hire someone as a coolhunter who was not, himself, cool, and it was a disaster.

"You can give them the boundaries," Piney explained. "You can say that if people shop at Banana Republic and listen to Alanis Morissette they're probably not trendsetters. But then they might go out and assume that everyone who does that is not a trendsetter, and not look at the other things."

"I mean, I myself might go into Banana Republic and buy a T-shirt," DeeDee chimed in.

Their non-cool coolhunter just didn't have that certain instinct, that sense that told him when it was O.K. to deviate from the manual. Because he wasn't cool, he didn't know cool, and that's the essence of the third rule of cool: you have to be one to know one. That's why Baysie is still on top of this business at forty-one. "It's easier for me to tell you what kid is cool than to tell you what things are cool," she says. But that's all she needs to know. In this sense, the third rule of cool fits perfectly into the second: the second rule says that cool cannot be manufactured, only observed, and the third says that it can only be observed by those who are themselves cool. And, of course, the first rule says that it cannot accurately be observed at all, because the act of discovering cool causes cool to take flight, so if you add all three together they describe a closed loop, the hermeneutic circle of coolhunting, a phenomenon whereby not only can the uncool not see cool but cool cannot even be adequately described to them. Baysie says that she can see a coat on one of her friends and think it's not cool but then see the same coat on DeeDee and think that it is cool. It is not possible to be cool, in other words, unless you are—in some larger sense—already cool, and so the phenomenon that the uncool cannot see and cannot have described to them is also something that they cannot ever attain, because if they did it would no longer be cool. Coolhunting represents the ascendancy, in the marketplace, of high school.

Once, I was visiting DeeDee at her house in Laurel Canyon when one of her L Report assistants, Jonas Vail, walked in. He'd just come back from Niketown on Wilshire Boulevard, where he'd bought seven hundred dollars' worth of the latest sneakers to go with the three hundred dollars' worth of skateboard shoes he'd bought earlier in the afternoon. Jonas is tall and expressionless, with a peacoat, dark jeans, and short-cropped black hair. "Jonas is good," DeeDee says. "He works with me on everything. That guy knows more pop culture. You know: What was the name of the store Mrs. Garrett owned on 'The Facts of Life'? He knows all the names of the extras from eighties sitcoms. I can't believe someone like him exists. He's fucking unbelievable. Jonas can spot a cool person a mile away."

Jonas takes the boxes of shoes and starts unpacking them on the couch next to DeeDee. He picks up a pair of the new Nike ACG hiking boots, and says, "All the Japanese in Niketown were really into these." He hands the shoes to DeeDee.

"Of course they were!" she says. "The Japanese are all into the tech-looking shit. Look how exaggerated it is, how bulbous." DeeDee has very ambivalent feelings about Nike, because she thinks its marketing has got out of hand. When she was in the New York Niketown with a girlfriend recently, she says, she started getting lightheaded and freaked out. "It's cult, cult. It was like, 'Hello, are we all drinking the Kool-Aid here?'" But this shoe she loves. It's Dr. Jay's in the Bronx all over again. DeeDee turns the shoe around and around in the air, tapping the big clear-blue plastic bubble on the side—the visible Air-Sole unit—with one finger. "It's so fucking rad. It looks like a platypus!" In front of me, there is a pair of Nike's new shoes for the basketball player Jason Kidd.

I pick it up. "This looks . . . cool," I venture uncertainly.

DeeDee is on the couch, where she's surrounded by shoeboxes and sneakers and white tissue paper, and she looks up reprovingly because, of course, I don't get it. I can't get it. "Beyooond cool, Maalcolm. Beyooond cool."

© 1997 Malcolm Gladwell

Spring: Doing

The Antigone Legend and The Prologue in Sophocles' *Antigone*

Bertolt Brecht

Translated by Judith Malina

[Brecht's poem, "The Antigone Legend," is a recapitulation of the drama in summary form. Brecht himself used it as a rehearsal device intended to develop objectivity in the actors' performances: his stage manager interrupted the rehearsal at intervals to read the relevant description of the action from the poem while the cast paused. The Living Theatre, on the other hand, used Brecht's poem for another purpose. Performing the play in English in different parts of the world, the company paused regularly to recite the poem's description of the action in the audience's own language. —J.M.]

But Antigone, the child of Oedipus, went with the jug
to gather dust to cover the body of Polyneikes
which the angry tyrant had thrown to the dogs and the vultures.

And her sister Ismene met her as she was gathering dust.

Bitterly, Antigone complained of their brothers' fate,
both fallen in the war, the one a hero, the other,
fleeing the battle, slain, not by the enemy, but killed by his own men.

But she did not persuade her sister to take the forbidden steps
towards the shamed and mangled corpse of their brother.

And the sisters parted in anger at the break of day.

But hearing at dawn of the victory-battle in the long war for metal,
the Elders of Thebes put on the wreaths of victory,
which are woven of the glittering leaves of the poisonous laurel,
which confuses the senses and makes the step uncertain.

Early in the morning they were already standing in front of Kreon's house.

And back from the battle, preceding the troops of Argos,
came the tyrant, and found them in front of the house at daybreak.

And, leaning on the saber, he described how over in Argos
vultures now hopped from corpse to corpse; it delighted the elders.

Quickly they crowned him with laurel, but he did not yet give them
the saber, but grimly gave it to his bodyguard.

Reviling the son of Oedipus, his showpiece, to frighten the people,
the tyrant spoke of a bloody clean-up, exterminating the enemies
under the Theban roof, when a messenger came: the horror
had not horrified, the mangled body was covered with dust.

Angrily the tyrant questioned the guard and all the others,
and so that they saw it, he tested the saber's blade with his thumb.

Wandering with bowed heads, the Elders considered man
and his monstrous power, how the sea with the keel, and the beast
with the yoke, and the horse with the bridle were conquered,
and yet he will, like a monster, also conquer his fellow man.

And how, as Antigone was brought in and questioned as to why
she broke the law, she looked around and turned to the Elders
and saw that they were appalled and said: 'To set an example.'

Then she asked support from the Elders, but the Elders
looked to Kreon. Antigone said: 'He who seeks power
is drinking salt water. He can't keep it down, yet
he has to drink more. I am not the first sacrifice, nor the last.'
But they turned their backs. Antigone called: 'Woe is you!'

'She wants to divide us!' cried the tyrant, 'and divided,
our city will fall to the invaders.' Said Antigone: 'Always,
the men in power make this threat, and we bring you sacrifices, and soon
the city, thus weakened and enslaved, falls to the invader.
He who bows down sees only the earth and the earth will get him.'

'Fresh girl, are you cursing your country? Listen, it's thrown you out!'
Said Antigone: 'Who throws me out? A place where I can't hold my
head up isn't my country. O, there are less in the city
since you are in power. The youngsters, the men,
aren't they coming back? You left with so many and now you return
all alone.' Then the tyrant was silent and had no answer.

'You're raving,' said the Elders and asked, 'Haven't you heard of the victory battle?'
'Because she is my enemy,' said the tyrant, 'she begrudges you the victory.'
Said Antigone: 'It would be better, and safer too, to sit
in the ruins of our own houses, than with you in the enemy's city.'
The Elders looked at her coldly and stood by the tyrant.

And Ismene, her sister, came out of the house and said:
'I am the one who did it.' But Antigone said: 'She's lying.'
And wiping the sweat off, he said: 'Work it out between you.'

But Antigone was overcome by weakness, and asked her sister
to go on living. 'I think it is enough if I die.'

Said the tyrant: 'When joyous Thebes begins the dances
of peaceable Bacchus, the cave shall receive her, living and dead.

And they led her away, who dared to face up to the ruler.

Obediently, the Elders handed the ruler the mask of Bacchus,
speaking the choral song: 'When you dress up for the victory dances,
don't stamp too hard on the ground, and not where it grows green.'

'May he who has troubled you, praise your victory.'

And the ruler's youngest son stepped forward, Hamon,
commander of the city's garrison, who was to marry Antigone,
to bring news of the unrest in the city because of the fate of Oedipus' child.

Reluctantly now the father reveals his hidden distress
with a show of force and hardness, but his son does not understand him.

Not minding the listening Elders, and wooingly circling the stubborn one,
the father asks his son to forget her who broke the law.

But when his son did not yield, Kreon mocked him,
whipping the straw mane of his mask in his son's face.

And his son left him. The Elders watched with alarm.

Grimly the victor went to the celebration.

And the music from the city alarmed the listening Elders.
The dancers of Bacchus are forming their circles.

And this is the hour too when Oedipus' child in her room
hears Bacchus in the distance and prepares for her last journey.
For now he calls to his own, and the city, thirsting for pleasure,
gives the peaceable god its joyous answer.

For victory is great and Bacchus irresistible,
when he approaches the mourners and hands them the drink of forgetfulness.
Then she discards the black robes she was sewing to mourn her sons in,
and runs to the orgy of Bacchus, seeking depletion.

And now, as Antigone was led out of Kreon's house,
she weakened at last and collapsed among her friendly servants.

Politely the Elders reminded her that she herself
chose her deeds and her death. She said: 'Are you making fun of me?'

And went on and complained of her fate: dreary childhood,
doomed parents, to whom she returns now, unmarried,
and also a brother who now draws her down to the grave.

The Elders set the bowl before her and the small jug of wine and
millet, the gifts for the dead, and recounted for her comfort the names
of the saints and heroes who died full of greatness and glory.

They sternly advise her to practice patience with godly resolution.

Then she got angry and called the Elders cowards.

And her own weakness vanished when she saw their weakness.
'You are expecting wagons' she cried, 'loaded with booty, and wagons
will come, but to carry booty away. You, the living' she cried,
'it is you whom I accuse' and tears of anger choked her.

And she looked around and saw beautiful Thebes'
roofs and hills and groves, and soberly bowed down before them,
taking her leave. But again her compassion turned to anger.

'Out of you, my native land, monsters have risen, and so you must
come to dust and ashes. Girls,' she said, 'if anyone
asks for Antigone, tell him: 'We saw her escape to the grave.'

Turned around and went, with light, secure steps.

Blindly the Elders watched her going, and recited the choral song:
'But she, too, once ate of the savory bread
that was baked in the dark caves. Not until her own kind
suffered and died, did she raise her voice loudly in protest.'

But she who warned them could not have yet reached the grave
when a somber awareness was sensed in the celebrant city.

For now the seer comes, the blind man, driven by rumors
of conflict in the ruler's house. And mocking, a mummer
leaps about him, and shakes the straw mane of the mask,
and rattles it over his head and pursues him across the plaza.
Lifting the sole of his foot to the tempo of the Bacchanalian dances,
he points a scornful thumb to show the elders the seer's failing.

Impudently tapping the ground with his staff before the seer's groping foot, and
it is Kreon, drunk with victory. The Elders watch in silence.

'Old fool, you don't seem to like celebrations. Why aren't you
wearing the laurel? It's ours!' And anger sharpened his voice.

'Does a blinder man follow the blind man?' asked the seer.
'Remember, Kreon, strife and sacrilege displease the gods.
Ugly birds rise up before me that have fed on Oedipus' son.'

The ruler laughed. 'I know that your birds fly at your pleasure,
obedient to your mood, and that your mood can be swayed by silver.'

'Please don't offer me any. What use is silver in wartime?'
said the seer. Said the ruler: 'The war is over.'

'Is it over?' asked the seer. 'Down by the harbor
they're drying fish for the troops, as though they won't be back by autumn.'
'You are cruel. Why? What mischief have you started?'
The tyrant stood silently by and had no answer.

And the seer got up and went.
And murmuring gloomily
the tyrant prepared to leave. The Elders watched astonished.
Fear answered fear, and they dared to ask the question:
'Well now, Kreon, how goes the war?' And he said, 'No good.'

And they stepped up to him, with the mask of peace in his hand,
and they too held the masks of peace in their hands.
And they argued with him whether it was their war or his.
'But it was you who sent me to get the metal in Argos!'
'But it was you who told us the victory was ours.' 'I said: In the end.'

And again he started to leave, and again the Elders
angrily pressed the ruler: 'Call the troops back home!'
because they were worried about the troops, and even more about their possessions.
And he drove the staff with the mask of peace into the ground.

'Certainly I'll call the troops, and my eldest son, Megareus,
will lead them, and, iron in hand, they will come to meet your ingratitude.'

And as the threatening name Megareus still hung in the air,
a messenger came: 'Sir, bow your head, Megareus
is no more, and your troops are besieged, and the enemy approaches.'

Gasping, he pictures the battle: how the troops, exhausted by brotherly
strife on account of Oedipus' son, half-heartedly lifted their spears,
while the people of Argos fought ferociously for their homes.

'And they come here ferociously now,' cried the messenger, and I'm
glad that I'm done for!' Held his stomach, and with fear on his face,
fell to the ground in front of Kreon's mask of peace.

But then Kreon screamed, too, but it was the father who was screaming.
Said the Elders: 'The enemy is advancing on us in fury, and Thebes,
drunk with joy, is dancing! Call up the troops of the home front!'

Then the Elders tore the victory wreaths from their heads,
and broke the masks of Bacchus, and covered the dead man
with the wreaths and masks and cried out: 'Woe is us!'

And the ruler remembered his other son, the younger one,
Hamon, leader of the troops of the home front,
and he hurried to forgive him and to pardon Antigone for him.

But the Elders stood up and struck the metallic cymbal
to waken the city from the deadly drunkenness of victory.
The stifling metal alarm disrupts the dancers of Bacchus,
and the stamping of triumph turns into terrified flight.

And through the raging city came a gentle messenger,
Antigone's youngest maid, who had led her to the grave.
'Hamon is dead and gone, bleeding by his own hand.
When he saw Antigone in the cave and saw that she was hanged,
he pierced himself with his sword in spite of the pleas of his father.'

And the Elders shudder to receive their leader, led by
Antigone's maids. He holds a bloody shirt in his hands.
'Hamon is dead and gone. Dead and gone is Thebes.
Because she betrayed me, she has become a meal for the vultures!'

And he showed the Elders the bloody shirt of his son,
who in anger denied him the sword. And rotten and gruesome,
unteachable, he staggers, he who was the leader of many,
toward the falling city. But the Elders
still follow the leader. Even now, in downfall and annihilation.

PROLOGUE

Berlin, April 1945

(DAYBREAK. TWO SISTERS COME OUT OF AN AIR-RAID SHELTER, RETURNING HOME.)

THE FIRST: And when we came out of the air-raid shelter
we saw that our house had not been destroyed, but looked brighter
than before, lit by the fire across the street; and then
my sister was the one who saw it first.

THE SECOND: Sister, why is our door open?

THE FIRST: The fire-storm pushed it open.

THE SECOND: Sister, what are these marks on the ground?

THE FIRST: Only the footprints of someone who tried to escape.

THE SECOND: Sister, what is that pack in the corner?

THE FIRST: Better to find something there than to find something missing.

THE SECOND: It's a loaf of bread, sister, and a whole ham!

THE FIRST: Well, that's nothing to be afraid of.

THE SECOND: But sister, who was here?

THE FIRST: How should I know?
        Someone who wants us to have a good meal.

THE SECOND: But we should have known! We have so little faith!
        What luck! Our brother is back!

THE FIRST: And we embraced each other and we were happy
        because our brother was in the war and he was all right.
        And we cut up the ham and ate the bread
        that he brought for our needs.

THE SECOND: Take more for yourself. The food is so bad
        in the factory lunchroom.

THE FIRST: No, you need it more.

THE SECOND: Take a bigger slice for yourself.

THE FIRST: No, no more for me.

THE SECOND: But how could he come here?

THE FIRST: With the troops.

THE SECOND: Where could he be now?

THE FIRST: Wherever the battle is.

THE SECOND: Oh.

THE FIRST: But we couldn't hear any sound of battle.

THE SECOND: I shouldn't have asked.

THE FIRST: I didn't want to worry you.
        And as we were sitting there silently, a sound struck
        our ears from the other side of the door that froze our blood.

(A SCREAM FROM OUTSIDE.)

THE SECOND: Sister, someone is screaming. Let's go see.

THE FIRST: Sit down, you. If you see you'll be seen.
        So we didn't go to the door, and didn't see
        the things that happened outside.
        But we didn't eat anymore, and didn't look
        at one another. We stood up and got ready
        to go to work, as we did every morning.
        And my sister did the dishes and I
        remembered and took our brother's pack to the closet

where his old things are kept.
And there it was, as though my heart had stopped.
There on a hook hung his field-jacket.
Sister, he is not in the battle.
He has run away.
He is not in the war anymore.

THE SECOND: There are some that are still in it. But he is not.
THE FIRST: He must have been condemned to death.
THE SECOND: And so he cheated them.
THE FIRST: And there was a little hole. . . .
THE SECOND: And that was what he crawled through.
THE FIRST: The others are still in it, but he is not in it.
THE SECOND: He is not in the war anymore.
THE FIRST: And we laughed and we were happy.
Our brother was out of the war and he was all right.
And we were still standing there when a sound struck
our ears that froze our blood.

(A SCREAM FROM OUTSIDE.)

THE SECOND: Sister, who's screaming outside the door?
THE FIRST: They are torturing people again for whatever their reason.
THE SECOND: Sister, shouldn't we go and see?
THE FIRST: Stay inside, you. If you see, you'll be seen.
So we waited awhile and didn't see
the things that happened outside.
But we had to go to work and then
it was I who saw what was outside the door.
Sister, sister, don't go out.
Our brother is in front of the house.
But he is not out of the thing.
He is hanging from the butcher's hook. Ahh.
But my sister did come out of the house
and she screamed.
THE SECOND: Sister, they have hanged him;
that's why he called out to us.
Give me the knife. Here, give me the knife
so that I can cut him down so he won't hang there.
So that I can carry his body inside
and bring him back to life.
THE FIRST: Sister, leave the knife alone.
You won't bring him back to life.
When they see us standing around him
they'll do to us what they have done to him.

THE SECOND: Let me go. I didn't go before
       when they hanged him.
THE FIRST: Just as she reached the door
      the officer approached.

(AN OFFICER ENTERS.)

OFFICER: I know him, but who are you?
      He stepped out of your door.
      So I figure it can be proved
      that you and this traitor knew one another.
THE FIRST: Please sir, don't arrest us.
      We don't know this person at all.
OFFFICER: Then what is she doing with the knife?
THE FIRST: Then I looked at my sister.
      Would she now under the penalty of death
      try to free her brother?
      If only he had not died.

Search for the Fallen in a Now-Quiet Forest

Jeffrey Fleishman, Times Staff Writer
May 2, 2007

A volunteer sifts the earth outside Berlin for forgotten soldiers. So far, he's uncovered the remains of 20,000.

QUIET OBSESSION: Erwin Kowalke collects the bones of a soldier who died in the last days of World War II south of Berlin.
(Petra Falkenberg/For the Times)

Hammer, Germany—The shallow hole widens and a man comes together like a puzzle: hips, fingers, ribs, vertebrae, teeth and crushed skull. A boot surfaces along with a rusted bullet clip. But no dog tags, no wedding ring, nothing to give him a name, so the bones go into a box where they are marked with a number written in white chalk: 1,968.

The one who filled the box is sweaty; his after-shave fades amid the dirt and the dust. His name is Erwin Kowalke. The villagers know him by his determined face and trim graying beard and the way he moves from shovel, spade to hoe. He collects the bones of the fallen from a world war that ended six decades ago, but one that, if you listen, still moans through the forests and across the marshes.

"I once dug a whole plane out of a swamp. The pilot was sitting in the cockpit. His leather jacket was pretty well preserved even after all those years, but he was burned," said Kowalke, a volunteer who has excavated the remains of 20,000 people, most of them German and Russian soldiers killed in fighting as Berlin collapsed toward defeat in the final days of April 1945.

EXCAVATION: Erwin Kowalke holds the jawbone of a soldier found buried in a forest close to Hammer, south of Berlin. "I can tell how old they were when I hold their bones," Kowalke says. "Bones have a different feel at different ages."
(Petra Falkenberg/For the Times)

The dead are hidden in this loamy earth, but they are his, and with quiet obsession he aims to find them, even if there are 20,000 more scattered beyond the windshield of his white station wagon, which bounces and swerves down forgotten country roads.

"People tell me to just let the bones sleep in the woods," said Kowalke, a member of the German War Graves Assn. who has been searching for skeletons for 43 years. "But I say to them that no matter what this generation did, without them you wouldn't be here."
(Phillippe Huguen/AFP/Getty Images)

"People tell me to just let the bones sleep in the woods," said Kowalke, a member of the German War Graves Assn. who has been searching for skeletons for 43 years. "But I say to them that no matter what this generation did, without them you wouldn't be here."

"In these bones you see what war is like. I know war now. I'll tell you what it is. War is young men killing other young men they do not know on the orders of old men who know one another too well."

And so he digs, this compact 65-year-old man with a briefcase holding ledgers of the dead and an amber-tinted photograph of his father, a German soldier killed somewhere in France. What a boy didn't have he invents; the bones Kowalke collects honor his father and those days in 1944 when the man returned briefly from the front to visit his 3-year-old son. It was the last time they saw each other.

"He was tall," said Kowalke, "I still remember my small arms around his black boots. He arrived home on June 3 and three days later it was D-day in Normandy and they called him back."

Kowalke grew into a fidgety man with two daughters and five grandsons; his wife, Gisela, calls him a "restless pensioner." His coveralls are neat and pressed and his boots, like those he recalls on his father, are shiny, as if each new day, despite the grime to come, must be faced with a meticulous spirit. When he brushes the dirt from a bone, he speaks of where joints and cartilage connect, and then his eyes, pale blue and flecked with brown, scan the parts of a man he never knew for clues to who he was.

He conjures old battles as if they've happened just last week, of how the Germans moved and how the Russians countered; for him history lies about 36 inches beneath the ground, the depth where he finds most of his bones.

The land he scours these days rolls out from the soldiers' cemetery in the town of Halbe toward the Polish border, about 30 miles south of Berlin. In this terrain thick with pine and broken by lakes and creeks, two Russian divisions closed in like pincers on the trapped 9th German Army. Tens of thousands died and the bodies of infantrymen were stacked along roadsides shadowed by starving dogs and storms of swirling flies.

Many were burned. Some were pushed into bomb craters, others were flung into rough graves dug by men in a hurry. The dead were lost, except their bones. Kowalke gathers them in black cardboard boxes the size and shape of an infant's coffin that he delivers to the cemetery. The earth claims much after 60 years, and if there are no identifying signs tangled amid the ribs, the bones are reburied, sometimes in a small ceremony, and given a marble marker that says: Unknown.

That mystery bothers Kowalke. Unknown. He hates the sound. But names often do survive, on zinc and aluminum dog tags, strangely preserved papers, trinkets zipped into shaving kits and in letters scratched on helmets.

"We identified one soldier awhile back. His 92-year-old widow from Berlin came to the cemetery in Halbe," Kowalke said. "When I saw that old woman in a wheelchair holding the box of bones that were her husband and saying, 'Oh, Werner, I know where you are. Now, I can have peace,' I knew that what I do matters."

He seems to understand that a man often finds his calling by chance. After the war ended, his mother married a farmer; Kowalke grew up in the fields, apprenticed as a carpenter and later worked as a machinist for irrigation equipment.

He knew the land, from the winter fields to the river grass. He unearthed his first German soldier in 1963, when his wife's father, who had asthma, asked him to help with some digging.

Until the fall of the Berlin Wall in 1989, the work went on quietly; the Soviet-backed leaders of East Germany didn't much care whether Hitler's army received a proper resting place. German fascist aggression killed millions of Russians and instigated the Holocaust—why, the thinking went, should the German army be granted even a semblance of respect?

"I excavate Russian soldiers too," Kowalke said. "Some Germans get mad at me for that. They say, 'How can you do it? Look what the Russians did to us.' But I tell them, 'Don't forget history. It was the Germans who marched into Poland and started all this.'"

"It doesn't matter whether they're Russian or German to me. The dead deserve a bit of honor. They were mostly all young, you know. I can tell how old they were when I hold their bones. Bones have a different feel at different ages."

Kowalke is, perhaps, the most frequent visitor to the cemetery. He knows it well, remembers how it flowed from a church graveyard and spread through the forest, taking shape the way a knitted shawl grows from a bag of yarn. He looked toward the tree line; beyond, cars raced north and south on the autobahn, their sounds a soft, distant thrum in a cemetery where rows read like this: Gottfried Puchinger, 5/7/1920 to April 1945. Unknown. Unknown. Unknown. Unknown. Unknown. Unknown. Unknown. Helmut Kruse 5/29/1916 to April 1945.

"I don't judge the dead," Kowalke said, "but God knows them all."

He has delved all over the east German map, but he has also turned soil from Romania to the Balkans, and is mystified by the breadth of a war that scattered German bones, and those of millions of others, across countries and continents. Collecting them all may never happen. Kowalke works with 20 or so other volunteer diggers, but the war veterans are dying out and the desire to remember, long a sensitive topic in Germany, has faded with younger generations.

On a clear morning not long ago, Kowalke left the cemetery to dig a shallow hole in a stand of pine at the rim of a farm field. He had gotten a call from the guys with metal detectors who hunt for munitions and bombs. The woods are full of unexploded things—bullets, grenades and tank shells. But there was something else out there, a faint ping as if from a belt buckle or a button. Kowalke arrived in his car and the guys nodded; he is like them, a scavenger of sorts.

They pointed. Kowalke worked his spade, slicing it easily into soil marbled with sand and clayish dirt. He broke shallow roots, breathing through his nose, finding a rhythm, muscles hardening beneath his zip-up fading green coveralls. Scrape, scrape, plunk.

"A bone," he said.

He pulled up a dark clump, a boot, German by make he could tell because of the nail studs in the heel. He lifted more, a shin bone. He brushed the dirt from it, put it into the box. He took his shovel, but went slower; the strange, dark harvest came.

"I'd say he was between 30 to 35 years old. No doubt he was a German," said Kowalke, holding the jawbone and examining the teeth. "Russians didn't have these kinds of fillings.

Given his age, you have to assume he was married and probably had children. They probably never knew where he ended up."

More digging. An ammunition clip, then another. And then a crushed skull, breaking apart in Kowalke's hands. He took a hoe, raked the dirt for small bits.

"I can't think about who he was or might have been," he said. "It's better not to speculate, but concentrate on details."

His hands work the soil, his fingers like rippling sieves. But nothing, nothing he had hoped for; no dog tags, no ring, no rifle, no wisp of identity. Kowalke piled the bones into the box and carried it to his car. He measured arm and leg bones and determined that "this man was 1 meter 68 centimeters tall. All of him fits in a small box."

He opened his briefcase, pushed aside the picture of his father and filled out the death ledger. By the space for a name he wrote 1,968. He stapled the lid on and slid the box into his car. He rubbed the dirt from his hands and drove toward the cemetery, and another marble marker chiseled with the word: Unknown.

jeffrey.fleishman@latimes.com

Before the Law

Translated from the German by Malcolm Pasley
Franz Kafka

Before the law stands a doorkeeper. To this doorkeeper there comes a man from the country and asks to be admitted to the law. But the doorkeeper says that he cannot at present grant him admittance. The man considers, and then asks whether that means he may be admitted later on. 'It is possible,' says the doorkeeper, 'but not at present.' Since the gate leading to the law stands open as always and the doorkeeper steps aside, the man bends down to look through the gateway into the interior. When the doorkeeper sees this he laughs and says: 'If it tempts you so, then try entering despite my prohibition. But mark: I am powerful. And I am only the lowest doorkeeper. In hall after hall stand other doorkeepers, each more powerful than the last. The mere sight of the third is more than even I can bear.' The man from the country has not expected such difficulties; the law, he thinks, should be accessible to everyone and at all times; but as he now takes a closer look at the doorkeeper in his fur coat, at his large pointed nose, his long, sparse, black Tartar beard, he decides that it is better, after all, to wait until he receives permission to enter. The doorkeeper gives him a stool and lets him sit down to one side of the door. There he sits for days and years. He makes many attempts to be admitted and wearies the doorkeeper with his entreaties. The doorkeeper often conducts little examinations with him, questioning him about his home and about much else; but they are impersonal questions such as dignitaries ask, and he always concludes by repeating once again that he cannot yet admit him. The man, who has equipped himself well for his journey, uses up all that he has, however valuable it is, in order to bribe the doorkeeper. The latter always accepts everything, but saying as he does so: 'I only accept so you won't feel there's anything you haven't tried.' Throughout the many years the man observes the doorkeeper almost without interruption. He forgets the other doorkeepers, and this first one seems to him the sole obstacle barring his admission to the law. He curses his misfortune, fiercely and loudly in the early years; later, as he grows old, he merely grumbles away to himself. He becomes childish, and since during his long study of the doorkeeper he has even discovered the fleas in his fur collar, he begs the fleas as well to help him and change the doorkeeper's mind. Finally his sight begins to fail and he does not know whether it is really growing darker around him or whether his eyes are just deceiving him. But he can indeed perceive in the darkness a radiance that streams out unquenchably from the doorway of the law. Now he has not much longer to live. Before his death all the experiences of the long years assemble in his mind to form a question which he has never yet asked the doorkeeper. He beckons to him since he can no longer raise his stiffening body. The doorkeeper has to bend down to him, for the difference in height has changed very much to the man's disadvantage. 'What is it that you still want to know?' asks the doorkeeper, 'you are insatiable.' 'Surely everyone strives to reach the law,' says the man, 'how does it happen that for all these many years no one except me has ever asked for admittance?' The doorkeeper recognizes that the man is at his end, and in order to reach his failing ears he raises his voice and bellows at him: 'No one else could ever have been admitted here, since this entrance was intended for you alone. Now I am going to close it.'

Selections from The Indian War of Independence 1857

Vinayak Damodar Savarkar

Author's Introduction

Fifty years having passed by, the circumstances having changed, and the prominent actors on both sides being no more, the account of the War of 1857 has crossed the limits of current politics and can be relegated to the realms of history.

When, therefore, taking the searching attitude of an historian, I began to scan that instructive and magnificent spectacle, I found to my great surprise the brilliance of a War of Independence shining in "the mutiny of 1857." The spirits of the dead seemed hallowed by martyrdom, and out of the heap of ashes appeared forth sparks of a fiery inspiration, I thought that my countrymen will be most agreeably disappointed, even as I was, at this deep-buried spectacle in one of the most neglected corners of our history, if I could but show this to them by the light of research. So, I tried to do the same and am able to-day to present to my Indian readers this startling but faithful picture of the great events of 1857.

The nation that has no consciousness of its past has no future. Equally true it is that a nation must develop its capacity not only of claiming a past but also of knowing how to use it for the furtherance of its future. The nation ought to be the master and not the slave of its own history. For, it is absolutely unwise to try to do certain things now irrespective of special considerations, simply because they had been once acted in the past. The feeling of hatred against the Mahomedans was just and necessary in the times of Shivaji—but, such a feeling would be unjust and foolish if nursed now, simply because it was the dominant feeling of the Hindus then.

As almost all the authorities on which this work is based are English authors, for whom it must have been impossible to paint the account of the other side as elaborately and as faithfully as they have done their own, it is perfectly possible that many a scene, other than what this book contains, might have been left unstated, and many a scene described in this book might be found to have been wrongly described. But if some patriotic historian would go to northern India and try to collect the traditions from the very mouths of those who witnessed and perhaps took a leading part in the War, the opportunity of knowing the exact account of this can still be caught, though unfortunately it will be impossible to do so before very long. When, within a decade or two, the whole generation of those who took part in that war shall have passed away never to return, not only would it be impossible to have the pleasure of seeing the actors themselves, but the history of their actions will have to be left permanently incomplete. Will any patriotic historian undertake to prevent this while it is not yet too late?

Even the slightest references and the most minute details in this book can be as much substantiated by authoritative works as the important events and the main currents of the history.

Before laying down this pen, the only desire I want to express is that such a patriotic and yet faithful, a more detailed and yet coherent, history of 1857 may come forward in the nearest future from an Indian pen, so that this my humble writing may soon be forgotten! —Vinayak Damodar Savarkar

The Original Publisher's Preface

This book on the history of 1857 was originally written in an Indian vernacular. But owing to the unique nature of the book which, for the first time ever since the great War was fought, proves from the English writers themselves that the rising of the Indian people in 1857 was in no way an insignificant chapter in, or a tale unworthy of, a great people's history, pressing requests were made from many quarters to translate the work into the English language, so that, by translations into the other vernaculars, the whole of the Indian nation might be enabled to read the history of the ever memorable War of 1857. Realising the reasonableness and importance of these requests and with the kind permission of the author the publishers undertook the translation of the original into the English language. With the patriotic co-operation of many of their countrymen, they are able to-day to place this work in the hands of Indian readers.

The work of translating an Oriental work into a western tongue has ever been a task of immense difficulty, even when the translator has all the facilities which leisure and training could afford. But when the translation had to be done by divers hands and within a very short time, it was clearly foreseen by the publishers that the translation would be defective and unidiomatic. But the main point before the publishers was not to teach the Indian people how to make an elegant translation nor to show them how to write correct English—points to which they were supremely indifferent—but to let them know how their nation fought for its Independence and how their ancestors died "for the ashes of their fathers and the temples of their Godds." So, the publishers decided to run the risk of publishing the book as soon as it could explain the facts it had to tell, though none could be more conscious of the faults of the language than they themselves. Fifty years have passed and yet those who died for the honour of their soil and race are looked upon as madmen and villains by the world abroad; while their own kith and kin for whom they shed their blood, are ashamed even to own them! To allow this state of public opinion, born of stupid ignorance, and purposely and systematically kept up by a band of interested hirelings, to continue any longer would have been a national sin. So, the publishers have not waited till the language of this translation could be rendered elegant, which would be more shameful—to let hideous calumny hover over and smother down the spirit of martyrdom, or to let some mistake creep into a book admittedly translated into a foreign tongue? The first, at the best, was a crime, and the second at the worst a venial literary offence. Therefore, the publishers owe no apology to, nor would one be asked for, by the Indian readers for whose special benefit, the work is published.

But, to those sympathetic foreign readers who might be inclined to read this book, we owe an apology for the faults of the language and crave their indulgence for the same.   —THE PUBLISHERS,
LONDON MAY 10, 1909

The Story of this History

"An honest tale speeds best
By being plainly told."
—Shakespeare

Apart from the splendid merits of the subject matter dealt with in the warlit pages of this history of "The Indian War of Independence of 1857," the story of the thrilling vicissitudes through which this book had to pass does by itself entitle it to be placed on the classical shelf in any world library.

The Object and the Name of the the Book

Veer Savarkarji, the famous author of this book, did himself explain in an article in the "Talwar," an organ of the Abhi Nava Bharat Revolutionary Society, which was started by him and published in Paris, that his object in writing this history was, subject to historical accuracy, to inspire his people with a burning desire to rise again and wage a second and a successful war to liberate their motherland. He also expected that the history should serve to place before the revolutionists an outline of a programme of organisation and action to enable them to prepare the nation for a future war of liberation. It would never have been possible to preach such a revolutionary gospel publicly throughout India or carry conviction so effectively as an illuminating illustration of what had actually happened in the nearest past would do. So he invoked the warriors of 1857 to deliver his message through their own mighty words and mightier deeds.

The ideal of absolute political Independence, and the conviction that the ultimate and inevitable means to realize that ideal could be no other than an *armed nationol revolt* against the foreign domination,—were concepts which in those day–lay even beyond the horizon of the then political thought and action in India. The very mention of them was brushed aside as chimerical by the then extremists, was denounced as criminal by the loyal moderates and was even anathematised as immoral by the half-witted moralists! But these self-same concepts formed the two fundamental tenets of the A. N. B. (Abhi Nava Bharat) Revolutionary organisation. "Reforms and a peaceful solution" formed the alpha and omega of the ambition of the then Indian National Congress itself. Independence, Revolution—let alone a War for Independence—were as a rule words almost unknown, unheard and inconceivably incomprehensible even to the highly patriotic Indian world. It was to familiarize this Indian patriotic world with at least these words in daily thought, and by their constant repetition, like that of a '*Mantram*,' to hypnotize the youthful political mind into a sub-conscious attraction for the noble concepts, which the words connoted—that Savarkar, who as a Historian would have called this book a history of the 'National Rising' or of the 'Revolutionary War of 1857', did, of a set design, name it the history of "The Indian War of Independence of 1857."

Veer Savarkar always emphasized the necessity in the Indian condition of carrying politics and patriotism to the camp, to the military forces in India, for rendering any armed revolt practical. The history of the Revolutionary War of 1857 proved beyond cavil or criticism that only some fifty years previously our ancestors had aimed to achieve absolute political independence, could bring about the active and armed participation in the National struggle of the military forces and could wage an inexorable war for the liberation of our motherland. He consequently felt that this history if told viewing it through such a revolutionary perspective was most likely to animate the rising generation of India with the faith that there was no reason why it should not be practicable and even more faithful to try again as, at any rate, there was no other way to salvation. How far this expectation of the author was realized will be seen as this story proceeds.

Originally Written in Marathi

This book was written originally in Marathi, in 1908, when Veer Savarkar was about twenty-four years of age. Some select chapters used to be reproduced in English, in speeches which Veer Savarkarji used to deliver at the open weekly meetings of the Free India Society in London. Perhaps through this channel or otherwise the detectives got some scent of the subject-matter of this book which their reports dubbed as revolutionary, explosive and highly treasonous. Soon a chapter or two of the Marathi manuscript were found missing, which, it was disclosed later on, were stolen by the detective agents, and found their way to the Scotland Yard, the headquarters of the British Intelligence Department in London. Nevertheless, the Marathi manuscript was sent to India by the revolutionists so secretly and cleverly that, foiling the strict vigilance of the customs authorities of the Indian Ports, it reached safely its destination. But the leading press-concerns in Maharashtra dared not run the risk of printing the volume. At last, the owner of a printing firm who was himself a member of the Abhi Nava Bharat Secret Society undertook to publish it. In the meanwhile, the Indian police too got some vague information that the volume was being published in Marathi. They, thereupon, carried a number of simultaneous surprise raids on some prominent printing houses in Maharashtra. But fortunately, the owner of the Press, where the book was being actually printed, got a hint through a sympathetic Police Officer and succeeded in smuggling out the Marathi manuscript to a safer place just before the search party arrived. The manuscript was later on sent back to Paris, instead of to London, and fell into the hands of its author.

Finding thus that it was impossible to get it printed in India, it was decided to get the Marathi book printed in Germany where some Sanskrit literature used to be published in the Nagari script. But after a lot of waste of money and time, the scheme had to be given up as hopeless, owing to the uncouth and ugly Nagari type cast in Germany, and to the fact that the German compositors were absolutely ignorant of the Marathi language.

The History Translated into English

The A. N. B. Revolutionary Party resolved thereupon to publish, at least, the English translation of this History of the Indian War of Independence of 1857 with a view to enabling the English speaking public, both in India and outside, to know its contents. A few highly intellectual Maratha youths in London, members of the A. N. B., distinguished graduates of Indian Universities studying Law and candidates for the I.C.S. Examination, volunteered to translate the voluminous work into English. After the translation was complete under the supervision of Sriyut V. V. S. Aiyer, efforts were made to get it printed in England. But the British detectives, too, were not idle, and made it impossible for any British printer to undertake the publication of it for fear of being prosecuted forthwith. The English manuscript was then sent to Paris; but the French Government at that time was so thoroughly under the thumb of England, with whom France had to ally herself in order to face combinedly the impending danger of a German invasion that the French detectives were working hand in hand with the British police to suppress the A. N. B. revolutionary activities in France; and under their threat even a French printer could not be found ready to run the risk of printing this history. At last by a successful ruse, the revolutionists persuaded a printing firm in Holland to print the book. The British Intelligence Department continued to grope in the dark, as the revolutionists publicly gave it out that the English translation was being printed in France. Before the British detectives could get any inkling, the volume was printed in Holland and the whole edition of the English translation was smuggled into France and kept secretly ready for distribution.

In the meanwhile, before the book was sent to Holland for getting it printed, the British and the Indian Governments got so nervous, and dreaded so much the effects of Savarkar's writings that they proscribed the book which they admitted was not yet printed! This was so high-handed a step on their part that the English papers themselves resented this action of proscribing a book before its publication—a case almost unprecedented in a land which boasted of its Freedom of the Press. Veer Savarkar also did not spare the Government and poured vials of ridicule on the proscribing order in a spirited letter which he wrote to "The London Times." He challenged in it, "It is admitted by the authorities that they were not sure whether the manuscript had gone to print. If that is so, how does the Government know that the book is going to be so dangerously seditious as to get it proscribed before its publication, or even before it was printed? The Goverment either possess a copy of the manuscript or do not. If they have a copy, then why did they not prosecute me for sedition as that would have been the only course legitimately left to them? On the contrary, if they have no copy of the manuscript how could they be so cocksure of the seditious nature of a book of which they do not know anything beyond some vague, partial and unauthenticated reports?" The "London Times" not only published the letter, but added a note of its own that the very fact that the Government should have felt it necessary to have recourse to such presumably high-handed and extraordinary executive steps proved that there must be "Something very rotten in the State of Denmark."

After getting the English translation printed in Holland, the revolutionists smuggled into India hundreds of its copies by ingenious devices. Many of them were wrapped in artistic covers specially printed with such innocuous and bogus names as "Pickwick Papers," "Scot's Works," "Don Quixote" etc. Several copies got smuggled in boxes with false bottoms. It will be interesting to note that one such box, containing a number of copies under a false bottom, was taken into India by a youthful member of the Abhi Nava Bharat named Shikandar Hayat Khan who later on was known to fame as Sir Shikandar Hayat Khan, the chief minister of the Punjab. Even the vigilance of the Argus-eyed monster of the Bombay Customs House failed to spot these devices and thousands of copies did thus reach their destinations in India addressed to many prominent leaders, members of Abhi Nava Bharat, leading libraries, colleges and especially to secret sympathisers who had access to several military camps throughout India. All these copies of this first edition of this history were sent free, even the postal charges being defrayed by the A. N. B. Revolutionary Society. It was then openly published in France, was freely circulated and widely read by leading English historians, politicians and revolutionary circles especially in Ireland, France, Russia, America, Egypt and Germany.

The "Gadar" in America and the Second English Edition

In the year 1910, the British and the Indian Governments launched a violent campaign of persecutions and prosecutions with a view to crushing the Abhi Nava Bharat Secret Society. Several Indian revolutionaries were hanged; several transported for life; hundreds sentenced to terms extending from ten to fourteen years of rigorous imprisonment. The heroic story of Veer Savarkar's arrest, escape, re-arrest, persecutions, prosecutions and consequent transportation to the Andamans for two life-sentences amounting to at least fifty years' imprisonment, is well-known to be recited here.

No sooner did the Abhi Nava Bharat organisation recover from this stunning blow than Madam Cama, the well-known brave Parsi lady, Lala Hardayal, Chattopadhyaya and other leaders of the A. N. B. Revolutionary Party decided to bring out the second English edition of this book, Lala Hardayalji organised the American branch of the A. N. B. and started his well-known newspaper "The Gadar"—(Rebellion) in America. Not only was the second English edition of this Indian War of Independence of 1857 published this time for regular sale to replenish the party funds; but translations of this History were published regularly in Urdu, Hindi and Punjabi languages secretly through the 'Gadar'. It aroused the Sepoys in the Army, as the "Gadar" reached several camps in India and especially the large number of the Sikh agriculturists settled in America. Soon after that, the First World War broke out. How the Indian revolutionists in India and outside joined hands with the Germans against England, how large amounts of arms and ammunitions were smuggled into India, how the '*Komagatamaru*' succeeded in landing revolutionary forces in India, how the Emden bombarded Indian ports, how mutinies broke out in Indian regiments stationed at Hong Kong, Singapore and Burmah under the leadership of Gader party and how this attempt by the Indian revolutionaries to invade India to liberate her was at last frustrated owing to the defeat of the Germans, is now a matter of history. Nevertheless, this revolutionary campaign proved to be a veritable rehearsal of the recent Military Invasion attempted on a mightier scale by Netaji Subhash Chandra Bose with the I. N. A. Throughout this later revolutionary movement, it became evident from the trials of hundreds of leaders and followers that this history of the first Indian War of Independence of 1857 proved to be a perennial source of inspiration, and even provided a detailed sketch of the programme of action. The demand for its copies was so great that they used to be sold and resold, in cases, for such fabulous prices as 300 Rupees each. Thousands of the arrested revolutionaries were found in possession of them, and possession of a copy of this book was taken to be a proof by itself of the complicity of the possessor in the revolutionary activities.

"The Original Marathi Book is Dead—Long live the Book!!"

After the arrest of Veer Savarkar, the manuscript of the original Marathi book was handed over to Madam Cama in Paris. She kept it in her safe in the Bank of France with a view to placing it beyond the reach of the Agents of the British Intelligence Department. But the invasion of France by the Germans threw the Government of France itself into a hopeless disorder. Madam Cama too, passed away. Consequently, when a searching enquiry was made regarding the whereabouts of the book no trace of the manuscript could be found. The great Marathi *tome* was lost— no hope of its recovery was left. Marathi literature had thus suffered an irreparable loss.[†]

The Third Known English Edition of the History

As we are noting down only those editions of which we have definite knowledge, leaving out of count those of which rumour alone informs us, the next English edition we must take cognizance of, is that which, after the re-emergence of the revolutionary party on an all India basis was printed and published in two parts, of course secretly, under Veer Bhagat Singh' lead. It was sold widely at high prices and the proceeds went to swell the party funds. The few copies, almost religiously preserved even at the risk of prosecution and persecution, which can be rarely found even today, belong, in the main, to this edition. The conspiracy cases which followed the arrest of Veer Bhagat Singh and his leading comrades revealed the fact that copies of 4th Edition of the book were found in searches in the possession of almost all the accused and that this History animated them to face martyrdom and guided them to chalk out the revolutionary programme—to organise an armed revolt to liberate our motherland!

The Indian National Army Organised by Netaji Subhash Chandra Bose and the Fifth English Edition

The well-ascertained fifth edition came to light in the days when the last and the most determined effort was made to organize an army on the largest scale, yet recorded, to invade India to free her from the British bondage, by Rash Bihari Bose, the President of the Hindu Maha Sabha branch in Japan, and which army was later on commanded by Netaji Subhash Chandra Bose. Unimpeachable evidence recorded by patriots and warriors who took an actual part in the invasion shows that this 'History' was read and re-read in their camps and was looked upon as a veritable text-book for the soldiers and officers in the army. A stray copy of a Tamil edition was also ransacked. Its tattered pages were glued and the volume was rebound and circulated in the army. But it is not known when or by whom the Tamil translation was made and published.[††]

[†]1. The original Marathi book is not dead; its manuscript changed hands after hands and was carried away to U.S.A by Dr. Cutino of Goa, himself a member of the Abhinava Bharat, and who was then in Europe, and settled in U.S.A. He kept the manuscript with him, till he came to know that the ban on it was lifted by the Government of Bombay Province (India) in 1946. He then sent the manuscript with Dr. Gohokar, that time studying in U.S.A. and now chairman Maharashtra State Public Service Commission and a follower of Late Dr. B.S. Moonje to India. Dr. Gohokar handed over the manuscript to Veer Savarkar in May 1949. That manuscript did not contain two chapter that were stolen by the British Intelligence before the book was banned. This Marathi manuscript has been published now with due corrections by Shri Balrao Savarkar.

[††]This Tamil Edition was edited by Shri Jayamani Subramhanyam one, of the publicity officers of I. N. A. A new Tamil Edition has been brought out now and Shri Jayamani Subramhanyam has himself disclosed how this book was blessed by Netaji Subhash!

The Sixth English Edition to Challenge the Ban on the Book

While throughout the last thirty or forty years the revolutionists were thus bringing out secretly, edition after edition of this history, an open public agitation was also going on in India demanding the raising of the Governmental ban not only on this history but on several other books written by Veer Savarkar. Public meetings and protests made by literary societies went unheeded by the British Government in England as well as in India. Even when the so-called National ministries formed by the Congressites came to power some ten years ago, they too did not raise the ban on Savarkarite literature as perhaps, it not only did not countenance but positively denounced the vagaries of the half-witted and even immoral doctrine of absolute non-violence to which the Congressites swore only verbal allegiance. But when the recent World War II was over and the present Congressite ministries came into power, the public demand for the raising of this ban grew so unruly that some enthusiastic patriots threatened to challenge and break the ban. They raised funds and secretly printed a new English edition in Bombay with a view to selling it openly and publicly courting arrests. They even informed the Congressite ministers of their intention.

The Ban Raised at Last after some Forty Years of Proscription

When matters came to this pass and as the Government too was inclined to reconsider the question, the ban on Savarkarite literature as a whole, which continued to be proscribed for some forty years in the past was raised by the Congressite ministry at long last, upon which sane act they deserve to be congratulated.

"The Book Became the Bible of the Indian Revolutionists"

It will be evident from the story as recited above that the book continued to be regarded as a veritable Bible by the Indian Revolutionists ever since the armed struggle for Indian Independence initiated by the Abhi Nava Bharat bands down to recent times when full-fledged armies marched to the battle-fields under Netaji Subhash Chandra Bose. Directly and indirectly the book has influenced, animated and guided at least two generations in India in their struggles to free the Motherland. That is why the Nation itself made it a point of honour to keep the book alive as a national asset in defiance of the violent efforts of the foreign government to suppress and kill it. Its survival despite of it all is almost miraculous.

Miraculous too is the survival of its illustrious author who, in spite of untold sufferings and sacrifices, trials, tribulations and transportations, has been spared by Providence to witness the triumphant march of the Revolutionary principles and programmes which he as a SEER preached and as a WARRIOR fought to carry out.

The Book Pays our National Debt to the Memory of the Warriors of 1857

We cannot do better than to quote Shrijut Subbarao, the gifted editor of the 'Gosthi' to illustrate the above truth:

"The British Raj in India has treated Savarkar's book as most dangerous for their existence here. So it has been banned. But it has been read by millions of our countrymen including my humble self. In trying to elevate the events of 1857, which interested Historians and Administrators had not hesitated to call for decades as an 'Indian Mutiny', to its right pose of 'Indian War of Independence.' All be it a foiled attempt at that! It is not a work of a Patriotic Alchemist turning base mutineering into noble revolutionary action. Even in these days what would the Mahatmic school have called the efforts of Subhash Bose's Azad-Hind-Fouj if Savarkas's alchemy had not intervened? True. Both the 1857 and 1943 'Wars' have ended in failure for our country. But the motive behind—was it mere Mutineering or War for Independence? If Savarkar had not intervened between 1857 and 1943, I am sure that the recent efforts of the Indian National Army would have been again dubbed as an Ignoble Mutiny effectively crushed by the valiant British-cum-Congress arms and armlessness. But thanks to Savarkar's book, Indian sense of a "Mutiny" has been itself revolutionised. Not even Lord Wavell, I suppose, can now call Bose's efforts as a Mutiny. The chief credit for the change of values must go to Savarkar—and to him alone. But the greatest value of Savarkar's Book lies in its gift to the Nation of that Torch of Freedom in whose light an humble I and a thousand other Indians have our dear daughters named after Laxmibai, the Rani of Jhansi. Even Netaji Bose in a fateful hour had to form an army corps named after Rani of Jhansi. But for Savarkar's discovery of that valiant heroine, Rani of Jhansi should have been a long-forgotten 'Mutineer' of the nineteenth century."

—Free Hindustan, Special, 28th May, 1946

This history has literally resurrected from continuing to be entombed in oblivion the spirits of the bravest of the leaders, warriors and martyrs who fell fighting in 1857, and taught us to pay our admiring and loyal tribute to Nana Sahib, Bala Rao, Kumar Singh, Mangal Pande, Ahmad Shah, the Queen of Jhansi, Senapati Tatia Tope and hosts of our warriors. The names could never have been on the lips of millions today but for the researches of Veer Savarkar guided by a gifted intuition and on a par with such excavations as at Mohenjodaro.

It cannot but be a source of satisfaction to Veer Savarkarji that the expectations he cherished about this History, when he wrote it in his youth, should have been realised before his eyes. But we are afraid that his satisfaction in this case must be only partial. For he never could conceive that the 'Rising of 1857' was an event complete by itself. He looked upon the war of 1857 as but a campaign in the war of Independence in its entirety. He did not, therefore, mean the book to serve as merely the annals of the past but also as a source of inspiration and guidance to the Future. Consequently he must be expecting this History to continue to discharge its mission yet further till the end in view is accomplished. This end is clearly marked out by Veer Savarkar himself as the following passage will show.

The special tribunal, which tried him in 1910 for waging war against the King (of course of England!) and sentenced him to transportation for life and forfeiture of his property quotes in its judgment as an overwhelming proof of his guilt' the following statement issued by Savarkar in 1908 from London:

"The war begun on the 10th of May 1857 is not over on the 10th of May 1908, nor can it ever cease till a 10th of May to come sees the destiny accomplished and our Motherland stands free!"

G. M. Joshi
Bal Savarkar

It is a simple truism patent even to the uneducated that the most tiny house cannot be built without a foundation strong enough to support its weight. When writers who profess to write the history of the Revolution that was enacted in India in 1857 ignore this common sense principle and do not try to discuss the real causes that led to it and impudently maintain that the vast edifice of the Revolution was built on a blade of straw, they must either be fools or, what is more probable, knaves. Anyway, it is certain that they are unfit for the holy work of the historian.

In all great religious and political revolutions, it is almost impossible to connect together links apparently inconsistent, without thoroughly understanding the principles which are at their root. On seeing a great work of machinery composed of innumerable screws and wheels doing work of tremendous magnitude if we do not understand how the power is produced, we may feel bewildering astonishment, but never the inner pleasure due to knowledge. When writers describe such stirring events as the French Revolution or the religious revolution of Holland, the very splendour and magnitude of the crises they paint, often, dassle and confuse their mind's eye and they rarely gather sufficient coolness and courage to go deep into the underlying principles. But without an exposition of the hidden causes and the mysterious forces that worked beneath, the essence of a revolution can never be made plain. And therefore it is that history attaches more importance to the exposition of principles than to mere narrative.

While searching after principles, historians often commit another mistake. For every act, there are various causes, direct and indirect, general and particular, accidental and necessary. In their proper classification lies the true skill of the historian. In this process of classification many historians get mixed up and make the accidental into a necessary cause. These make themselves as ridiculous as the judge in the story who, in a case of arson, put all the responsibility on the match instead of the man who struck it. The real importance of any event can never be understood by this confusion of causes. Not merely that, but mankind begins positively to curse the memory of men who are represented as having started, with a light heart and private selfish motives, a Revolution in the course of which countless lives are lost and immense expanses of country devastated. And therefore, in writing the history of any event in general, and of revolutionary movements in particular, a writer cannot give a true idea of them by means of simple description or by tracing them backwards to accidental causes. An upright and impartial historian must try to discover the foundations on which the revolutionary structure was erected. He must try to discover and discuss fundamental causes.

Mazzini, in a critical article on Carlyle's *French Revolution,* has said that every revolution must have had a fundamental principle. Revolution is a complete rearrangement in the life of historic man. A revolutionary movement cannot be based on flimsy and momentary grievance. It is always due to some all-moving principle for which hundreds and thousands of men fight, before which thrones totter, crowns are destroyed and created, existing ideals are shattered and new ideals break forth, and for the sake of which vast masses of people think lightly of shedding sacred human blood. The moving spirits of revolutions are deemed holy or unholy in proportion as the principle underlying them is beneficial or wicked. As in private life, so also in history, the deeds of an individual or a nation are judged by the character of the motive. If we forget this test, we cannot appreciate the vast difference between the empire-building wars of Alexander the Great and Italy's fight for liberty under Garibaldi. Just as to decide about the merits of these two different events one has to consider the prime motive of the chief actors in those wars, so also to write a full history of a revolution means necessarily the tracing of all the events of that revolution back to their source,—the motive, the innermost desire of those who brought it about. This is the telescope which will show clearly the lights and shadows obscured by the blurred presentation of partial and prejudiced historians. When a beginning is made in this manner, order appears in the apparent chaos of inconsistent facts, crooked lines become straight, and straight lines appear crooked, light appears where darkness is, and darkness spreads over light, what appeared ugly becomes fair and what looked beautiful is seen to be deformed. And expectedly, or unexpectedly, but in a clear form, the Revolution comes into the light of real history.

The history of the tremendous Revolution that was enacted in India in the year 1857 has never been written in this scientific spirit by any author, Indian or foreign. And hence there are current throughout the world most extraordinary, misleading, and unjust ideas about that Revolutionary War. English authors have committed, in this respect, all the faults noted above. Some of them have not made any attempt beyond merely describing the events, but most of them have written the history in a wicked and partial spirit. Their prejudiced eye could not or would not see the root principle of that Revolution. Is it possible, can any sane man maintain, that that all-embracing Revolution could have taken place without a principle to move it? Could that vast tidal wave from Peshawar to Calcutta have risen in flood without a fixed intention of drowning something by means of its force? Could it be possible that the sieges of Delhi, the massacres of Cawnpore, the banner of the Empire, heroes dying for it, could it ever be possible that such noble and inspiring deeds have happened without a noble and inspiring end? Even a small village market does not take place without an end, a motive: how, then, can we believe that that great market opened and closed without any purpose—the great market whose shops were on every battle field from Peshawar to Calcutta, where kingdoms and empires were being exchanged, and where the only current coin was blood? No, no. The market was neither opened nor closed without a purpose. English historians have always ignored this point, not because it is difficult to ascertain it, but because it is against their interests to admit the truth.

Even more deceptive than this indifference, and one which changes or distorts the whole spirit of the Revolution of 1857 is the other device of English historians copied by their Indian sycophants,—the device, namely, of describing the rumour as to the greased cartridges as the moving cause of the Revolution. An Indian writer[1] drawing inspiration from English history and English money says, "Foolish people went mad simply at the rumour that cartridges were greased with cows' and pigs' fat. Did anyone inquire as to whether the report was true? One man said and another believed; because the second became disaffected, a third joined him, and so like a procession of blind men, a company of inconsiderate fools arose, and rebellion broke out." We propose to discuss later on whether people blindly believed the rumour about cartridges. But it will be plain to anyone who has read even the English historians closely and thought about the matter, that a great attempt has been made to father all the responsibility of the Revolution on this rumour. It is not surprising that to one, who thinks that a mighty rising like that of '57 can be produced by such trifles, it was only 'a company of inconsiderate fools.' If the Revolution had been due only to the cartridges, why did Nana Sahib, the Emperor of Delhi, the Queen of Jhansi, and Khan Bahadur Khan of Rohilkhand join it? These were not surely going to serve in the English army, nor were they compelled to break the cartridges with their teeth! If the rising were due wholly or chiefly to the cartridges, it would have stopped suddenly as soon as the English Governor-General issued a proclamation that they should not be used any more! He gave them permission to make cartridges with their own hand. But instead of doing so, or ending the whole by leaving the Company's service altogether, the sepoys rose to fight in battle. Not only the sepoys but thousands of peaceful citizens and Rajas and Maharajas also rose, who had no direct or indirect connection with the army. It is therefore clear that it was not these accidental things that roused the spirit of the sepoy and the civilian, king and pauper, Hindu and Mahommedan.

Equally misleading is the theory that the rising was due to the annexation of Oudh. How many were fighting, taking their lives in their hands, that had not interest whatsoever in the fortunes of the Oudh dynasty? Then, what was their motive in fighting? The Nabob of Oudh himself was imprisoned in the fort of Calcutta; and according to the English historians, his subjects were very much disaffected under his regime. Then, why did Talukdars, soldiers, and almost every one of his subjects unsheath their swords for him? A 'Hindu' of Bengal wrote an essay in England at that time about the Revolution. In it the 'Hindu' says, 'You have no idea how many simple and kind-hearted people who had never seen the Nabob, nor were ever again likely to see, wept in their huts when the sorrows of the Nabob were being related before them. And you do not also know how many soldiers were daily taking an oath, after the tears had flown, to avenge this insult on Wajid Ali Shah, as if a calamity had fallen on themselves in person.' Why did the Sepoys feel this sympathy with the Nabob and why did eyes which had never seen the Nabob glisten with tears? It is plain, therefore, that the Revolution did not break out simply on account of the annexation of Oudh.

The fear of greased cartridges and the annexation of Oudh were only temporary and accidental causes. To turn these into real causes would never help us in understanding the real spirit of the Revolution. If we were to take them as the real moving causes, it would mean that, without these, the Revolution would not have taken place—that without the rumour of greased cartridges and without the annexation of Oudh, the Revolution would not have been there. It would be impossible to find a theory more foolish and more deceptive. If there had been no fear of the cartridges, the principle underlying that fear would have cropped up in some other form and produced a Revolution just the same. Even if Oudh had not been annexed, the principle of annexation would have manifested itself in the destruction of some other kingdom. The real causes of the French Revolution were not simply the high prices of grain, the Bastille, the King's leaving Paris, or the feasts. These might explain some incidents of the Revolution but not the Revolution as a whole. The kidnapping of Sita was only the incidental cause of the fight between Rama and Ravana. The real causes were deeper and more inward.

What, then, were the real causes and motives of this Revolution? What were they that they could make thousands of heroes unsheath their swords and flash them on the battlefield? What were they that they had the power to brighten up pale and rusty crowns and raise from the dust abased flags? What were they that for them men by the thousand willingly poured their blood year after year? What were they that Moulvies preached them, learned Brahmins blessed them, that for their success prayers went up to Heaven from the mosques of Delhi and the temples of Benares?

These great principles were Swadharma and Swaraj. In the thundering roar of 'Din, Din,' which rose to protect religion, when there were evident signs of a cunning, dangerous, and destructive attack on religion dearer than life, and in the terrific blows dealt at the chain of slavery with the holy desire of acquiring Swaraj, when it was evident that chains of political slavery had been put round them and their God-given liberty wrested away by subtle tricks—in these two, lies the root-principle of the Revolutionary War. In what other history is the principle of love of one's religion and love of one's country manifested more nobly than in ours? However much foreign and partial historians might have tried to paint our glorious land in dark colours, so long as the name of Chitore has not been erased from the pages of our history, so long as the names of Pratâpâditya and Guru Govind Singh are there, so long the principles of Swadharma and Swaraj will be embedded in the bone and marrow of all the sons of Hindusthan! They might be darkened for a time by the mist of slavery—even the sun has its clouds —but very soon the strong light of these self-same principles pierces through the mist and chases it away. Never before were there such a number of causes for the universal spreading of these traditional and noble principles as there were in 1857. These particular reasons revived most wonderfully the slightly unconscious feelings of Hindusthan, and the people began to prepare for the fight for Swadharma and Swaraj. In his Proclamation of the establishment of Swaraj, the Emperor of Delhi says, 'Oh, you sons of Hindusthan, if we make up our mind we can destroy the enemy in no time! We will destroy the enemy and will release from dread our religion and our country, dearer to us than life itself.'[2] What is holier in this world than such a Revolutionary War, a war for the noble principles propounded in this sentence, 'release from dead our religion and our country, dearer to us than life itself'? The seed of the Revolution of 1857 is in this holy and inspiring idea, clear and explicit, propounded from the throne of Delhi, THE PROTECTION OF RELIGION AND COUNTRY. In the Proclamation issued at Bareilly, he says "Hindus and Mahomedans of India! Arise! Brethren, arise! Of all the gifts of God, the most gracious is that of Swaraj. Will the oppressive Demon who has robbed us of it by deceit be able to keep it away from us for ever? Can such an act against the will of God stand for ever? No, no. The English have committed so many atrocities that the cup of their sins is already full. To add to it, they have got now the wicked desire to destroy our holy religion! Are you going to remain idle even now? God does not wish that you should remain so; for he has inspired in the hearts of Hindus and Mahomedans the desire to turn the English out of our country.

And by the grace of God, and your valour, they will soon be so completely defeated that in this our Hindusthan there will not remain even the least trace of them! In this our army, the differences of small and great shall be forgotten, and equality shall be the rule; for, all who draw the sword in this holy war for the defence of religion are equally glorious. They are brethren, there is no rank among them. Therefore, I again say to all my HINDI BRETHREN, 'Arise and jump into the battlefield for this divinely ordained and supreme duty!'" The man who, after seeing such magnificent utterances by the Revolutionary leaders, does not understand its principles is, as we said, either a fool or a knave. What stronger evidence is needed to prove that Indian warriors drew their swords at the time for Swadharma and Swaraj, feeling it the duty of every man to fight for the rights given to man by God? These Proclamations issued at different times and places during the war make it unnecessary to dilate more on its principles. These Proclamations were not issued by nonentities; but they were orders issued from adorable and powerful thrones. They were burning expressions of the agitated feelings of the time. In these the real heart of the Nation had spoken out, when at the time of war, there was no occasion to conceal real sentiments through pressure or fear. This tremendous, heroic shout, 'Swadharma and Swaraj,' proclaims to the world the character of the Revolution in which 'all who draw the sword are equally glorious.'

But were these two principles understood as different and exclusive of each other? At least, orientals have never had the idea that Swadharma and Swaraj have no connection with each other. The Eastern mind has maintained a full and traditional belief, as is also said by Mazzini, that there is no vast barrier between Heaven and earth but that the two are ends of one and the same thing. Our idea of Swadharma, too, is not contradictory to that of Swaraj. The two are connected as means and end. Swaraj without Swadharma is despicable and Swadharma without Swaraj is powerless. The sword of material power, Swaraj should always be ready drawn for our object, our safety is the other world, Swadharma. This trend of the Eastern mind will be often found in its history. The reason why, in the East, all revolutions take a religious form, nay more, the reason why Eastern history knows of no revolutions unconnected with religion, lies in the all-embracing meaning that the word 'Dharma' has. That this dual principle of Swadharma and Swaraj, always seen in the history of India, appeared also in the Revolution of 1857, should be a matter of no surprise. We have already referred to the first Proclamation of the Emperor of Delhi. Afterwards when Delhi was besieged by the English and the war was at its height, the Emperor issued another Proclamation addressing all Indians thus: 'Why has God given us wealth, land, power? They are not for individual pleasure, but they are given for the holy object of defence of our religion'. But where are now the means to attain this holy end? As said in the Proclamation given above, where is the gift of Swaraj, the greatest of all the gifts of God?

Where is wealth? Where is land? Where is power? In the plague of slavery, all this divine independence is all but dead. In the above Proclamation, in order to show how the plague of slavery was destroying India, full descriptions are given as to how the Kingdoms of Nagpur, Ayodhya, and Jhansi were trampled down into dust. And it awakens the people to the fact that they are guilty of the sin of destroying religion in the house of God, having lost these means of defending religion. The command of God is, Obtain Swaraj, for that is the chief key to the protection of Dharma. He who does not attempt to acquire Swaraj, he who sits silent in slavery, he is an atheist and hater of Religion. Therefore, rise for Swadharma and acquire Swaraj!

"Rise for Swadharma and acquire Swaraj!" What divine events in the history of India are due to the realization of this principle! The poet-saint Ramdas gave the same dictum to the Mahrattas 250 years ago. "Die for your Dharma, kill the enemies of your Dharma while you are dying; in this way fight and kill, and take back your kingdom!"[3]

This alone is the principle in the Revolutionary War of 1857. This is its mental science. The true and only telescope which will show it in its true and clear form is the above verse of Ramdas.

Seeing at it through this telescope, what a spectacle comes into view! The war fought for Swadharma and Swaraj does not lose its lustre by defeat. The splendour of Guru Govind Singh's life is none the less, because his efforts did not immediately succeed at the time. Nor do we think the less of the rising of 1848 in Italy, because the Revolution failed completely at that time.

Justin McCarthy says: "The fact was that throughout the greater part of the northern and north-western provinces of the Indian peninsula, there was a rebellion of the native races against the English power. It was not alone the Sepoy who rose in revolt—it was not by any means a merely military mutiny. It was a combination of military grievance, national hatred, and religious fanaticism against the English occupation of India. The native princes and the native soldiers were in it. The Mahomedan and the Hindu forgot their old religious antipathies to join against the Christian. Hatred and panic were the stimulants of that great rebellious movement. The quarrel about the greased cartridges was but the chance spark flung in among all the combustible material. If that spark had not lighted it, some other would have done the work. . . . The Meerut Sepoys found, in a moment, a leader, a flag and a cause, and *the mutiny was transformed in to a revolutionary war*. When they reached the Jumna, glittering in the morning light, they had all unconsciously seized one of the great critical moments of history and converted a military mutiny into *a national and religious war*!" [4]

Charles Ball writes: "At length, the torrent overflowed the banks, and saturated the moral soil of India. It was then expected that those waves would overwhelm and destroy the entire European element and that, when the torrent of rebellion should again confine itself within bounds, patriotic India, freed from its alien rulers, would bow only to the independent sceptre of a native prince. The movement, now, assumed a more important aspect. It became *the rebellion of a whole people* incited to outrage by resentment for imaginary wrongs and sustained in their delusions by hatred and fanaticism."[5]

White writes in his Complete History of the Great Sepoy War:—"I should be wanting in faithfulness as an historian if I failed to record with admiration the courage displayed by the Oudhians. The great fault of the Oudh Talukdars from a moral point of view was their having made a common cause with the murderous mutineers. But for this, they might have been regarded as noble patriots, fighting in a good cause, *pro rega pro patria*, for the King and the Motherland"—for Swaraj and Swadesh!

NOTES

1. वि. कॉ. ओक "शिपायांचें बंड".
2. Leckey's *Fictions Exposed* and Urdu works.
3. धर्मांसाठीं मरावें । मरोनि अवघ्यांस मारावें ।
   मारितां मारितां घ्यावें । राज्य आपुलें
4. *History of Our Own Times*, Vol. III.
5. *Indian Mutiny*, Vol. I, page 644.

Letter Regarding the Temple of Ranchodji

Introductory Text by Vinayak Chaturvedi for Letter by Ranchod Vira

Ranchod Vira was a 50-year-old peasant who, along with his wife, son and grandson, tilled over four acres of the village headman's land in Chaklasi, located in the plains of central Gujarat in western India. Little is known about the early years of Ranchod's life, except that he was a *bhagat* (village priest) who belonged to an agricultural community known as the Baraiyas. Indeed, he would probably have left no trace in the annals of history, but for the fact that on 9 January 1898 he declared the end of the British Raj and proclaimed himself the king of a new polity. By 12 January, five or six hundred armed Baraiya peasants had gathered in Chaklasi in support of Ranchod. Within a few hours, news of the activities in Chaklasi had reached colonial officials in the neighbouring town of Nadiad, and a group of eighteen constables led by Police Inspector Jagannath Sagun and the *mamlatdar* (a district revenue official) quickly departed to prevent any disturbance in the village. Around 4.30 in the afternoon, Inspector Jagannath and his men arrived in Chaklasi with the intention of speaking to Ranchod; however, they were stopped by the armed peasants. Jagannath insisted on meeting their leader and requested the crowd to disperse. In reply, the peasants told him to worship and asked him if he was a Gujarati or a *topiwallah* (literally, a hat-wearer). Ranchod sent a message to Jagannath demanding that the inspector communicate with him by writing a letter specifying his queries and concerns. Jagannath's refusal to comply with the request was viewed as a sign of hostility: Ranchod emerged to the resonating sounds of a trumpet and booming drums, and signalled his supporters to attack all representatives of the colonial government.

The battle lasted a few short hours, being quickly suppressed by the police. Constables began shooting into the large crowd, killing five peasants. Ranchod and most of his supporters escaped, while other peasants began chasing constables through the village: one constable was killed and three others were stripped of their uniforms and weapons. On the following day, 13 January, two hundred troops of the Fourth Bombay Rifles were dispatched from Ahmedabad to quell any further conflict in Chaklasi. Ranchod was captured as he was attempting to flee, and among his possessions confiscated by the police were weapons, police uniforms, two letters, moneylenders' account ledgers, a loose bundle of account registers, a small collection of books, twenty-two pieces of blank paper and a list of twenty-one villages.

Colonial power had stopped a small peasant movement from coalescing into something larger. The introduction of the military and police ensured that the peasants of Chaklasi could no longer gather for political or other reasons. Local representatives such as the village headman and village accountant were quickly replaced with individuals viewed as loyal to the government. Surveillance practices were enforced in the village and peasants were required to attend a daily roll-call as a way to monitor their everyday activities. Yet, despite the swift conclusion to Ranchod's reign as a king, colonial power was not able to suppress the circulation of ideas. Officials reported that a letter dictated by the peasant leader declaring the end of the government was spreading throughout the region: the 'letter is finding its way in the province . . . [the] people are enjoining to keep copies and forwarding to the next village'.

For an individual who could neither read nor write, Ranchod was well aware of the power of the written word. Although peasants in colonial India had often destroyed writings as symbols of elite dominance, especially those documents recording peasants' debts, Ranchod chose to confiscate, collect, preserve, produce and distribute writings as a way to establish his own authority and leadership. His desire to receive a written message from a colonial official such as Jagannath suggests that he was behaving in consonance with the norms of courtly traditions that required formal communication from representatives of other states. In addition, it indicates that Ranchod had appropriated the written form at a time when the bureaucratization of the colonial state had advanced to the point where peasants were keenly aware of the significance and impact of rent notes, legal documents and account ledgers in their everyday lives. The assimilation and use of writing was interpreted as a practice that symbolically affirmed Ranchod's ascendancy. And, as we shall see, this was not the only way in which Ranchod turned to courtly practices and traditions found throughout western India as a means of establishing his legitimacy as a king and to uphold a new social order.

—Vinayak Chaturvedi

SOURCE: Maharashtra State Archives (Mumbai), Judicial Department, 1899, volume 78, composition 457.

Letter Regarding the Temple of Ranchodji

The following is a letter composed by a peasant named Ranchod Vira in 1898:

The temple of Ranchodji is coming into existence in the middle of the lands of Chaklasi on the east side. The authority of the Government ceased from the full moon of Madgh-Samwat 1956. Therefore the satyug of Ranchodrai has commenced. Therefore no one should tell a lie, or do a wrongful act. If anyone does so transgress the wheel of Ram will pass above the ground and cut off the heads. The mandwa a sugarcane press will be put up by Ranchodrai and he who would pass through it and stand will rule. All people are hereby informed that no one should pay the Government installment. The money is due by the command of Ranchodrai. Patel Kashibhai is informed that—"If you want to inform your Government you may do so."

GLOSSARY

Ranchodji/Ranchodrai	A form of the Hindu deity Krishna
Chaklasi	A village in Gujarat, western India

Madgh	The name of a lunar month in the Hindu calendar.
Samwat 1956	A reference to the Vikram Samwat era adopted in the Hindu calendar. The year 1956, which corresponds to 1898
Satyug	Era of Truth
Ram	A Hindu deity
Mandwa	A temporary structure for worship; temple
Patel	Village Headman

Vinayak and Me: *Hindutva* and the Politics of Naming*

Vinayak Chaturvedi

During the spring of 1969, my grandmother Bai had taken me to Dr Dattatrey Sadashiv Parchure for a physical examination. Apparently, as an infant I had been quite ill and Bai had given up on standard remedies prescribed by my paediatrician. She had convinced my parents that a consultation with Dr Parchure might reveal alternative therapies for my illness, as he specialized in Ayurvedic medicine and had acquired a prominent reputation as a local healer in the central Indian city of Gwalior. After a brief examination, as I am told, Dr Parchure queried my grandmother about my name when he was filling out a prescription for some medication. Bai replied that the family had not given me an official first name as yet, but that I had an informal household name. Dr Parchure asked if it would be possible for him to give me the name Vinayak, and my grandmother accepted the doctor's request.

Unfortunately, Bai passed away before I could speak to her about the interaction with Dr Parchure. In a recent conversation, my mother stated that Bai was initially resistant to the idea of giving me any official name, Vinayak or otherwise, but she only agreed out of respect for Dr Parchure. It is common practice in India for families to wait several years before giving formal names to children: some argue this has to do with wanting to give a name that matches a child's personality; others say these are the cultural practices of a society that has high infant mortality rates.[1] In my case, I suspect that Bai was concerned about the latter, especially as I was regularly ill.

Throughout my childhood, aunts and uncles had often recounted the story of my name and I had grown accustomed to the idea that it had somewhat of an unusual origin. Relatives also had reminded me that Vinayak was another name of the elephant-headed god Ganesh, who was an auspicious deity celebrated as the remover of obstacles.[2] It was a common name among some communities in western and southern India, but certainly not within my clan in north India. I had long accepted that Dr Parchure, as a Marashtrian Deshastha brahmin, had probably favoured the popular Ganesh and felt the need to give the name Vinayak to sick children who needed many obstacles to be removed: after all, it had been an age-old practice to name children after Hindu deities. The story of my name could have ended here and I often wish it had. But those who are more familiar with the complexities of studying oral

*I would like to thank Dr Upendra Parchure for his generosity in narrating his father's life-story on two separate occasions in Gwalior, India, in April 2001 and May 2001. I have greatly benefited from advice and important comments from Tom Mertes, Bina Parekh and David Washbrook. Warm thanks are due to Geoff Eley and Gina Morantz-Sanchez for a valuable reading of an earlier draft, and especially for suggesting that I develop the ideas in the article within a wider social historical context. Finally, I would like to thank my parents Yogeshwar and Kusum Chaturvedi for patiently answering my questions about the historical nature of family life and nationalist politics in central and western India: themes central to the arguments discussed in this paper.

narratives will know that 'hidden transcripts' and silences often have a history of their own: this was especially true in the uncovering of the secret origins of my name. At some point in the mid-1980s, one of my aunts revealed a piece of information about Dr Parchure's past that had never been voiced to me before, even though it was clear that the entire family was well aware of its significance: Dr Parchure had been arrested and convicted as a conspirator in the 1948 murder of Mohandas K. Gandhi—the Mahatma.

From that day, I began to wonder if Dr Parchure's desire to name male children Vinayak had anything to do with his involvement in Gandhi's murder. I remember quickly searching through my books for any information about the murder and the trial. I was looking for a clue that would satisfy my curiosity, when I came across a copy of a book I had kept from my first undergraduate course in modern Indian history—*Freedom at Midnight* by Larry Collins and Dominique LaPierre. I recalled that somewhere within the text were the names of the men tried for killing Gandhi: Nathuram Vinayak Godse, Gopal Vinayak Godse, Vinayak Damodar Savarkar, Narayan Apte, Vishnu Karkare, Digamber Badge, Madan Lal, Shankar Kisayya and Dattatrey S. Parchure. As I read over the names of the accused, I began to see how the story of my name may have had less to do with the god Ganesh, and more to do with a legacy of the Mahatma's murder. Yet, at the same time, I also felt that my suspicion might have been unfounded; after all, Savarkar was the only one with the name Vinayak, and the Godse brothers had inherited their father's first name following a practice common in western India. Additional conversations with my parents and relatives about the links between Parchure, the accused and the naming issue left me dissatisfied, with no additional information. However, for reasons that continue to evade me, I had decided not to investigate further into this story.

In April 2001, I returned to Gwalior after a long interval. I cannot remember how Uma Bua— my father's sister—and I began speaking of Dr Parchure one afternoon, but it must have had something to do with recounting stories about Bai. Uma Bua, as a secular, lifelong supporter of the Congress Party, had regularly condemned the rise of the Hindu nationalist Bharatiya Janata Party (BJP), and for her the conspirators to Gandhi's assassination were some of the earlier 'trouble-makers' in a lineage leading up to today's right-wing leadership.[3] She argued that Dr Parchure's politics were fundamentally problematic, if not completely corrupt, especially as he had supplied the automatic pistol used by Nathuram Godse to kill Gandhi. As much as I had chosen to avoid the subject of my name, I now felt that it was impossible to do so. I wanted to meet Dr Parchure; I wanted to ask him about the significance of naming; I wanted to know why the name Vinayak was so important; I wanted to know who was Vinayak.

Unfortunately, I had waited too long: Dr Parchure was dead. In fact, he passed away in 1985, a couple of years before I first discovered his links to Gandhi's murder. Uma Bua suggested that I could speak to one of his two sons who still lived in Gwalior. I contacted Upendra Dattatrey Parchure: he was trained as an Ayurvedic doctor, like the senior Dr Parchure, and continued to practise in his father's office. I wanted to retrace Bai's steps and return to the location where the story of my name began. This seemed like the obvious place to start. Initially, I was apprehensive about how to introduce myself and explain why I was interested in speaking about Dr Parchure. There were important problems to be considered prior to the meeting: some intellectual, some political, some ethical and some personal. An interview to secure oral testimony about the past is generally a difficult, complex process in itself, but in this case, the nature of the problem was linked to some desire to come to terms with my own subjectivity: that is, not only a subjectivity of an oral historian, but also that I was somehow the passive subject of some historical and ideological processes intertwined with the life-story of Dr Parchure.[4]

My first meeting with Upendra Parchure was brief, barely lasting ten minutes. I introduced myself as someone whom his father had named Vinayak; I narrated how my grandmother had consulted his father when I was ill; I explained that I was hoping to have a conversation about his father. I also made clear that I was researching modern Indian history and that I was interested in writing about the intellectual development of Hindu nationalism. The doctor's first question was whether my parents had decided to keep the name Vinayak, or replace it with another. I assured him that my grandmother had promised his father back in 1969 that the family would not change the name, and that my formal first name was Vinayak. He was obviously pleased, but now wanted to know my surname. Those who are familiar with the legacies of India's multicultural politics will know that family names often reveal a great deal about one's background: caste, language, region and even class.[5] I was aware that my Chaturvedi kinship-affiliation would identify me as an educated, middle-class, local, Hindi-speaking brahmin, but I was also acutely cognizant of the fact that, in this situation, my position of social privilege would be welcomed by Upendra Parchure, who came from a similar, but Marashtrian background. After a few additional questions about my father and grandfather, establishing a patriarchal genealogy, the doctor asked if it would be possible for us to meet in his home where we could speak privately and at length; he stated that the kinds of things I wanted to know were best discussed outside the purview of his patients and staff. We agreed to meet the following week.

From the onset of the second meeting, I realized that Upendra Parchure was uncertain about the nature of the interview. He repeated his questions from our first meeting, and wanted to know what I intended to do with the information about his father. I stated that I was interested in knowing more about his father for two primary reasons: first, I had long wondered about the origins of my name; and, second, I wanted to write about his father's political activities in the locality as part of a research study on Hindu nationalist intellectuals. Apparently satisfied with my explanation, Upendra Parchure pursued an in-depth conversation about his father's public and private life for the next three hours. It began with a narrative of some major events about the senior Dr Parchure's life.

Upendra Parchure wanted me to know that more than anything else, his father, who was born in 1902, was a strong man, a strong nationalist and a strong Hindu. He described his father with awe and pointed out that he was a big, powerful man with broad shoulders, thick thighs and large arms.[6] His physical strength and martial prowess were also illustrated by the fact that he was a skilled wrestler, winning the Gwalior State title in his late teens. Although specific details of Dr Parchure's training were not discussed, what can be inferred is that the process of becoming a local, or regional wrestling champion, would have involved years of regimented and disciplined training with a guru and a cohort throughout childhood.[7] The Indian wrestler is typically dedicated to a distinct ideology that is centred on somatic principles, and requires an acceptance of an ethos of wrestling as a way of life.[8] Initially, I was unclear why Upendra Parchure emphasized his father's masculinity, until later in the conversation it occurred to me this was a consistent theme of how Dr Parchure was remembered in his personal and public life. This point was further clarified when Upendra Parchure celebrated the values and ethics his father learned while training as a wrestler, linking them to the development of his politics as a nationalist. It is not clear whether Dr Parchure intended to make this connection himself, or this is how his son remembered him. However, recent scholarship suggests that central to Hindu nationalism from the 1920s has been the need to set political agendas which relied upon power, masculinity and strength, both discursively and institutionally.[9] Dr Parchure's political career may have had a beginning during his teens in ideologies of 'wrestling nationalism,'[10] but according to his son, the application of some of these strategies later in his life translated into brutal forms of violence, at home and in the public sphere. At another level, as I was soon to discover, the assertion of masculinity was also at the centre of naming male children Vinayak.

In 1935, Dr Parchure founded the Gwalior Branch of the All-India Hindu Mahasabha (literally, the Great Hindu Association), an organization first established in 1915 to defend and protect Hindu interests. The idea of creating the national-level Hindu Mahasabha, however, emerged out of a regional collective known as the Punjab Hindu Sabha, which had originally incorporated a wide range of ideas of high-caste Hindu thinkers on the themes of nationalism and patriotism.[11] By the 1920s, the All-India Hindu Mahasabha had transformed its image to a 'hardline' organization, marginalizing the moderate Hindu leadership from within. This marked an important conjuncture in nationalist politics of the early twentieth century, as the development of Hindu nationalism was firmly established, incorporating the idea of creating a powerful and militant Hinduism that was both anti-British and anti-Muslim.[12] For Upendra Parchure, his father ranked among a group of elite Hindu nationalists in India during this period, with Dr Parchure establishing himself as President of the local branch of the organization for the purpose of promoting an independent Hindu nation. He led a grass-roots movement travelling to villages and small towns in central India—between Gwalior, Bhind, Sheopur and Guna—with the aim of 'injecting a pure Hindu spirit' and creating a pan-Hindu jati, including both high and low castes. It occurred to me during the conversation that the ideas expressed about Dr Parchure's politics appeared consistent with those articulated by Vinayak Savarkar, and it came as little surprise when Upendra Parchure described his father as a 'true Savarkarite,' who had for many years followed Savarkar's writings on revolutionary politics, Hindutva and anti-colonial nationalism. I felt that the mystery of my name had finally been solved: Dr Parchure was evoking Vinayak Savarkar when naming male children. I wanted to know more about the naming issue, but Upendra Parchure continued on more important themes: his father's place within an emergent Hindu nationalism and his connections with Savarkar, Nathuram Godse and Gandhi's murder. I remained silent and listened.

Dr Parchure had trained as a medical student and received his M.B.B.S. from Grant Medical College in Bombay during the 1920s. According to Upendra Parchure, his father continued to practise medicine in Bombay until 1935, when he was dismissed for insubordination from the Jamsetjee Jeejeebhoy Hospital. By 1937 he had become disillusioned with the methods of 'western' medicine and began a study of Ayurvedic medicine, specializing in paediatrics.[13]

The narrative of Dr Parchure's professional life appeared rather fragmented, and little else was discussed about the significance of the events around being fired, or why Ayurveda acquired such an important role. However, it may be worth saying something about the relationship between the medical profession and nationalism as a way to further contextualize the development of Dr Parchure's politics in the mid-1930s.[14]

The decades of the late nineteenth century were marked by the 'return of Hindu science,' especially in reviving the fields of indigenous medicine, especially Ayurveda.[15] It has been argued that this revivalist movement in medicine was predominantly a 'corollary' to the emergence of Hindu nationalism in the 1890s.[16] At one level, Ayurveda represented a type of 'authentic' response to colonial intervention in medicine, especially in a period when state policies to control epidemic diseases, like the bubonic plague, were popularly considered coercive and draconian.[17] Ayurvedic medicine was viewed as a legitimate replacement to the western system which had come to dominate with British colonial expansion in India. At another level, though, Ayurveda also provided a complementary direction to the development of western medicine that could rely upon Indian contributions to the making of modern science.[18] Indian nationalists, like Bal Gangadhar Tilak and M. K. Gandhi, had engaged in public debates on the importance of the medical profession in India, but neither wholeheartedly accepted the claim of the 'revivalists' who sought to replace western medical practices with the 'indigenous' Ayurveda.[19] However, there were doctors trained in western medicine who were inspired by the Ayurvedic revivalism and sought to professionalize and modernize the 'indigenous' tradition by publishing textbooks, and opening colleges, hospitals and clinics, while also participating in the 'Freedom Movement.'[20] It has been suggested that the participation of these doctors in formal nationalist politics increased during the inter-war period.[21] According to Upendra Parchure, his father's decision to take up Ayurveda after abandoning western medicine occurred in this period, a time when medical politics became increasingly significant in public debates throughout India. Dr Parchure's decision to study Ayurvedic medicine was in consonance with the practices of other doctors throughout India, most of whom were also inspired by the ideology of Hindu revivalism, a key component of the emergent Hindu nationalism.

In 1939, Dr Parchure met Vinayak Savarkar for the first time at a Hindu Mahasabha conference. According to Upendra Parchure, the meeting was an important moment for his father, who, by this point, considered himself a 'disciple' of Savarkar. Dr Parchure, like many other Indian nationalists, had followed Savarkar's illustrious political career as a 'freedom-fighter' against the British raj. Biographical accounts of Savarkar posit that he had participated in underground revolutionary activities from a young age, in organizations like the Mitra Mela and the Abhinava Bharat Society (ABS), for the purpose of politicizing Hindus for nationalist aims.[22] Savarkar remained active in the ABS as a law student in Bombay, and became a prolific writer during his college years. In 1906, Savarkar arrived in London for an advanced law degree, but his collaboration with his patron Shyam Krishnavarma furthered Savarkar's involvement in underground activities against British rule.[23] Intellectually, Savarkar had developed an interest in the revolutionary ideas of the Italian thinker Giuseppe Mazzini, and published a Marathi translation of his autobiography in 1907. In fact, it has been suggested that the ABS was modelled after Mazzini's group Young Italy and underground organizations in Russia.[24] The following year, Savarkar completed his opus titled *Indian War of Independence, 1857,* a text with a polemical flair adopted from Mazzini's writings on Italy in the nineteenth century, and combined with claims of a universal Hindu identity for India's past in the form of swaraj and swadharma.[25] The British government banned the book but, nevertheless, it achieved wide circulation among revolutionaries in India.

Savarkar was finally arrested in London on 13 March 1910 on five separate charges, ranging from 'delivering seditious speeches,' 'procuring and distributing arms,' to 'waging war against the King Emperor of India.'[26] Savarkar was extradited to India, and convicted of seditious activities for which he was sentenced to fifty years in the infamous penal settlement in Port Blair located in the Andaman Islands.[27] In 1922, Savarkar was transferred to a prison in Ratnagiri due to ill health, and in 1937 he was finally released, after twenty-seven years' imprisonment. However, during his term of incarceration, Savarkar had continued to write extensively on the issues which had initially landed him in trouble with the British authorities.[28] Savarkar's prison writings were centrally informed by debates in European social theory, especially the literature on German ethnic nationalism.[29] Yet his claim for independence from colonial rule was at the centre of his work, as was the articulation of resurrecting a powerful Hindu nationalism that had lain dormant for centuries. Savarkar had acquired an important public reputation throughout India, especially within the Hindu Mahasabha, for his nationalist and anti-Muslim writings, for his patriotic actions in India and Britain, and for having spent the bulk of his adult life as a political prisoner. Shortly after Savarkar's release from prison, he officially joined the All-India Hindu Mahasabha and served as its President between 1937 and 1944.[30] Savarkar came to power on a platform that had certainly appealed to Dr Parchure and the entire Hindu Mahasabha: 'Hinduize Politics and Militarize Hindudom.'[31]

Although Upendra Parchure emphasized his father's dedication to Savarkar's principles, there was very little discussion about the specific details of these ideas. He may have believed that the intellectual connections with Savarkar were too obvious to discuss with me, or perhaps simply chose not to explain them. However, for me, this point marked an important transition in the interview. Upendra Parchure had thus far celebrated his father's accomplishments, but now the nature and tone of the conversation changed as it moved towards the topic of violence. In 1939, Dr Parchure formed a paramilitary-style organization in Gwalior known as the Hindu Rashtra Sena (literally, Hindu National Army), which boasted a cadre of three thousand volunteers.[32] The development of this organization probably had something to do with the meeting with Savarkar in the same year but, according to Upendra Parchure, his father had specifically grown tired of what he believed to be Muslim persecution of Hindus in Hyderabad State, and felt that local retaliation was necessary. In fact, the Hindu Mahasabha, under Savarkar's leadership, had been agitating against the Nizam of Hyderabad in southern India between October 1938 and July 1939 to secure demands for Hindus, arguing that a Muslim ruler was suppressing their 'civil liberties' and 'culture.'[33] Dr Parchure, as the President of the Hindu Rashtra Sena, subsequently began organizing Hindu attacks on Muslim localities,[34] and, in the process, acquired the notoriety of being 'the most controversial political figure in Gwalior.'[35]

Nathuram Godse was a frequent visitor to the Parchure family home in Gwalior. They may have had long-standing ties, but during the interview I was unable to establish the origins of Dr Parchure's relationship with Godse. However, a brief examination of Godse's activities reveals important parallels relevant to the discussion here. Some time during the early 1930s, Nathuram Godse joined the Poona branch of the Hindu Mahasabha and a paramilitary unit known as the National Volunteer Association, or Rashtriya Swayamsevak Sangh (RSS).[36] It has been suggested that for Godse—and the argument can be expanded to include Dr Parchure— participation in these organizations represented a 'Hindu search for self-esteem' and 'political potency' through the use of power and violence.[37] Godse abandoned the RSS after some years, claiming that it lacked proper levels of militancy, and co-founded the Hindu Rashtra Dal (Hindu National Party), an organization whose name and objectives closely matched Dr Parchure's Hindu Rashtra Sena.[38] In 1942, Savarkar had promoted the idea of establishing the Dal as a secret volunteer organization among a small group of disciples in the Poona Hindu Mahasabha, who, like Godse, shared similar opinions about the RSS.[39] Savarkar required volunteers to take an oath of loyalty to him and perform underground activities that could not be sanctioned by the Mahasabha.[40] The group's primary objective was to propagate 'Savarkarism' as a way to 'protect Hindudom and render help to every Hindu institution in their attempt to oppose encroachment on their rights and religion.'[41] Training camps were set up throughout western and central India, advocating villagers to take up arms, teaching individuals 'Indian games, physical exercises, [and] shooting exercises,' in addition to spreading Savarkar's ideology.[42]

Dr Parchure and Naturam Godse are said to have met on several occasions to discuss the activities of the Hindu Mahasabha.[43] In fact, it has been argued that Dr Parchure, while on a political lecture tour in Poona, approached Godse with the aim of merging the Sena and the Dal. The deliberations failed, but both agreed to proceed with their respective, yet intimately connected projects. Further links between Dr Parchure's Hindu Rastra Sena and the Dal remain unclear, especially in understanding the exact nature of the collaboration between Dr Parchure, Savarkar and Godse. I asked Upendra Parchure if his father had kept any personal letters, diaries or writings about the activities in this period, especially related to his interactions with Godse and Savarkar; he argued that Dr Parchure did not believe in keeping any evidence that could potentially incriminate him, and, more importantly, the government had confiscated all the documents in the house when his father was arrested in 1948. However, it might still be suggested that there were important intellectual and personal ties that were forged in this period. An individual by the name of Panna Lal Chaube told government officials that Dr Parchure and Nathuram Godse were travelling companions, who arrived in Alwar, located in Rajasthan, around October 1947 for the specific purpose of acquiring a handgun from comrades in the local Hindu Mahasabha.[44] Chaube claimed to have met Dr Parchure and Godse, and discussed the plan to murder Gandhi with them. According to Chaube, Dr Parchure argued that it 'was not in the interest of the country that the Mahatma should live and that Godse alone could assassinate Gandhi.'[45] The two left Alwar dissatisfied with the quality of pistols offered to them.

On 2 December 1947, Dr Parchure returned to Poona as the main speaker at a Hindu Mahasabha meeting in the Tilak Samarak Mandir,[46] where Godse and Savarkar were certainly present. An official report of Dr Parchure's speech provides further insight into his position:

> He was described as a second Savarkar and that so great was his influence that on every mosque in Gwalior flew the Bhagwa flag. In his speech Dr Parchure, after referring to the state of affairs in Gwalior, advocated the use of force to achieve whatever they wanted. He also said that Gwalior Army was full of Muslims who were in a majority and that the State was increasing the Muslim elements. . . . The trend of speech was anti-Congress and extremely anti-Muslim. He criticized Pandit Nehru's policy as regards Kashmir and pointed out the quiescence of Hindus in the face of Mohammedan aggressiveness. In the end he made a significant remark, the importance of which was perhaps not then appreciated, that Gandhiji and Nehru would surely reap the fruits of their sins in a short time.[47]

Dr Parchure appears to have achieved a prominent status within the inner circle of the organization by this point, especially as he was now being compared with Savarkar. His anti-Muslim and anti-Congress positions were consistent with those advocated by Savarkar and the Hindu Mahasabha, even though Savarkar had by then resigned from the presidency of the organization. However, Dr Parchure's other intellectual and political connections with the Mahasabha, Sena or Dal are not as apparent in this period. Nevertheless, Dr Parchure's public profile increased enormously when he was convicted for helping Nathuram Godse to arrange for the handgun that was used to assassinate Gandhi.

Upendra Parchure shifted the discussion away from his father's public life at this point in the conversation and began talking about some personal details. The separation between the public/private sphere, or the spiritual/material domain, has been a topic of much scholarly debate, especially with regard to thinking about Indian politics within this framework.[48] At the time the debates had little to offer as I was faced with a dilemma of interpreting the private details within the context of Dr Parchure's public life, as President of the Gwalior Hindu Mahasabha and Hindu Rashtra Sena. Moreover, as my questions never even broached the subject of Dr Parchure's private life, I was surprised when Upendra Parchure openly narrated an incident about family abase. Dr Parchure spent three-quarters of his income from his medical practice on funding his two organizations. One day Upendra Parchure's mother Sushilabai required some money to purchase items for the family.[49] Dr Parchure was apparently unavailable, and the mother decided to take a few rupees from his organizational fund. Upon realizing that Sushilabai had taken the money. Dr Parchure proceeded to beat his wife till she was unconscious. Upendra Parchure stated: 'It is only by the grace of god that my mother did not die that day.'

This was the only time his mother was mentioned in the conversation, but it was clear that this was not an isolated incident. The conversation appeared to have triggered a son's memory about his parents' conflictual relationship that often resulted in violence against the mother. I asked myself why Upendra Parchure wanted to ensure that his father's abuse was included in the narrative of Dr Parchure's politics. There are at least two ideas which can be offered as explanations. First, Upendra Parchure wanted to establish a continuity between his father's activities in the public sphere and his violence at home; and, second, the discussion of attacks against innocent Muslims and against his mother was one way to prevent the construction of a hagiographical account of his father's life, especially as he knew I was conducting the interview for the purpose of writing about Dr Parchure. At another level, Hindu nationalists in western India had already developed discourses on the themes of domesticity, 'the home' and family life by the end of the nineteenth century.[50] Inscribed within the debates was a view that the 'domestic sphere' was central for the preservation of Hindu spiritual values, and a necessary space for 'respectable women' to serve their duty as 'devoted wives' and 'enlightened mothers' in the making of the nation.[51]

It has been suggested that these processes were corollaries to the re-emergence of Maharashtrian brahmans in the nineteenth century, when forms of brahmanic Hinduism became important determinants for social behaviour, especially on the 'woman's question.'[52] Tilak and other conservatives writing in the 1880s argued against the education of Hindu women on the grounds that reading was likely to encourage 'immorality' and 'insubordination' and, thereby, challenge Hindu traditions and religion.[53] Savarkar later contributed to these debates in an essay titled 'Woman's beauty and duty,' arguing that 'the primary duty of a woman is to the home, children, and the nation.'[54] Although Savarkar was not against formal education for women, he felt that they should be trained in areas suited to their 'temperament': that is, women primarily needed to be educated as mothers to create a new generation of patriots for the betterment of the nation.[55] For example, in a speech given in 1937, he encouraged women 'to be mothers of fine, healthy progeny,' while the 'kitchen and children were the main duties of women.'[56] However, any woman who digressed from her duty in the domestic sphere, as prescribed by Savarkar, was declared 'morally guilty of a breach of trust.'[57] Public debates on the topic of female improprieties that violated the emergent Hindu norms within the domestic sphere often concluded with harsh resolutions, like advocating the use of violence against 'weak' and 'wicked' women.[58] Were Sushilabai's actions of taking a few rupees from Dr Parchure's organizational fund an immoral act and a transgression from her duty as a devoted wife? Unfortunately, Upendra Parchure did not have an answer to this question.

The conversation next turned to Mahatma Gandhi's murder. The leadership of the Hindu Mahasabha and its affiliates had declared the partition of India and the creation of Pakistan a failure. It had been condemned by Savarkar, for example, on the grounds that the 'vivisection of the Motherland' was an insult to all Hindus, and the idea of Pakistan was a threat to the making of a Hindu nation in the aftermath of the British raj.[59] For Savarkar's followers, like Godse and Dr Parchure, Mahatma Gandhi and the Congress Party were to blame for the turn in political developments leading up to the partition in 1947, a period in which it was argued that the rights of Hindus were not being protected. Godse echoed Savarkar's claims by arguing:

> *Gandhiji failed in his duty as the Father of the Nation. He has proved to be the Father of Pakistan. It was for this reason alone that I as a dutiful son of Mother India thought it my duty to put an end to the life of the so-called Father of the Nation who had played a very prominent part in bringing about vivisection of the country—our Motherland.*[60]

According to Upendra Parchure, Nathuram Godse and Narayan Apte travelled from Delhi to Gwalior by train on 28 January 1948.[61] They arrived at the Parchure family home for the purpose of securing a gun, which was to be used to assassinate Gandhi. Godse was unhappy about the gun he already had in his possession because it was not an automatic and it frequently locked up without firing a round. Upendra Parchure remembers his father showing a pistol to Godse, and says that he even saw Godse firing it outside. The pistol was said to have originated in Europe, and only came to Gwalior when a Mr Deshmukh, a military officer in the Gwalior State Army, acquired it while on a training exercise in Germany.[62] The connection between Dr Parchure and Deshmukh remains unclear in this narrative. Upendra Parchure's only other comment about Godse was that he was someone who was shy and afraid of being in the presence of women. Although this point has been made by scholars studying Godse's life, it is unclear why the comment was inserted at this point in the conversation, except as a way of highlighting some seeming tension or paradox within Godse's personality.[63] On 29 January Godse and Apte left Gwalior for Delhi, and on the following evening Nathuram Godse walked up to Mahatma Gandhi and fired three rounds from the automatic pistol into his body.

Dr Parchure reportedly celebrated Gandhi's death by distributing sweets in Gwalior.[64] On 3 February Dr Parchure was detained by the police, and then formally arrested for conspiracy to commit murder two weeks later.[65] He confessed to his role in Gandhi's murder on 18 February while being interrogated by R. B. Atal, the First Class Magistrate of Gwalior,[66] but later retracted his confession arguing that it was 'untrue' and forcefully extracted.[67] Dr Parchure, along with five others, was found guilty of the conspiracy to murder Mahatma Gandhi and sentenced to 'transportation for life.'[68] Nathuram Godse and Narayan Apte were determined to be the primary perpetrators, and were ordered to be executed, while Savarkar was acquitted of all charges with no direct evidence linking him to the murder. Digamber Badge became the official 'approver' in the case and was released after the trial. Dr Parchure filed an appeal in the Punjab High Court, arguing that he had no role in the conspiracy, even though he had met Godse and Apte prior to the murder.[69] He stated that the two had arrived in Gwalior to recruit volunteers from the Hindu Rashtra Sena for some demonstrations in Delhi. Apte and Godse corroborated with Dr Parchure's testimony during the trial, and Nathuram argued that the automatic pistol used to kill Gandhi was purchased through an arms dealer in a Delhi refugee camp.[70] The High Court accepted Dr Parchure's claim that coercion was used to extract his initial confession, and that there was enough doubt about the exact nature of his interactions with Godse and Apte to warrant an acquittal of all charges.[71] According to Upendra Parchure, his father was banned from Gwalior for two years following his release from prison, but he finally returned in 1952 on the condition that he would no longer participate in public politics.[72] He re-established his medical practice and continued to live in Gwalior until his death in 1985.

Upendra Parchure did not mention that there was a controversy about his father's involvement in Gandhi's murder. Officially, Dr Parchure was acquitted of all charges, but within the family he has continued to be celebrated as one of the conspirators. Dr Parchure's original confession described how he had instructed an individual by the name of Dandavate to purchase a gun from one Jagdishprasad Goel.[73] Dandavate returned to Dr Parchure's house with a 9-mm Beretra automatic and about ten rounds of ammunition. Nathuram Godse tested the weapon in Dr Parchure's yard, and agreed to purchase it for 300 rupees. Upendra Parchure's narrative of events generally appears to be consistent with his father's original confession, except that there is no discussion of Dandavate and Goel, but there is an addition of a Mr Deshmukh (who was not mentioned by Dr Parchure). Yet Dr Parchure's exact role remains unresolved today, although it is popularly accepted that he assisted Godse with the purchase of the gun. 'The Official Mahatma Gandhi eArchive' even has a brief history of the murder weapon entitled 'The gun: a 9-mm Beretta automatic' and states that Dr Parchure had organized Godse's acquisition of the weapon.[74] In a recent interview, Gopal Godse claims that Dr Parchure did help his brother, but was not part of the inner circle who plotted Gandhi's murder: 'Nathuram managed to get an automatic pistol from Dr Dattatrey Parchure from Gwalior, though he was not a part of the conspiracy, and was later released by the High Court.'[75]

Upendra Parchure finally turned to the question of naming children. He argued that his father had probably named 'dozen upon dozens of children Vinayak' if not 'hundreds upon hundreds.' He stated he personally knew seven Vinayaks presently living in Gwalior who had acquired the name while patients in his father's clinic; I happened to be number eight. Upendra Parchure was very clear that his father's desire to name boys Vinayak was in honour of Savarkar. Dr Parchure had spent his adult life promoting the ideologies of his guru, initially through the Hindu Mahasabha and the Hindu Rashtra Sena, and then later in his life, when forced out of public politics, he adopted alternative strategies to promote Savarkarism. Upendra Parchure argued that I should feel very proud to have been named after such a strong, powerful nationalist who spent his entire life fighting for Hindu rights, and stated that 'the spirit of Savarkar now lives through you.'

After that moment in the interview, I began questioning why my family decided to keep the name Vinayak, especially as they knew Dr Parchure's background. Were they aware of his hidden agenda which was directly tied to Savarkar? I have repeatedly asked my parents about this topic over the past few months, but the answers fail to explain the intricate details that interest me. My mother states that I was named after Ganesh, the decision was not political and she was unaware that Dr Parchure had an agenda. She reminds me that Bai was not interested in giving me any name; I was too ill. In one conversation, she stated that Dr Parchure told Bai that my health would improve, and because it did, the family decided to keep the name. My father repeats my mother's explanation, but reminds me that he was not even living in Gwalior when I was named. I find it difficult to probe my parents any further about my name, not least because they have grown frustrated with my questions. I certainly get a sense that my illness was very serious, my recovery was a tremendous relief for a family that had already lost one child through ill-health, and Dr Parchure was thanked for his medical advice and honoured by naming me Vinayak. Needless to say, Savarkar does not emerge anywhere in their narratives.

Dr Parchure's strategy of naming children as a way of promoting Savarkarism initially appeared rather innocuous, especially for someone who had achieved national-level notoriety for his public politics. It is not clear when Dr Parchure began giving the name Vinayak, but it may be suggested that the process began after Savarkar's death in 1966. However, it is important to note that Dr Parchure was not the first to take up the idea of using the name Vinayak for political purposes. In fact, he may have been following a pattern set by other disciples of Savarkar, namely, Nathuram Godse and the conspirators to Gandhi's murder. In the months leading up to the assassination these individuals regularly used half a dozen or so aliases when travelling, mostly centring on the name Vinayak in honour of Savarkar.[76] Dr Parchure, who in 1947 was described as a 'second Savarkar,' would have been well versed in his guru's writings, especially the seminal text *Hindutva: Who is a Hindu?*. Since its first publication in 1923, *Hindutva* has acquired a reputation as a defining treatise for the development of Hindu nationalism in the twentieth century. The editor's introduction to the fifth edition of *Hindutva* furthers this point by arguing that 'the concept of Hindutva is Savarkar's own . . . [that] the Hindus are tied together by bonds of a common fatherland, ties of blood, a common culture and civilization, common heroes, common history and above all, the will to remain united as a nation.'[77] Savarkar intended to use the text to clarify divergent opinions on how to define 'Hindu,' 'Hinduism' and 'Hindutva' by establishing a history of the term 'Hindu,' demonstrating links between territoriality and Hindu identity, and answering the question 'Who is a Hindu?.' His main focus in the text, nevertheless, was to argue that the conceptualization of Indian national identity must, at its foundation, be based within the political philosophy of Hindutva.[78]

I would suggest that Dr Parchure's desire to give names was a return to the basic principles outlined by Savarkar in *Hindutva*, especially when considering that the first section of the book begins with the title 'What is in a name?' and others following include 'Name older still,' 'Other names' and 'How names are given.'[79] In *Hindutva*, there does not appear to be a specific prescription for naming individuals; instead, the focus is on the importance of naming a society and a nation.[80] Savarkar, of course, was focusing on these issues as a way of identifying the etymology of 'Hindu' and 'Hindustan,' and in order to establish a genealogy of names connecting Hindus and Hindustan with India and Indians. However, an examination of Savarkar's argument for 'what is in a name' provides a clue to Dr Parchure's tactics:

> *For, things do matter more than their names, especially when you have to choose one only of the two, or when the association between them is either new or simple. The very fact that a thing is indicated by a dozen names in a dozen human tongues disarms the suspicion that there is an invariable connection or natural concomitance between sound and the meaning it conveys. Yet, as the association of the word with the thing it signifies grows stronger and lasts long, so does the channel which connects the two states of consciousness then allow an easy flow of thoughts from one to the other, till at last it seems almost impossible to separate them. And when in addition to this a number of secondary thoughts or feelings that are generally roused by the thing get mystically entwined with the word that signifies it,* the name seems to matter as much as the thing itself.[81]

Upon reading this passage, I was reminded of Upendra Parchure's vivid declaration that 'the spirit of Savarkar' was now living through me and, by extension, through the dozens or hundreds of other Vinayaks. It certainly might be argued that Dr Parchure held the belief that inscribed within the name Vinayak was a signifying system tied to Savarkar and the principles of Hindutva. Those versed in semiotics would suggest that Dr Parchure was aware of the power of the name-sign, so by naming children he had hoped to evoke a mental image of Savarkar as an icon in everyday life.[82] Indeed, the name Vinayak has become more popular in India over the past generation than in previous ones, although, at the same time, it would be incorrect to assume that all links go back to Savarkar My own parents say that they had no clue about Dr Parchure's interest in naming boys, and I wonder if other parents whose sons are named Vinayak have also remained oblivious to this information over the years and think that the origins of the name are only tied to Ganesh. But here too there is a 'hidden transcript,' with a history intertwined with the ideological development of Hindu nationalism.

It may be worth saying something more about the long-term significance of Ganesh, as every conversation about the name Vinayak usually begins here. The worship of Ganesh in western India began as early as the sixth or seventh century, although primarily limited to Maharashtrian Brahmins, the Deshastha and Konkanastha.[83] By the eighteenth century Ganesh was popularized in temples and festivals around Pune through the patronage of the Maratha Peshwas, but there was a significant decline with the subsidence of Peshwa power after 1818 and the arrival of the British in the area.[84] In the 1890s, Ganesh's popularity had a resurgence under the leadership of Bal Gangadhar Tilak, who began mobilizing large numbers of Hindus from upper and lower castes around an annual Ganesh festival.[85] Tilak was concerned about harnessing mass support against colonial rule, while simultaneously using the symbol of Ganesh to articulate a political agenda linking 'Hindu revivalism' with Indian nationalism. It was considered an 'extremist' form of nationalism for its celebration of Maharashtrian 'martial prowess'[86] and for its militant anti-Muslim character.[87] In fact, it has been argued that Tilak's invention of a Ganesh tradition was primarily in response to, and corresponded with, the annual Muslim festival of Muhharam.[88] This point is generally obscured in today's popular memory of the Ganesh festival's origins, especially as it has achieved national appeal throughout India, moving beyond the local and regional centres in Maharashtra. Tilak's role is also important in this discussion for another reason: namely, that Dr Parchure, Savarkar and the others in the Hindu Mahasabha and its affiliated organizations were heavily influenced by his nationalist politics.[89]

The fact that over the years neither my parents nor I were cognizant of Dr Parchure's naming practice is irrelevant for the politics of Hindutva. It may be argued that, for Dr Parchure, the celebration of Vinayak as Ganesh, or as Savarkar, was equally powerful because inscribed in both were the legacies and inspirations of Hindu nationalism. As I write this article, I sit in a room with a dozen or so idols of Ganesh—recent gifts I have received from friends and family, each of whom stated that they purchased the idol because of my name. I often wonder how many other Vinayaks are out there who share a similar story, but part of me simply does not want to meet a Vinayak who actually embodies the myriad characteristics which would make Dr Parchure proud.[90] For Savarkar and his contemporary disciples, the creation of a Hindu nation was a long, multi-generational process which could not be achieved in their lifetime. Savarkar was keenly aware of the risks and limitations of his political strategies, but advocated that his followers promote the ideals of a Hindu nation, even in minute ways, for the benefit of future generations:

The seed of the banyan tree is so trivial as to be smaller than the mustard seed. But it holds within itself the rich promise of luxuriant expanse. If we are to live with honour and dignity as a Hindu

Nation . . . that nation must emerge under the Hindu flag. This my dream shall come true—if not in this generation, at least in the next. If it remains an empty dream, I shall prove a fool. If it comes true, I shall prove a prophet.[91]

Savarkar's principles of *Hindutva* are very much alive today, and the new generation of Hindu nationalists have been openly working towards the goal of creating a Hindu fatherland by following Savarkar's prescription:

The nation that has no consciousness of its past has no future. Equally true it is that a nation must develop its capacity not only for claiming a past but also for knowing how to use it for the further-ance of its future.[92]

In India, there are many who have been inspired by the writing and activities of Savarkar and his disciples, and one does not need to look very hard to find these individuals and groups, especially as their public presence cannot be avoided in everyday life. The discursive project of Hindutva, led by the Bharatiya Janata Party (BJP) and its subsidiaries, for example, promotes the changing of names in consonance with Savarkar's ideals.[93] In November 1995 the Maharashtrian state government led by the Shiv Sena (Shivaji's Army) changed the official name of Bombay to Mumbai.[94] The Shiv Sena as a nativist organization had been demanding the ver-nacularization of the city's name since its founding in 1966, but could only change it once it had secured the partonage of the BJP government at the centre.[95] The process was extended to replacing the names of streets, buildings, railway stations, neighbourhoods and anything deemed necessary to rid the city of its Portuguese and British titles, and as a way to reinscribe a Hindu identity into the city. Institutionally, the project has played an important role in targeting Muslims, Christians and other minorities: the incarnations of the Hindu Rashtra Sena and the Hindu Rashtra Dal frequently make their presence felt, as in the case of the Bombay riots in 1992–3,[96] and most recently leading to the killing of an estimated 2000 Muslims in Gujarat.[97]

I asked Upendra Parchure about his views on the direction of today's Hindu nationalism, BJP style. To my surprise, he was dissatisfied with the current leadership and their national pro-gramme. He argued that today's politicians were corrupt, and consequently they did not live up to the ideals of creating a 'Hindu Nation' as articulated by Savarkar, his father and the oth-ers involved in the Gandhi murder case. Upendra Parchure reiterated that the assassination was necessary for the betterment of the nation, to ensure that India could develop into a strong, powerful homeland for Hindus. For Upendra Parchure, I was part of the future generation his father and Savarkar had hoped would serve as the messengers of *Hindutva*. As Vinayak, I could embody the characteristics of power, strength and masculinity inscribed in my name, and participate in the making of a Hindu nation. As I stated from the outset, I wish the story of my name had ended many years ago and did not require such a long, unsettling journey.

I thanked Upendra Parchure for his time and for sharing memories of his father's life-story. My last request however, was to see a photograph of Dr Parchure, whose image was the only one conspicuously missing among the numerous photographs of the group arrested for Gandhi's murder. Upendra Parchure stated that he only had two photographs of his father in his house. I was taken into his bedroom where they were hanging: the first was a picture of

Dr Parchure as a young wrestler, flexing his chest and arms; the second showed Dr Parchure with his wife, probably taken shortly after their wedding. As I was leaving, Upendra Parchure asked if I had noticed the third photograph in the room which had been carefully positioned above the door. I imagined that this was a reference to a picture of Ganesh, who is often placed in such a location as an auspicious symbol for all those who pass through the doorway. Instead, it was a large image of the assassin Nathuram Godse, who was being celebrated as an incarnation of Vinayak and the remover of obstacles.

University of California, Irvine

Notes

1. I thank Heidi Tinsman for reminding me of this point. Also, see Dipesh Chakrabarty, *Provincializing Europe: Postcolonial Thought and Historical Difference* (Princeton, 2000), 242.

2. For an etymology of the name Vinayak, see A. K. Narain, 'Ganeśa: a protohistory of the idea and the icon' in Robert L. Brown (ed.), *Ganesh: Studies of an Asian God* (Albany, 1991), 21–5. Narain argues that by the fifth century A.D. Ganesh was popularly referred to as Vinayak, a name literally meaning 'a leader or guide for regulating, controlling, or implementing order and discipline' (21–2). Ganesh also acquired additional names in this period, some based on the physical characteristics of an elephant, others determined by his position as the lord or leader of deities. In all, the literature on this topic suggests that Ganesh has 108 names. For a list of the names and definitions in English, Gujarati and Marathi, see <http://www.rediff.com/gujarati/2002/feb/20ganesh.htm>; <http://www.esakal.com/ganeshutsav/names.htm>; <http://www.mantraonnet.com/108ganeshnames.html>.

   For a brief discussion on the significance of the number 108 within Hindu traditions, see <http://www.zen-forum.com/a13/b2001/c12/d3/e783/z7>.

   For a collection of Ganesh images and forms, see <http://www.eprathana.com/html/iganesh.asp>; <http://astrology.indianinfo.com/festivals/ganesh/ganesh_names.html>. Also, see Paul B. Courtright, *Ganeśa: Lord of Obstacles, Lord of Beginnings* (New York, 1985).

3. See Bruce Graham, *Hindu Nationalism and Indian Politics: The Origins and Development of the Bharatiya Jana Sangh* (Cambridge, 1990).

4. On a similar theme, see Amitav Ghosh, *In an Antique Land: History in the Guise of a Traveler's Tale* (New York, 1994).

5. For a useful discussion on related themes, see James C. Scott, John Tehranian and Jeremy Mathias, 'The production of legal identities proper to states: the case of the permanent family surname.' *Comparative Studies in Society and History*, XLIV, 1 (2002), 4–44.

6. For a further physical description of Dr Parchure, see Manohar Malgonkar, *The Men Who Killed Gandhi* (Madras, 1978), 135.

7. See Joseph S. Alter's, *The Wrestler's Body: Identity and Ideology in North India* (Berkeley, 1992), especially chap. 7 on 'Wrestling tournaments and the body's recreation.'

8. *Ibid.*, 1. This point is also discussed in Nita Kumar, *The Artisans of Banaras: Popular Culture and Identity*, 1880–1986 (Princeton, 1988), 111–24; John Rosselli, 'The self-image of effeteness: physical education and nationalism in nineteenth-century Bengal,'

Past & Present, LXXXVI (1980), 121–48: Phillip B. Zarrili, 'Repositioning the body, practice, power, and self in an Indian martial art' in Carol A. Breckenridge (ed.) *Consuming Modernity: Public Culture in a South Asian World* (Minneapolis, 1995), 183–215.

9. See Tapan Basu, Pradip Datta, Sumit Sarkar, Tanika Sarkar and Sambuddha Sen, *Khaki Shorts Saffron Flags: A Critique of the Hindu Right* (New Delhi, 1993); Ashis Nandy, 'Final encounter: the politics of the assassination of Gandhi' in his *At the Edge of Psychology* (Delhi, 1980), 70–98; Alter, *op. cit.,* 237–55. Related themes outside the social context of India are also discussed in John Kasson, *Houdini, Tarzan, and the Perfect Man: The White Male Body and the Challenge of Modernity in America* (New York, 2001); Peter Filene, *Him/Her/Self: Gender Identities in Modern America* (Baltimore, 1998, 3rd edn); Stephen Garton, 'The scales of suffering; love, death and Victorian masculinity,' *Social History,* XXVII, 1 (2002), 40–58.

10. Alter, *op. cit.,* 261–3. For a comparative perspective on the related themes of military aspects of national character and the construction of manliness see, for example, Sam Pryke, 'The popularity of nationalism in the early British Boy Scout movement', *Social History,* XXIII, 3 (1998), 309–24; Robert Morell (ed.), *Changing Men in South Africa* (Pietermaritzburg, 2001); Jonathan Rutherford, *Forever England: Reflections on Race, Masculinity and Empire* (London, 1997); Michael Kimmel, *Manhood in America* (New York, 1996); Mrinali Sinha, *Colonial Masculinity: The 'Manly Englishman' and the 'Effeminate Bengali' in the Late Nineteenth Century* (Manchester, 1995).

11. Christophe Jaffrelot, *The Hindu Nationalist Movement and Indian Politics 1925 to the 1990s* (London, 1996), 17–25; Stuart Corbridge and John Harriss, *Reinventing India: Liberalization, Hindu Nationalism and Popular Democracy* (Cambridge, 2000), 182–3.

12. See Gyanendra Pandey, 'Which of us are Hindus?' in Gyanendra Pandey (ed.), *Hindus and Others–The Question of Identity in India Today* (New Delhi, 1993), 238–72.

13. The specialization of Ayurvedic paediatrics is called Kaumarabhritya. Its origins date back to the ancient text Artharvaveda, defining the branch of Ayurveda as 'the management of infants and advises . . . to the means of rectifying the morbid conditions of milk of the wet-nurses and of curing various diseases caused by unwholesome milk and planetary influence.' Cited in Girindranath Mukhopadhyaya, *History of Indian Medicine: From the Earliest Ages to the Present Time,* vol. 1 (New Delhi, 1974, 2nd edn; original edition 1922), 3. Also, see Dr C. Chaturvedi, Dr Romesh Sharma and Prof. P. V. Tewari, *Advances in Ayurvedic Pediatrics* (Varanasi, 1988).

14. See David Arnold, *Colonizing the Body: State Medicine and Epidemic Disease in Nineteenth-Century India* (Berkeley, 1993); Roger Jeffery, 'Doctors and Congress: the role of medical men and medical politics in Indian nationalism' in Mike Shepperdson and Colin Simmons (eds), *The Indian National Congress and the Political Economy of India 1885–1985* (Aldershot, 1988), 160–73.

15. David Arnold, *Science, Technology and Medicine in Colonial India, The New Cambridge History of India,* III, 5 (Cambridge, 2000), 169–210. I thank Douglas Haynes for this reference.

16. *ibid.,* 176. For a related discussion on the shifts in the field of medicine in Britain during the nineteenth century, see Robert Gray, 'Medical men, industrial labour and the state in Britain, 1830–50'. *Social History,* XVI, 19–43.

17. See Vinayak Chaturvedi, 'Colonial Power and Agrarian Politics in Kheda District (Gujarat), c. 1890–1930' (Ph.D., University of Cambridge, 2001), 103–48; David Arnold, 'Touching the body: perspectives on the Indian plague, 1896–1900' in Ranajit Guha (ed.), *Subaltern Studies V* (Delhi, 1985), 55–90.

18. Gyan Prakash, *Another Reason: Science and the Imagination of Modern India* (Princeton, 1999), 149–52; Arnold, *Science, Technology and Medicine, op. cit.,* 169–70, 176–7. Also, see Charles Leslie, 'The ambiguities of medical revivalism in modern India' in Charles Leslie (ed.), *Asian Medical Systems: A Comparative Study* (Berkeley, 1976), 356–67. On related themes, see Ashis Nandy, *Alternative Sciences: Creativity and Authenticity in Two Indian Scientists* (Delhi, 1995).

19. In 1897, Tilak called for a 'judicious combination' of the two systems of medicine, while Gandhi remained altogether troubled with all fields of medicine. Arnold, *Colonizing the Body, op. cit.,* 321. n. 100. On the other hand, Gandhi condemned 'European medicine', arguing that 'the English have certainly effectively used the medical profession for holding us . . . [and] for political gain, and 'to study European medicine is to deepen our slavery'. M. K. Gandhi, *Hind Swaraj or Indian Home Rule* (Ahmedabad, 1990, 8th edn), 52–4. Also Partha Chatterjee, *Nationalist Thought and the Colonail World: A Derivative Discourse* (Minneapolis, 1993), 93.

20. Leslie, *op. cit.,* 363.

21. Jeffery, *op. cit.,* 166.

22. Dhanajay Keer, *Veer Savarkar* (Bombay, 1988), 23, 28–51. Also, see Lise McKean, *Divine Enterprise: Gurus and the Hindu Nationalist Movement* (Chicago, 1996), 71–96; Pandey, *op. cit.,* 239–72; Jaffrelot, *op. cit.,* 19–33; Amalendu Misra, 'Savarkar and the discourse on Islam in pre-independent India', *Journal of Asian History,* XXXIII, 2 (1999), 142–84; Vidya Sagar Anand, *Savarkar: A Study in the Evolution of Indian Nationalism* (London, 1967); Jyoti Trehan, *Veer Savarkar: Thought and Action of Vinayak Damodar Savarkar* (New Delhi, 1991); Chitra Gupta, *The Life of Barrister Savarkar* (New Delhi, 1939); Harindra Srivastava, *The Epic Sweep of V. D. Savarkar* (New Delhi, 1993).

23. See Harindra Srivastava, *Five Stormy Years: Savarkar in London, June 1906–June 1911* (New Delhi, 1983).

24. Keer, *op. cit.,* 23.

25. See Vinayak Damodar Savarkar, *Indian War of Independence, 1857* (Delhi, 1986, 10th edn).

26. Keer, *op. cit.,* 73.

27. See Satradru Sen, *Disciplining Punishment: Colonialism and Convict Society in the Andaman Islands* (Delhi, 2000).

28. S. S. Savarkar, 'Preface by the publisher of the second edition' in Vinayak Damodar Savarkar, *Hindutva: Who is a Hindu?* (Bombay, 1989, 6th edn), v–vi. Also, see *An Echo from Andamans: Letters Written by Br. Savarkar to his Brother Dr Savarkar* (Nagpur, n.d).

29. Jaffrelot., *op. cit.,* 32. Jaffrelot cites Savarkar's *My Transportation for Life* (Bombay, 1984), 271–2, where he argues that Johann Casper Bluntschli's *The Theory of the State* (Oxford 1885) was influential in developing ideas of a Hindu nationalism.

30. See A. S. Bhide (ed.), *Veer Savarkar's 'Whirl-Wind Propaganda': Statements, Messages and Extracts from the President's Diary of his Propagandistic Tours, Interviews from December 1937 to October 1941* (Bombay, 1941); Keer, *op. cit.,* 225, 230, 360.

31. Bhide, *op. cit.*, v.

32. The size of the Sena is given in Manohar Malgonkar, *The Men Who Killed Gandhi* (Madras, 1978), 136.

33. Nathuram Godse, *May It Please Your Honour* (Pune, 1977), 23, 93, 100; Bhide, *op. cit.*, 57–88. 101–14, 180–1; Keer, *op. cit.*, 240–5.

34. Gopal Godse, 'Events and accused' in Godse, *op. cit.*, xv. M. K. Gandhi is reported to have received a telegram from 'some Muslims in the Gwalior State' stating, 'The Hindus attacked our village and beat us, destroying our houses and crops and the State authorities take no notice in spite of requests.' The date of the telegram is not given, but the incident appears to correspond with the activities of the Hindu Rashtra Sena. Full details are given in Government of India, *Report of the Commission of Inquiry into Conspiracy to Murder Mahatma Gandhi*, part II, vol. IV, 72 (henceforth, *RCI*).

35. Malgonkar, *op. cit.*, 135.

36. Godse, *op. cit.*, 15–16; Nandy, 'Final encounter', *op., cit.*, 81. On the development of the RSS's politics, see Basu, Datta, Sarkar, Sarkar and Sen, *op. cit.*; Jaffrelot, *op. cit.*; Sumit Sarkar, 'Fascism of the Sangh Parivar,' *Economic and Political Weekly*, XXVIII, 5 (1993), 163–7; Sumit Sarkar, 'Indian nationalism and the politics of Hindutva' in David Ludden (ed.), *Contesting the Nation: Religion, Community, and the Politics of Democracy in India* (Philadelphia, 1996), 270–93.

37. Nandy, 'Final encounter', *op. cit.*, 81.

38. Godse, *op. cit.*, 18, 37.

39. *RCI*, part II, vol. IV, 66–7.

40. *ibid.*, 67.

41. *ibid.*, 67.

42. *ibid.*, 67: *RCI*, part I. vol. III, 263.

43. The discussion of the interaction between Dr Parchure and Nathuram Godse is given in Malgonkar, *op. cit.*, 135–6.

44. Evidence of Panna Lal Chaube, Witness Number 47, *RCI*, part I, vol. II, 239–41.

45. *ibid.*, 239.

46. *RCI*, part I, vol. III, 265.

47. *ibid.*, 265 (italics in original).

48. Here I am thinking of Partha Chatterjee's argument in *The Nation and Its Fragments* (Princeton, 1993).

49. For a brief discussion about Sushilabai Parchure, see P. L. Inamdar, *The Story of the Red Fort Trial 1948–49* (Bombay, 1979).

50. See Rosalind O'Hanlon, *A Comparison between Women and Men: Tarabai Shinde and the Critique of Gender Relations in Colonial India* (Delhi, 1994). The literature on this theme is extensive for India, especially in the context of Bengal: see Antoinette Burton, 'House/Daughter/Nation: interiority, architecture, and historical imagination in Janaki Majumdar's "Family History"', *Journal of Asian Studies*, LVI, 4 (1997), 921–46; Antoinette Burton, 'Thinking beyond the boundaries: empire, feminism and the domains of history', *Social History*, XXVI, 1 (2001), 60–71; Tanika Sarkar, 'The Hindu wife and the Hindu nation: domesticity and nationalism in nineteenth century Bengal,' *Studies in History*,

---

VIII, 2 (1992), 213–34: Judith E. Walsh, 'What women learned when men gave them advice: rewriting patriarchy in late nineteenth-century Bengal,' *Journal of Asian Studies*, LVI 2, (1997), 371–90; Mary Hancock, 'Home science and the nationalization of domesticity in colonial India', *Modern Asian Studies*, XXXV, 4 (2001), 871–903; Pradip Kumar Bose, 'Sons of the nation: child rearing in the new family' in Partha Chatterjee (ed.), *Texts of Power: Emerging Disciplines in Colonial Bengal* (Calcutta, 1996), 118–44; Uma Chakravarti, 'Whatever happened to the Vedic *Dasi*? Orientalism, nationalism, and a script for the past' and Partha Chatterjee, 'The nationalist resolution of the woman's question' in Kumkum Sangari and Sudesh Vaid (eds), *Recasting Women: Essays in Indian Colonial History* (New Brunswick, 1990), 27–87, 233–53. Also, see Kamala Visweswaran, 'Small speeches, subaltern gender: nationalist ideology and its historiography' in Shahid Amin and Dipesh Chakrabarty (eds), *Subaltern Studies* IX (Delhi, 1996), 83–125; Gayatri Chakravorty Spivak, 'The new subaltern: a silent interview' in Vinayak Chaturvedi (ed.), *Mapping Subaltern Studies and the Postcolonial* (London, 2000), 324–8; Partha Chatterjee and Pradeep Jeganathan (eds), *Subaltern Studies XI: Community, Gender and Violence* (Delhi, 2000); and Pandey, *op. cit.,* 260–2.

51. O'Hanlon, *op. cit.,* 51.

52. *ibid.,* 10.

53. *ibid.,* 16.

54. Keer, *op. cit.,* 210, 213.

55. *ibid.,* 213–14. For examples of comparative perspectives on related debates outside the Indian case, see the discussion on the relationship between nationalist politics and motherhood in Argentina in Daniel James, *Doña María's Story: Life, History, Memory, and Political Identity* (Durham, NC, 2000), 241. I thank Heidi Tinsman for this reference. On the themes of nationalism and the female body, Marcelo Bergman and Mónica Szurmuk, 'Gender, citizenship, and social protest: the new social movements in Argentina' in Ileana Rodríguez (ed.), *The Latin American Subaltern Studies Reader* (Durham, NC, 2001), 383–401; Elsa Barkley Brown, 'Negotiating and transforming the public sphere: African American political life in the transition from slavery to freedom' in The Black Public Sphere Collective (ed.), *The Black Public Sphere* (Chicago, 1995), 111–50. Joan B. Landes, *Women and the Public Sphere in the Age of the French Revolution* (Ithaca, 1988) is also relevant for a discussion of the above themes. I thank Sharon Block for this reference. Also, see the following contributions in Craig Calhoun (ed.), *Habermas and the Public Sphere* (Cambridge, 1966): Nancy Fraser, 'Rethinking the public sphere: a contribution to the critique of actually existing democracy,' 109–42; Mary P. Ryan, 'Gender and public access: women's politics in nineteenth century America,' 259–88; and Geoff Eley, 'Nations, publics, and political cultures: placing Habermas in the nineteenth century,' 289–339.

56. Keer, *op. cit.,* 230. Also, see Lise, *op. cit.,* 86–7; Pandey, *op. cit.,* 260–1.

57. *ibid.,* 214.

58. O'Hanlon, *op. cit.,* 36–8.

59. Keer, *op. cit.,* 386–7.

60. Gopal Godse, *Gandhihartya ani Mce* (Poona, 1967), 306. Originally cited in Nandy, 'Final encounter,' *op. cit.,* 83.

61. For the official narrative of events relevant to Gandhi's assassination, see *RCI*, part I, vol. I. Also, see Inamdar, *op. cit.*; Malgaonkar, *op. cit.*; Ghosh, *op. cit.*

62. Malgaonkar suggests that the gun was manufactured in Italy in 1934, and was in the possession of an officer in Mussolini's army. An officer in the 4th Gwalior State Infantry, fighting in Abyssinia, acquired the gun when his Italian counterpart had surrendered. Malgaonkar, *op. cit.*, 137.

63. See Nandy, 'Final encounter', *op. cit.*, for further development on this theme.

64. Tapan Ghosh, *The Gandhi Murder Trial* (New York, 1973), 100.

65. *RCI*, part I, vol. I, 57.

66. Ghosh, *op. cit.*, 115.

67. *ibid.*, 119.

68. *RCI*, part I. vol. I, 60.

69. For a full discussion on Dr Parchure's case and subsequent appeal, see the reflections on the trial by his lawyer in Inamdar, *op. cit.*

70. Godse, *op. cit.*, 7, 13–14.

71. See Inamdar, *op. cit.*

72. Inamdar suggests that Dr Parchure's period of absence was set at six months through an 'order of Externment from the Gwalior division of the state of Madhya Bharat,' *ibid.*, 220.

73. See *RCI*, part 1, vol. 1.

74. See 'Dr Dattatraya Sadashiv Parchure' and 'The gun' at <http://www.mahatma.org.in/conspirators>.

75. 'The men who killed Gandhi,' *Asian Age Online* (18 August 2001) at <http://www.helinfinet.com/2001/AUG/WEEK3/7/AOSCS2frame.jsp>.

76. Nandy, 'Final encounter', *op. cit.*, 96–7, n. 36. For example, Nathuram Godse used the aliases Vinayakrao and N. Vinayak Rao. *RCI*, part I, vol. 1, 59, 78. Also, see Malgonkar, *op. cit.*, 115; Ghosh, *op. cit.*, 90.

77. G. M. Joshi, 'Introduction' in Savarkar, *Hindutva, op. cit.*, xi.

78. Savarkar articulates this point in *Hindutva, op. cit.*, 3. He states: 'The ideas and ideals, the systems and societies, the thoughts and sentiments which have centered round this name are so varied and rich, so powerful and so subtle, so elusive and yet so vivid that the term Hindutva defies all attempts at analysis. . . . Hindutva is not a word but a history. Not only the spiritual or religious history of our people as at times it is mistaken to be by being confounded with the other cognate term Hinduism, but a history in full. Hinduism is only a derivative, a fraction, a part of Hindutva.'

79. Savarkar, *Hindutva, op. cit.*, 1–16.

80. See Lise, *op. cit.*, 79–80; Pandey, *op. cit.*, 247–9. The literature on the politics of naming is extensive; for a comparative perspective, see Dietz Bering, *The Stigma of Names: Antisemitism in German Daily Life*, trans. Neville Place (Cambridge, 1992); bell hooks, *Yearning: Race, Gender, and Cultural Politics* (Boston, 1990); and Malcolm X, *The Autobiography of Malcolm X*, with the assistance of Alex Haley (New York, 1988 edn).

81. Savakar, *op. cit., Hindutva*, 1–2 (emphasis mine).

82. For example, see Anna Makolkin, *Name, Hero, Icon: Semiotics of Nationalism through Heroic Biograhy* (Berlin, 1992).

83. Paul B. Courtright, 'The Ganesh Festival in Maharashtra: some observations' in Eleanor Zelliot and Maxine Berntsen (eds), *The Experience of Hinduism* (Albany, 1988), 76–7.

84. Courtright, *Ganeśa, op. cit.*, 226.

85. See Richard Cashman, 'The political recruitment of God Ganapati,' *Indian Econnomic and Social History Review*, VII (1970), 347–73.

86. C. A. Bayly, *Origins of Nationality in South Asia: Patriotism and Ethical Governance in the Making of Modern India* (Delhi, 1998), 108–9.

87. S. Tejani, 'A Pre-History of Indian Secularism: Categories of Nationalism and Communalism in Emerging Definitions of India, Bombay Presidency, c. 1893–1932' (Ph.D., Columbia University, 2002), especially chap. 1, 'Cow protection and Tilak's Ganpati'; Thomas Blom Hansen, *Wages of Violence: Naming and Identity in Postcolonial Bombay* (Princeton, 2001), 29–30.

88. Tejani, *op. cit.*, 113–26.

89. Gopal Godse, 'Events and accused' in Godse, *op. cit.*, xii. Also, see Richard Cashman, *The Myth of the Lokamanya: Tilak and Mass Politics in Maharashtra* (Berkeley, 1975); Dhananjay Keer, *Lokamanya Tilak, Father of the Indian Freedom Struggle* (Bombay, 1969); Ram Gopal, *Lokamanya Tilak: A Biography* (New York, 1965); T. V. Parvate, *Bal Gangadhar Tilak: A Narrative and Interpretive Review of his Life, Career and Contemporary Events* (Ahmedabad, 1958); Dattatraya Parashuram Karmarkar, *Bal Gangadhar Tilak: A Study* (Bombay, 1956); Theodore Shay, *The Legacy of the Lokamanya: The Political Philosophy of Bal Gangadhar Tilak* (Bombay, 1956); D. V. Tahmankar, *Lokamanya Tilak: Father of Indian Unrest and Maker of Modern India* (London, 1956); Stanley Wolpert, *Tilak and Gokhale: Revolution and Reform in the Making of Modern India* (Berkeley, 1961).

90. Savarkar develops this idea in *Hindutva* under the heading 'How names are given'. He states:

    A name by its nature is determined not so much by what one likes to call oneself but generally by what others like to do. In fact a name is called into existence for this purpose. Self is known to itself immutable and without a name or even without a form. But when it comes in contact or conflict with a non-self then alone it stands in need of a name if it wants to communicate with others or if others persist in communicating with it. It is a game that requires two to play at. If the name chosen by the world for us is not directly against our liking then it is yet more likely to shadow all other names. But if the world hits upon the world by which they would know us as one redolent of our glory or our early love then that word is certain not only to shadow but to survive every other name we may have.

    (Savarkar, *Hindutva, op. cit.*, 15–16)

91. Vinayak Damodar Savarkar. 'This my legacy' cited in *Savarkar Darshan Pratishthan, Savarkar: Commemoration Volume* (26 February 1989), 3.

92. Vinayak Damodar Savarkar, *Samagra Savarkar Vangmaya,* vol. V (Poona, 1987), 1. Originally cited in Misra, *op. cit.*, 142.

93. On the theme of 'naming like a state,' see Scott, Tehranian and Mathias, *op. cit.*

94. Hansen, *op. cit.,* 1. Also, see Pauline Rohatgi, Pheroza Godrej and Rahul Mehrotra (eds). *Bombay to Mumbai: Changing Perspectives* (Mumbai, 1997); Meera Kosambi, 'British Bombay and Marathi Mumbai: some nineteenth century perceptions' in Sujata Patel and Alice Thorner (eds). *Bombay: Mosaic of Modern Culture* (Bombay, 1995) 3–24.

95. See Mary Fainsod Katzenstein, Uday Singh Mehta and Usha Thakker, 'The rebirth of the Shiv Sena: the symbiosis of discursive and organizational power,' *Journal of Asian Studies,* LVI, 2 (1997), 371–90; Mary Fainsod Karzenstein, *Ethnicity and Equality: The Shiv Sena Party and Preferential Policies in Bombay* (Ithaca, 1979); Vaibhav Purandare, *The Sena Story* (Mumbai, 1999); Sikata Banerjee, *Warriors in Politics: Hindu Nationalism, Violence, and the Shiv Sena in India* (Boulder, 2000); Shripad Amrit Dange, *Shiv Sena and the Bombay Riots* (New Delhi, 1969); Dipankar Gupta, *Nativism in a Metropolis: The Shiv Sena in Bombay* (New Delhi, 1982). Also, see Arjun Appadurai, 'Spectral housing and urban cleansing: notes on millennial Mumbai,' *Public Culture,* XII, 3 (2000); Satish Deshpande, 'Communalizing the nation-space: notes on spatial strategies of Hindutva', *Economic and Political Weekly,* XXX, 50 (1995), 3220–7.

96. See the Indian People's Human Rights Commission, *The People's Verdict. An inquiry into the December 1992 & January 1993 riots in Bombay by the Indian People's Human Rights Tribunal Conducted by Justice S. M. Daud and Justice H. Suresh* (Bombay, 1993).

97. A large number of journals in India have devoted special issue to the Gujarat riots of 2002. For example, see 'Genocide, Gujarat 2002,' *Communalism Combat,* VIII, 77–8 (2002); and 'In bad faith', *The Little Magazine,* III, 2 (2002). Also, see *A Joint Fact Finding Team Report. A Continuing Crime: The relief and rehabilitation measures, the attitude of the judiciary and police investigation and arrests with regard to the genocide in Gujarat* (Mumbai, 2002).

Retro-Nationalism? Rock Music in the Former German Democratic Republic (GDR) (Excerpts)

Patricia Simpson

. . . . . .

In the early nineteen-fifties, the SED [Socialist Unity Party] realized that rock music was a phenomenon that demanded attention, then condemnation, followed by some careful management. References to the dangers of American barbarism, cultural imperialism, and the undermining influence of rock music abound in official publications.2 Party policy toward rock, what it would call Unterhaltungsmusik (entertainment music), became a high-profile political issue.

In 1953, official intervention began. Walter Ulbricht called for an end to the influx of "mass produced musical products."3

These, he argued, would be replaced by music that would contribute to *Bewußtseinsbildung*, or the cultivation of consciousness.4 During the plenary session of the Central Committee meeting of the SED in December 1965, Erich Honecker went so far as to analyze Beat music and its influence on the class struggle. He recognized the capacity of rock music to shape youth culture, and he warned against a music that would inspire "excesses" in its listeners. Honecker insisted that production of "rock music was not and could not be in accordance with the goals of a socialist society."5

Later, however, when rather laughable attempts to impose ballroom-like dances (the Lipsi, for example) to keep the young people from doing the twist failed, the Party took another course of action: it began throwing the party itself. Deploying the leadership of the organization Free German Youth (FDJ),6 the SED's action became paradigmatic for the interaction between politics and popular music. The nationalization of rock music effectively enlisted the help of bands in constructing *socialist personalities*. Rock, too, the men at the top realized, could participate in the pedagogical process of training the next generation to be good citizens of socialism.

During the nineteen-sixties and seventies, FDJ undertook various initiatives to foreground singing and dancing, conceptualized under the rubric of *Jugendtanzmusik* (youth dance music). The folk-song movement helped produce many *Liedermacher* (singer-songwriters), some of whom would turn their critical edge on the state, and not without consequences. All the while, FDJ continued a careful negotiation between the desire for Anglo-American capitalist imports and native bands.

After the X Party Congress of the SED, the Party's ideologue Jürgen Hagen could entitle his comments: "Entertainment art—firmly tied to socialist life."7 In summarizing the success of the GDR musicians, Hagen explicitly mentions their engagement with everyday life

These references to reality are constitutive of the socialist components in our entertainment art and contribute to its great resonance with the audience, especially with young people.

Themes such as: honesty, happiness, politically active lifestyles, love of children, understanding for the elderly, but also questions of creative dreaming, a happy future, the preserving of life on earth, and the desire for peace. It is also obvious that certain outmoded or destructive behavior be identified and artistically exposed. Alcohol abuse, smoking children, and insensitive treatment of the other sex are, for this reason, just as important, as is the persuasive representation of other themes, such as the fight against greed, ego-centrism, and narrow-minded bourgeois thought.[8]

The focus on daily life as the legitimate domain of popular culture and rock music, as described by Hager, has roots in socialist cultural traditions that overlap with GDR ideology. Hagen essentially advocates a national culture, albeit in a socialist, therefore international, context. The SED meant to steer a national popular culture in a direction that would be in alignment with its goals: socialist daily life was not, however, as equal for some as it was for Hagen, the SED, and FDJ.

Throughout the nineteen-eighties, the last decade of the GDR's existence as a sovereign state, the initiatives continued. In 1983, FDJ inaugurated the movement Rock for Peace, and all themes revolved around the escalation of Cold War tensions prompted by the threat posed to Western and Eastern Europe by nuclear missiles from the Soviet Union and United States respectively. Many believed that Germany, East and West, would be the theater for the nuclear war that would inevitably ensue from Cold War politics. Later, FDJ sponsored large concerts, on the model of the musical event as great spectacle.[9]

While the grand-scale concerts sounded in the service of peace, rumbles of discontent could be heard, in various musical genres, from professional (officially sanctioned bands with a license to perform and be paid) and official amateur bands (allowed to perform and make a certain amount of money, but the musicians had to prove employment), and from the underground or subculture, and the vinyl grooves of Amiga products. (Amiga was the official, and only, GDR record company.)

By the early nineteen-eighties, punk was visible on at least some streets of the GDR. The music and attitude had an intense (though circumscribed) impact. The response in the GDR's official reception of this music was initially divided. Some GDR critics pointed out the need for such a form of critique in the capitalist West, but punk's *excesses* were too much for the Party. As some recent publications document with poignant immediacy, punks were harassed, repeatedly arrested, forced to go to the West, or conscripted.[10]

Some bands, however, in part because they compromised or never transgressed into the territory of the state's official taboos, survived, and brought a fierce critique of socialist society to the foreground. Even more established bands echoed the spirit of critique that is unarguably constitutive of punk. Even though only few bands in the former GDR were strictly hard-core punk (the state took pains to keep this number to a minimum), the music, reduced to the bare bones of in-your-face attitude, insult, and rapid rhythms, exerted an influence that disrupted the equipoise of the GDR's production of music.[11]

. . . . . .

In their introduction to *Culture/Power/History*, Dirks, Eley, and Ortner write

> . . . [T]here is the sense that everyday life and culture, in which people implicitly "conform to" or "accept" their situation, should not always be contrasted with dramatic "social movements," in which people question and challenge the status quo. Instead, while organized social movements remain enormously important in understanding large-scale transformations, much can be learned by attending to "everyday forms of resistance" as well.[23]

Rock and punk rock music constituted one such form of daily resistance in the GDR. The authors go on to designate popular culture as the realm "in which people strive to define their identities, their boundaries, their self-respect, their 'space' against the established order."[24] This definition of popular culture, in conjunction with the emergence of a larger social movement that helped breach the Berlin Wall, best describes the role of rock and punk in the former GDR. The bands, the music, the performances, and the state's response to all of the above, offer an alternative model to the socialist lifestyle in which work and obedience dominated. In a society known for its development of niches, pockets of private life where the state had no place (*Nischengesellschaft*), music marked a "safe" zone in which alternative identities could be constructed.[25]

How did government policies affect the East German music scene? The SED made every effort to resist the infiltration of capitalist music from the West and to foster the production and consumption of acceptable sounds from the East. FDJ controlled the clubs; there was a sixty/forty quota (sixty percent music from the East and forty percent from the West). The record company, Amiga, was the only label in the entire country. There was a black market (people on bikes with records from Hungary; cassette tapes of concerts, etc., and the DT 64 *Mitschnittservice*; a DJ would play an entire album for the audience to tape), but it was not without risk.

The best effort, however, was the state's investment in bands. Imported rock was not welcome, but tolerated in controlled doses. But when it came to sound waves, the border was permeable. In the mid-nineteen-seventies, German (and German-language) rock came into its own. With bands like the Puhdys, this music acquired an East German profile that included melancholy ballads, arranged and performed with rock artistry. They became the representatives of New German Wave in the East, and the title song "Computerkarriere" became the agit-prop song for the FDJ peace movement.[26] Their popularity waned in the late nineteen-eighties, partly as a result of the inevitable comparison to critical punk bands.

They came out of retirement after the fall of the Wall. I attended a concert in 1995, complete with the sponsorship of Berliner Pilsner, which flowed from ads, "Das Bier von hier!" Still, the Puhdys stayed pretty strictly within the established limits of GDR rock. Their type of music bore the GDR national music signature, the SED's stamp of approval. Though the popularity of GDR bands did not dampen the interest in music from the West, it did create a space for somewhat different expectations in the audience through a process of identification with German language rock.

The band Pankow, named after a fairly upper-class section of East Berlin, full of villas and diplomats, departs from the established norm of the professional GDR rock band. The group was founded in 1981 by the singer André Herzberg. Throughout the nineteen-eighties, Pankow became known as one of the most successful and the most credible of bands. It enjoyed widespread notoriety in the GDR, produced many albums, performed many concerts, and managed to walk a fine line between criticism and censorship. The band thematized the difficult daily life of the average GDR youth.

The band sticks with strict rock. In their first "rock spectacle" "Paule Panke," Pankow brought the grim reality of life in the working world to the stage.[27] In Rauhut's estimate, Pankow was one of three professional bands (from a field of about 110)[28] who were critical, who pushed the envelope of the speakable. For instance, the band referenced the censorious presence of the Stasi in a 1986 concert at a time when "Rock for Peace" was in ideological jeopardy.[29]

Throughout the nineteen-eighties, Pankow maintained a devoted audience, and managed to retain the sponsorship of the state. In one famous song, *Langeweile* (boredom), from 1988, they came close to open critique. On an official exchange in the West, Pankow performed its tribute to negativity. In the text, the singer laments the lack of anything to do: he has read an old detective novel too often, eaten the same bad food, been there and done that many times too often. The refrain underscores the deadening repetition

> I've been run around
> run around so much
> run around too much
> still nothing happened.

In the second stanza, the text turns to passive gazing at women and monotonous relationships, sexual rejection, too much drinking, too much talking, and more boredom. After the refrain, the final stanza connects the dots between the personal and the political

> Dasselbe Land so lange gesehen
> Dieselbe Sprache zu lange gehört
> Zu lange gewartet
> Zu lange gehofft
> Zu lange die alten Männer verehrt.
>
> Seen the same country too long
> Heard the same language too long
> Waited too long
> Hoped too long
> Honored the old men too long . . .

Before the final refrain goes up an octave, the band moves from an enforced discipline of the body, through eating uncooked spaghetti and failed contact to women, to a generalized failure of political action. Using incremental repetition, "Boredom" celebrates a moment of recognition; that there is a reason for all of the nothing that happens. It proclaims disenfranchisement at what the audience can only assume is the end of waiting. With this, Pankow signals an end to silent tolerance of the country (and not being able to travel), the language, the carefully managed positive emotions of hope and endurance.[30] The final line, "Honored the old men too long," leaves them responsible for the fatal status quo.

In an interview with Radio Bremen, the band soft-pedaled the potential for explosive criticism in that last line. Again, the relationship to the West mediates the semiotics of critique. With regard to the identity of the "old men," the moderator queries, "The ones in the Politbüro, perhaps?" The response follows, "It's possible that one hangs onto to his old ideals too long, certainly that is the case, it has something to do with me (the singer), I wrote it."[31]

The performance of this song in the western media unleashed a debilitating debate within the SED and FDJ. As a result, the band was boycotted in the GDR media. In an attempt to break the silence, Pankow wrote an exculpatory letter to Erich Honecker (without response), and insisted that they were misquoted in the interview with Radio Bremen. But it was not the fine points of the dialog (regarding official GDR permissions, for example) that disturbed certain functionaries so much that the performance of that song was discussed at the meeting of the Central Committee in December 1988.[32] The old men apparently knew who they were, even while the band foregrounded the polyvalence of its text.

Noteworthy is the band's impulse to write to the head of state. Even under these circumstances—critique, political friction, boycott—the band identifies with the GDR and its institutions to the extent that it assumes access to them in a quest for justice; it does not insist on the right to criticize the Party, no matter what the song says. They plead guilty only to ambiguity. Later the band was instrumental in drafting a declaration of the need for reform, and participated in various discussions about the role of culture in the GDR. Ultimately, the members of Pankow were *Hierbleiber*, those who would stay in the GDR and perform in the GDR.[33]

The reforming impulse is predicated on a positive identification with the GDR state, against the historical background of a divided Germany; it implies a choice to remain (the exodus had begun) as cultural ambassadors of political reform, within the borders of the nation. Indeed, in a published interview, Pankow's guitarist Jürgen Ehle[34] invokes the national to describe the role of GDR rock in the new, harsh market economy, "It is important for us to secure the presence of national rock music in the public-legal media as well. The dominance of Anglo-American pop music in the broadcast media from the Federal Republic cannot be a model").[35]

Again, the idea of a national culture emerges as defensible at a time without nation, a strategy to protect the local from the encroachment and dominance of the imported.

While professional bands like Pankow performed their high-wire act with the state institutions of the GDR, other bands brought a version of punk to the studios of the state. As early as the late nineteen-seventies, punk became a presence in the former East. Punk in the GDR differed radically from that in the capitalist West: it was for the most part not open to the same degree of co-modification, for example, in part because it was repressed, in part because consumer culture was limited.

Thinking, Making, Doing

The visible signs of punk in the East, at least in the early nineteen-eighties, were home-made. On another, semiotic level, East German punk emptied out such socially acceptable values as the ethic of hard work, the importance of socialist education, the praise of the collective. However, GDR punk was criminalized for stating social facts, such as the existence of the Wall, the Stasi, or Neo-fascism.

The "No future" attitude so common to international punk stood in impudent opposition to the state ideology of an illustrious socialist future. What may have blended into the streetscape or escaped as punk cliché in Düsseldorf or Brixton or West Berlin violated the GDR's self-definition. In the months prior to the fall of the Berlin Wall, the trend toward open protest and public criticism of the state gained momentum: punk participated. In the reunified Federal Republic, punk does share an aesthetic of aggression against the potentially repressive social and political forces of bourgeois institutions. But the music played a particular role in fostering explicit critique of the GDR.

In the GDR, official media first acknowledged punk's place in the capitalist West where young people had no work and no future. In his lexicon of rock, H.P. Hofmann emphasizes the "social causes on which punk is based," and he mentions youth unemployment, dim prospects for the future, racism, and neo-fascism.[36] But, as Rauhut notes, "For a long time in the East of Germany, punk was officially a total taboo."[37] GDR society itself came under attack, and some bands named names in utterly unambiguous references to the institutions of state socialism.[38] GDR punk quickly exceeded any familiar characterizations of the music and signifying practices associated with western punk, in which political impulses and governmental responses were present and persistent, though in most cases to a lesser extent. Punk was rapidly and radically politicized by the state's nervous response to the critique of society and the fantasy of anarchy voiced in the music.

In their book on alternative music scenes in the GDR, Manfred Stock and Philipp Mühlberg insist that GDR punk was "a 'declaration of war' on the state."[39] Given the SED's efforts to impose order by erasing punk from the landscape, it is surprising, the authors and other scholars suggest, that punk survived and persisted at all in the East. When punk drew strength from the negative relationship to authority, the state changed its approach and strategically co-opted key musicians, thereby deflating the music's potential critical force. In the mid-nineteen-eighties, according to Stock and Mühlberg, punk was mainstreamed in a kind of *Scheinöffentlichkeit* (apparent public sphere) where the state could police it more easily.[40]

Since the publication of Stock and Mühlberg's book in 1990, other documents of punk music and punks' lives have appeared, extending and deepening the discourse about the role of popular culture in the GDR and the state's management of its production and reception. GDR punk was in part shaped by the power it criticized. For this reason, it is important to examine not only the fans' and musicians' self-perceptions, but also the individuals and institutions that influenced their fates.

As the polarization between left and right wing musicians and fans was established in the late nineteen-eighties, punks moved to the left, and with that into a more sustained engagement with the fascist past and the neo-Nazi present. Thus external forces that changed with the fall of the Berlin Wall and the demise of the GDR affected punk. Historical shifts transformed East German punk. While the critique of established power and irreverence toward social norms are constitutive of punk as a transnational phenomenon, GDR punk theorized a place for itself in the meta-narrative of German history both before and after the fall of the Wall.

In the GDR of the late nineteen-eighties, popular amateur bands[41] demonstrated punk impulses: Herbst in Peking parodied the SED State's rhetoric of triumph (*Sieg* or victory) in the song "Bakschischrepublik;" and Sandow, a band from Cottbus, produced the banner song of a generation "Born in the G.D.R.,"[42] intended as a form of ridicule directed against fellow citizens who continued to toe the ideological line in the age of glasnost.

The political critique—sometimes encoded, often transparent—created a community of fans. For many (certainly not all) musicians, success, or "making it" meant producing music that strengthened a sense of shared experience: successful communication meant more than making records, and in some cases, even money. In other cases, live concerts became occasions for genre-crossing, forums for general venting that attracted fans of all types. The state's strenuous efforts to break the bonds forged between bands and fans resulted in the politicization of the music as a form of communication, for it empowered the bands to create communities potentially beyond the state's reach.

For a brief period after the collapse of the GDR, this music flourished without restraint. Some bands used this opportunity to extend their criticism beyond a contemporary context to include the representation of Germany, German identity, and German history. Some former East German groups, such as the Skeptiker, Feeling B, and Freygang,[43] continued to criticize contemporary, reunified Germany for its imperial past and fascist history with their respective songs in the beat of post-punk and blues/rock. Freygang is the only band that still performs concerts and produces CDs. The images that rise and converge from the rock music scene of mid-eighties to mid-nineties are of a failed socialist experiment (GDR), an unkept promise of paradise (Bundesrepublik Deutschland, or BRD), and the recycled (and ridiculed) nationalistic symbols of a country "with a past." The bands responded to what they perceived as repressive systems under both German flags with a vision of anarchy and apocalypse, and these images still abound.[44] In a society stereotyped for order, industriousness, and domestic comfort, disorder still signifies defiance.

Punk is still the popular genre with the longest record of disorderly conduct.

As one form of political resistance—and this neither it's exclusive province nor purpose—punk threatened the socialist public sphere,[45] which could not countenance either the aesthetics or politics of its existence. For many disgruntled citizens, real political activity took place behind the scenes, often under the roof of the Protestant church, which began its "open work" of providing space to marginalized social and political groups in the nineteen-eighties.[46] Churches provided a stage for punk bands. The state proved intolerant of this culture in which, as Rauhut points out, the names of bands were themselves sufficient provocation.[47] As Galenza and Havemeister write in their introduction

In 1983, the 'punk problem' was to be solved with every means possible. Mielke, the Minister for State Security, ordered 'toughness against punk.' His troop fought the punk movement with an unconditional severity that destroyed peoples' personalities. Punks were deliberately criminalized, intimidated, taken into custody, deported to the West, or rounded up into the National Peoples Army.[48]

This is just one sign, more of a symptom, of the SED's reaction to the perceived homology between punk and protest. According to autobiographical essays by punks published in the Galenza and Havemeister volume, the state feared the revolutionary capacity of punk. In fact, as Klaus Michael observes at the end of his contribution

That the history of GDR punk was relatively short and not nearly as distinctive as the punk movements in the West had less to do with the inconsistency or lack of creativity of those involved. Instead it can be attributed to the totality of the state's claim, which did in fact lose some power during the nineteen-eighties, but for a longer time did not tolerate the formation of independent cultural milieus or alternative public spheres. That it existed at all can still be a source of astonishment today.[49]

Michael acknowledges a sense of amazement that punk survived in any capacity, given the severity of measures taken against it. That punk was anything more than ephemeral in the GDR is of historical concern. That it constituted a form of resistance seems uncontestable in light of the state's vigorous and vituperative response.[50] . . . two bands, both of which had official status and that survived the *Wende* (change) at least until the turn of the century.

The first is Feeling B. In 1983, Aljoscha Rompe founded the band with Paul Landers (guitar) and Christian "Flake" Lorenz (keyboard). Aljosha, as he was widely known, enjoyed certain privileges unfamiliar to the average GDR citizen. Through a unique set of circumstances (his grandfather left Switzerland and emigrated to the GDR in 1947 with his pregnant daughter), Aljosha acquired a Swiss passport in 1978, which meant he could travel beyond the borders of "socialist brother countries," which he did, but he returned repeatedly to East Berlin from his various sojourns. Among other things, he brought punk with him, and eventually, instruments, a Swiss stipend to study theater in West Berlin (he never actually pursued this course of study), and needed equipment.

Aljosha had another buffer zone of sorts; his stepfather was the GDR's leading atomic physicist, and also a member of the National Security Council and the Central Committee of the SED. In some sense, Aljosha was untouchable. All agree, he was the center and impulse for Feeling B. The band acquired a dedicated following throughout the nineteen-eighties. They performed everywhere they possibly could, including at unauthorized open-air concerts on the Baltic Sea, drawing fans from all over to pogo in the sand.

In his filming of the 1988 documentary *flüstern & SCHREIEN*, the director Dieter Schumann[51] followed Feeling B as the band devised its songs, repaired the van, cooked breakfast, discussed the response of the audience, and so on. One band member, Paul, also helped with the editing, and became involved in the project. Controversy ensued with any official, state-sponsored project. It was clear: Aljosha saw an opportunity to promote his philosophy of fun and party, perhaps with the vague hope of testing larger political-institutional structures. Others would see any cooperation with the state as betrayal: the state was beyond repair.

One signature song has become an anthem for the band: "Mix mir einen Drink." The song assumed the status of a folk song for the disgruntled in the GDR. Aljoscha's expressed mission to spread fun in the state of boredom and bourgeois conformity involved a dangerous amount of alcohol. Aljoscha's unique personality and life have been well documented in the extraordinary volume *Mix mir einen Drink*.[52] As it happened, Aljoscha brought this song to the band; it stemmed from "camp fire" drinking and singing in Romania from the mid- nineteen-seventies.[53]

As Paul and Flake report, Aljoscha brought this song, apparently of collective origin, to Feeling B, and it became along with "Wir wollen immer artig sein" the band's most performed piece.[54] According to Flake, "Wir wollten auch volkstümlich sein, wir wollten nie gut sein" ("We also wanted to be folkloric; we never wanted to be good").[55] This band represented punk of a certain stamp in the East. It is often described as *fun* punk to distinguish it from *political* punk.[56] The appeal of bad music and simple texts, however, cannot be underestimated: the band's records sold 100,000 copies.[57] In the drinking song, the lyrics point to a desire to be anywhere but the GDR, "Mix mir einen Drink, mix mir einen Drink. Mix mir einen Drink, der mich woanders hinbringt." (Mix me a drink, mix me a drink, mix me a drink that brings me somewhere else.")[58] The garbled singing and hiccuping are self-exemplary. And the keyboard's high pitch from Flake's Casio penetrates the deep rhythms. Yet, in an aggressive, angry stanza, Aljosha's grating, nasal voice proclaims, "Ich will nicht mehr bleiben unter diesen Leichen" (I won't stay here among these corpses"). He rhymes "Leichen" with "Weichen" (weak, soft people) in the official text, but in one recorded performance, he seems to sing the word "Gleichen" (the equals, the same), a code for GDR citizens, those who are equal and the same under state socialism. The absurdity and hilarity of the vocal gestures are grounded with some seriousness on the bodies of the GDR. The critique is not subtle.

. . . . . .

. . . . To return to the example of Feeling B: in one song, the band sings about the narcotic cocktail that would transport the consumer to some other, any other place. And while all the drunken gestures of the song prevent anyone from taking it too seriously, the subject matter inevitably references the severe problems the population in general—and the lead singer in particular—had with alcohol consumption (no reliable statistics exist).

Stories abound of Aljoscha falling drunk from the stage during concerts, and he was not alone. Still, one in turn looks for the cause of such reckless celebration, and Aljoscha expressed the imperative to party. There is at least a possible relationship between politics and alcohol consumption. The equation of *party* and drinking could even be conceived as a way out of the grim reality of life in the land of pathological *boredom*, though this correlation is not particular to socialism. Then History happened. In the wake of that juggernaut that came to be known as unification, the band engaged in a bit of post-Wall land reclamation.

. . . . . .

. . . . For a decade, Feeling B walked a tight rope between the critical and the harmless. Nonetheless, the band had an impact. . . .

Thinking, Making, Doing

. . . . . .

In the early nineteen-nineties, Feeling B fell apart as a band for a variety of reasons, among them the end of a political era in which boredom was the enemy and the band the guerilla fighters[67] who sang and ran. Paul and Flake broke away to form Rammstein. Aljoscha carried on with various projects until his death in 2000. In the mid-nineteen-nineties, Aljosha became involved with a guitar band; he insisted the sound was not "techno" but rather new rhythms with new technology. As far as Feeling B, the band, he hoped they would play together and produce a record, but not for a large record company. As Aljosha emphasized in an interview, "Wir machen es in einem Zimmer. Wir haben heutzutage alle Geräte zu Hause" (We can do it all in one room. Nowadays we have everything we need at home.).[68]

. . . . . .

I want to turn now to one other band in order to take this narrative a bit further. Die Skeptiker were also known as a "punk" band in the GDR, though, as I have pointed out elsewhere, that term is relative. The band performed fast songs about the inner lives of the GDR's discontents.[70] The lyrics responded to contemporary conditions of life with visions of anarchy and apocalypse, performed to the beat of punk and post-punk. The band had been giving concerts for several years when Amiga, the state's record company, included the band in the anthologies *Rock-Bilanz '89*, a mixed collection that included songs from the Puhdys and other more established GDR bands, and *Parocktikum* (1989), a compilation of "new" music.

The label then released *Skeptiker, Die anderen Bands* in 1989.[71] Lyrics often leveled explicit social critique. "Strahlende Zukunft" (radiating future), for example, appeared on the first album *Harte Zeiten* (1990), an Amiga co-production with a West German label. This song—the title is a play on the dangers of nuclear power, the need for political-environmental activism, and the rhetoric of a glorious future espoused by the SED—was anthologized after the *Wende*. In the lyrics, Balanskat charges the adjective *strahlend* in its double meaning as "radiating" and "radioactive." The first line, "Strahlend soll die Zukunft sein, hat man uns erzählt" (the future is supposed to be radiant, so they've told us) echoes the SED rhetoric of the future. The refrain makes this critique more explicit, "Glück und Ruh' alle Zeit / Arbeit und Sicherheit / Sicherheit Glück und Ruh' / woran zweifelst du?" (Happiness and peace always / work and security / security happiness and peace / what do you doubt?). The refrain is sung in mock reverence, a self-impugning parody of those values held so dear in the vocabulary of the GDR. Since the band could not sing about unemployment, they sang instead about superficial security and the lack of adequate pay. The text disrupts the endlessly rehearsed narrative of some indefinite future toward which everyone must work—though the band never explicitly critiques any GDR institution.

While the lyrics of this song indict the rhetoric of the future, they also call in the debts of the past, the promises that have not been and will never be kept. However, the fans were able to get past the critique of the past and interpret the song for the present in post-Wall Berlin. In 1995, I attended a concert in the Kesselhaus in (East) Berlin to celebrate the release of a new CD. The large hall was packed with a range of fans from the visibly punk to unremarkably average. The lyrics to Die Skeptiker songs are rapid-fire and complex. Many, if not most, of the people in the audience were mouthing, if not singing, the words. When the band performed this song, the fans shouted the refrain, "Arbeit und Sicherheit," some with raised fists. I heard and saw in this gesture an expression of anger at the rising unemployment in the East since the fall of the Wall, a demand for precisely that which was lost with the GDR.

There is a behind-the-scenes story of the band and its relationship to the state. The Skeptiker, and punk in general, articulated criticism in the GDR and post-*Wende* Germany. The response to the band shifted once it had signed with the GDR record label and was cast in the role of a "token" punk band. The band's relationship to the official GDR media and to FDJ posed problems for some fans, though not for others. The politics of music production in this segment of GDR cultural history are crucial. In *Kassetten als Kassiber* (cassettes as secret messages), Susanne Binas quotes Matthias Hofmann, an editor at Amiga/VEB Deutsche Schallplatten,[72] about his involvement in the official attempt to attract new bands to the label.

As he reports, he was hired in 1989 in part because he was young and had connections to the new music scene, which included such bands as the Skeptiker, Feeling B, and others. He suggests that the record company was hoping for an "instrumentalization"[73] of alternative music, in other words, a co-optation of the music to suit official purposes, which included maintaining some kind of credibility with a young audience. While Hofmann attributes this effort to Amiga's survival instincts, he does note the rather cynical attempt to embrace and control the music, thus mitigating its potentially subversive effects.[74] Lutz Schramm from DT 64 also mentions the Skeptiker as a band that lost its "Street-Credibility" after becoming known as an FDJ band.[75] The official cultural strategy appeared successful. By the end of 1987, for example, fans that adorned their jackets with Die Skeptiker labels were subject to the insult "FDJ-Punks" by the others.[76]

The Skeptiker, however, did not become a state-sponsored band by accident. In an interview with Rainer Börner, an FDJ functionary and Stasi-IM who first approached the Skeptiker about state support, he expresses regret for his role in the co-optation of their music. He confessed to a feeling of regret about his intervention with the band, "The fans confronted the Skeptiker and criticized them for selling out to FDJ."[77]

In "Strahlende Zukunft," the critique remains implicit, generalized to a topic, the dangers of nuclear power, that was politically accepted as worthy of blame in the former GDR of the late nineteen-eighties. The band underwent a process that was closely linked both to historical events and a relationship to German history. The band's earlier work (*Harte Zeiten*, 1990; *Sauerei*, 1991) is frequently categorized as punk, while the later releases (*Schwarze Boten*, 1993; *Live*, 1994; *Stahlvogelkrieger*, 1995; *Wehr dich*, 1998) retain certain vocal and musical gestures. The music remains insolent and aggressive, but there is more explicit engagement with German history. On *Sauerei* (obscenity, scandal), the lyrics reflect the violence of the times. Several songs express outrage at the measures taken by the state: "Deutschland halt's Maul" (Germany, shut up), "Sauerei," and "Straßenkampf" especially function as a call to arms. In "Deutschland halt's Maul," the Skeptiker take the offensive against the contemporary state from the moral high ground of historical consciousness. The first track on *Sauerei* (which sold fairly well in both the Eastern and Western parts of Germany), the song accuses Germany of expanding its power in order to overcome a worldwide inferiority complex. The words command the country to leave the world alone, to leave the foreigners alone, to remember that violence from above will be met with violence from below. The song's title echoes the motto of a demonstration, "Halt's Maul Deutschland," which took place on Alexanderplatz on Unification Day, October 3, 1990. That event ended in tear gas and police truncheons.[78]

 . . . . . .

Further, cultural vehicles, such as rock and punk rock music, must be considered in any discourse about intellectual life in a society in which print culture was a monopolized instrument of the state, by and large, excluding the various self-published literary and political projects of the nineteen-eighties. This music set individuals against institutions, criticized if not the GDR explicitly, then its stifling political and social practices. Or singers demonstrated care and/or craziness to avert the fate of hard-core political critics who ended up in jail.

 . . . . . .

BIBLIOGRAPHY

ADN/Junghänel. "Keine Schonzeit mehr für DDR-Rock." In *Melodie und Rhythmus.* 7/1990.

Bathrick, David. *The Powers of Speech: The Politics of Culture in the GDR.* Lincoln: University of Nebraska Press, 1995.

Binas, Susanne. "Kassetten als Kassiber." In *Wir wollen immer artig sein. Punk, New Wave, HopHop. Independent-Szene in der DDR 1980–1990.* Ronald Galenza and Heinz Havemeister, eds. Berlin: Schwarzkopf & Schwarzkopf, 1999: 248–258.

Dirks, Nicholas B., Geoff Eley, Sherry B. Ortner, eds. *Culture/ Power/ History: A Reader in Contemporary Social Theory.* Princeton: Princeton University Press, 1994.

Friedrich, Jasper André and Ray Schneider. "Leipzig von unten: Punk- und Independent-Szene, Aktionen, Zeitschriften und Bands." In *Wir wollen immer artig sein. Punk New Wave, HipHop, Independent-Szene in der DDR 1980–1990.* Ronald Galenza, and Heinz Havemeister, eds. Berlin: Schwarzkopf & Schwarzkopf, 1999: 102–145.

Hagen, Jürgen. "Unterhaltungskunst—fest mit dem sozialistischen Leben verbunden." In *Praktische und theoretische Fragen der Entwicklung von Unterhaltung und Unterhaltungskunst in der DDR.* Edited by Informationszentrum beim Ministerium für Kultur. Berlin: Ministerium für Kultur, no date, ca. 1982.

Hecht, Heinrich. "Bewußtseinserweiterung. Feeling B: Verrückt für jedermann, der zahlen will und das auch kann." In *Junge Welt.* 28.3.1998.

Galenza, Ronald and Heinz Havemeister, eds. *Wir wollen immer artig sein. Punk, New Wave, HipHop, Independent-Szene in der DDR 1980–1990.* Berlin: Schwarzkopf & Schwarzkopf, 1999.

———. "Singende Gaukler und metallene Langeweile." Interview with André Herzberg (Pankow) and Sebastian Baur (Keks). In *Wir wollen immer artig sein. Punk, New Wave, HipHop, Independent-Szene in der DDR 1980–1990.* Berlin: Schwarzkopf & Schwarzkopf, 1999: 300–308.

———. *Mix mir einen Drink. Feeling B. Punk im Osten. Ausführliche Gespräche mit Flake, Paul Landers und vielen anderen.* Berlin: Schwarzkopf & Schwarzkopf, 2002.

Greiner-Pol, André. *Peitsche Osten Liebe—Das Freygang Buch.* Edited by Michael Rauhut. Berlin: Schwarzkopf & Schwarzkopf, 2000.

Jarausch, Konrad H. and Michael Geyer. *Shattered Past: Reconstructing German Histories.* Princeton: Princeton University Press, 2003.

Kraushaar, Elmar. "Tingeln für den Sozialismus," In *tageszeitung*. August 10, 1991.

Kenntemich, Wolfgang, Manfred Durniok and Thomas Karlauf, eds. *Das war die DDR. Eine Geschichte des anderen Deutschland*. Berlin: Rowohlt, 1993.

Kurby, Christina and Martin Miersch. "Das Mißtrauen hat mich krankt gemacht. Ein FDJ-Funktionär zwischen Kulturförderung und –verhinderung." Interview with Rainer Börner. In *Junge Welt,* 19.12.92: 12–13.

Müller, Jan-Werner. *Another Country: German Intellectuals, Unification and National Identity*. New Haven and London: Yale University Press, 2000.

Preuß, Torsten. "Stasi, Spaβ und E-Gitarren: Die Geschichte der Berliner Punkband Namenlos." In *Wir wollen immer artig sein . . . Punk, New Wave, HipHop. Independent-Szene in der DDR 1980–1990*. Ronald Galenza and Heinz Havemeister, eds. Berlin: Schwarzkopf & Schwarzkopf, 1999: 51–61.

Rauhut, Michael. *Beat in der Grauzone: DDR-Rock 1964–1972—Politik und Alltag*. Berlin: BasisDruck, 1993.

———. *Schalmei und Lederjacke: Udo Lindenberg, BAP, Underground: Rock und Politik in den achtziger Jahren*. Berlin: Schwarzkopf & Schwarzkopf, 1996.

Rauhut, Birgit and Michael Rauhut, eds. *AMIGA. Die Diskographie aller Rock- und Pop-Produktionen 1964–1990*. Berlin: Schwarzkopf & Schwarzkopf, 1999.

Schneider, Peter. *The Wall Jumper*. Chicago: University of Chicago Press, 1998. Translated by Leigh Hafrey, Random House, 1983.

Schramm, Lutz. "Spule, Feedback und Zensur. Interview mit Lutz Schramm." In *Wir wollen immer artig sein. Punk, New Wave, HipHop, Independent-Szene in der DDR 1980–1990*. Ronald Galenza and Heinz Havemeister, eds. Berlin: Schwarzkopf & Schwarzkopf, 1999: 288–295.

Simpson, Patricia A. "Germany and Its Discontents: The Skeptiker's Punk Corrective." In *German Matters in Popular Culture*. Christoph Lorey and John L. Plews, eds. Special Issue of *Journal of Popular Culture,* Vol. 34.3 (Winter 2000): 129–140.

———. "Soundtracks: GDR Music from 'Revolution to 'Reunification'," in *The Power of Intellectuals in Contemporary Germany*. Michael Geyer, ed. Chicago: University of Chicago Press, 2001: 227–248.

Stock, Manfred and Philipp Mühlberg. *Die Szene von Innen: Skinheads, Grufties, Heavy Metals, Punks*. Berlin: LinksDruck, 1990.

Žižek, Slavoj. *Tarrying with the Negative: Kant, Hegel, and the Critique of Ideology*. Durham: Duke University Press, 1993.

Discography

Compilations

Aufbruch, Umbruch, Abbruch. Rock aus Deutschland, 1992. Vol. 20, (liner notes, Olaf Leitner), Deutsche Schallplatten LC 6065.m.

Engerling[83]

Egoland, 1992. SPV Records SPV 008–88654.

Feeling B

Wir kriegen euch alle, 1991. CD Piratmusik SPV 084–38112.

Pankow

Pankow: 10 Jahre, 1991. Deutsche Schallplatten GmbH. LC 6446.

Die Skeptiker

Harte Zeiten, 1990. CD 80262; 303.1026.2. 41.
Sauerei, 1991. Our Choice / Rough Trade CD 195.1177.2.40.
Schwarze Boten, 1993. Our Choice, Rough Trade CD 195.1378.2 42.
Die Skeptiker Live, 1994, Our Choice / Rough Trade CD 195.1730.2 30.
Stahlvogelkrieger, 1995. Our Choice / Rough Trade CD 195.3010.2 42.
Wehr dich!, 1998. Rausch Records CD 07902–2.

Film

flüstern & SCHREIEN, 1988. DEFA documentary, dir. Dieter Schumann; co-written by Dieter Schumann and Jochen Wisotzki.

NOTES

2. See Michael Raubut, *Rock in der DDR,* 6f. for a cogent and concise narrative of the SED's response to rock music in the early 1950s. I allude here only to a few representative perspectives.

3. Quoted in Elmar Kraushaar, "Tingeln für den Sozialismus," *tageszeitung* (10.8.91), 12.

4. Michael Rauhut, *Beat in der Grauzone, DDR-Rock 1964–1972—Politik und Alltag,* (Berlin: BasisDruck, 1993), 34.

5. Quoted on the CD *Aufbruch,* track 17, and liner notes (by Olaf Leitner).

6. Michael Rauhut, "Schalmei und Lederjacke: Udo Lindenberg," *BAP, Underground: Rock und Politik in den achtziger Jahren,* (Berlin: Schwarzkopf & Schwarzkopf, 1996), 8f.

7. Jürgen Hagen, "Unterhaltungskunst—fest mit dem sozialistischen Leben verbunden," in *Praktische und theoretische Fragen der Entwicklung von Unterhaltung und Unterhaltungskunst in der DDR,* (Berlin: Ministerium für Kultur), 1. All translations, unless otherwise noted, are my own.

8. Hagen, "Unterhaltungskunst," 15–16.

9. Rauhut, "Schalmei und Lederjacke," 128f.

10. See the most significant volume published to date: Ronald Galenza and Heinz Havemeister, eds. *Wir wollen immer artig sein.* (Berlin: Schwarzkopf & Schwarzkopf, 1999).

11. Yet, even with punk, the Party and FDJ eventually embraced the music of "disaffected youth" in an attempt to invite even Mohawks and safety pins into the socialist mainstream. See my "Germany and Its Discontents: The Skeptiker's Punk Critique," in *German Matters in Popular Culture,* Special Issue, *Journal of Popular Culture,* 34.4 (Winter 2000), 129–140.

23. Nicholas B. Dirks, Geoff Eley, Sherry B. Ortner, eds. *Culture/ Power/ History: A Reader in Contemporary Social Theory* (Princeton: Princeton University Press, 1994), here from the editors' "Introduction," 5.

24. Dirks, Eley and Ortner, *Culture/ Power/ History,* 5.

25. While most citizens were well aware of the Stasi presence in daily life, the true extent of the IM network was revealed only after the fall of the Wall. Private spaces were well within the Stasi's panoptic view.

26. Wolfgang Kenntemich, Manfred Dumiok and Thomas Karlauf, eds. *Das war die DDR. Eine Geschichte des anderen Deutschland,* (Berlin: Rowohlt, 1993), 158.

27. Rauhut documents the official political discussion about this performance and other Pankow projects, *Schalmei,* 259f.

28. Rauhut, *Schalmei und Lederjacke,* 59.

29. Rauhut, *Schalmei und Lederjacke,* 40.

30. Herzberg discusses his frustrations with the GDR in "Singende Gaukler und metallene Langeweile. Interview mit André Herzberg (Pankow) und Sebastian Baur (Keks)" in *Wir wollen immer artig sein,* 300–308.

31. Letter from Pankow to Erich Honecker, quoted in Rauhut, *Schalmei,* 266.

32. Rauhut, *Schalmei und Lederjacke,* 263.

33. Rauhut, *Schalmei und Lederjacke,* 301.

34. In 1996 Ehle was "outed" as a Stasi-IM. See *Wir wollen immer artig sein,* 308.

35. Ehle, *No more close time for GDR skirt,* http://www.ostmusik.de/pankow_presse21.htm. INTERNET

36. H.P. Hofmann, *Rock,* (Berlin: VEB Lied der Zeit, Musikverlag, 1983), 186.

37. Rauhut, *Schalmei und Lederjacke,* 217.

38. See especially Torsten Preuß, "Stasi, Spaß und E-Gitarren: Die Geschichte der Berliner Punkband Namenlos," in Galenza and Havemeister, *Wir wollen immer artig sein,* 51–61.

39. Manfred Stock and Phillip Mühlberg, *Die Szene von Innen: Skinheads, Grufties, Heavy Metals, Punks,* (Berlin: LinksDruck, 1990), 168.

40. Stock and Mühlberg, *Die Szene von Innen,* 174.

41. Bands were obliged to obtain a permit to perform, and were evaluated by a committee of musicians, music teachers, and functionaries, which bestowed a grade, known as the *Einstufung* or classification. Thus all performing bands were categorized from *Grundstufe* through *Sonderstufe,* and their rank determined their pay. For a more thorough presentation of this system, see Leitner's history of GDR rock, *Rockszene DDR,* 137f.

42. See my "Born in the Bakschischrepublik," *Transformations of the New Germany,* ed. Ruth Starkman (forthcoming), in which I focus on the two bands, Sandow and Herbst in Peking, whose respective songs "Born in the GDR" and "Bakschischrepublik" became anthems of and defined GDR music of the *Wende.*

43. The first band signed with a West German label soon after the *Wende* and was with Rausch Records in Rostock until it broke up in 2000. Though Feeling B regrouped occasionally to perform locally within Berlin, the founder of the band died in November 2000. Prior to that, two former split off and formed Rammstein. Freygang, which released another CD in 2002, and the band continues to perform as a core group with a lively constellation of musicians. The lead singer and founder of the group, André

Greiner-Pol, has also published a book about his life as a musician and the band, *Peitsche Osten Liebe.*

44. I treat the image of the apocalypse in East German rock music briefly in a piece about the concert staged for the *Währungsunion.* See my "Soundtracks: GDR Music From 'Revolution' to 'Reunification'," in *The Power of Intellectuals in Contemporary Germany,* ed. Michael Geyer (Chicago: University of Chicago Press, 2001), 227–248.

45. See David Bathrick, *The Powers of Speech: The Politics of Culture in the GDR* (Lincoln: University of Nebraska Press, 1995), on the concept of a public sphere in the former GDR.

46. See Ulrike Poppe, "Citizens' Movements in the GDR: Their Past and Future," *Michigan Germanic Studies,* special issue on Gegenwartsbewältigung: *The GDR after the Wende,* Vol. XXI 1/2 (Spring/Fall 1995), 37–43. See also Stock and Mühlberg, *Die Szene von Innen,* 170; and Rauhut, *Schalmei und Lederjacke,* 218.

47. Rauhut, *Schalmei und Lederjacke,* 222.

48. Ronald Galenza and Heinz Havemeister, eds. Introduction, *Wir wollen immer artig sein . . . Punk, New Wave, HipHop, Independent-Szene in der DDR 1980–1990,* (Berlin: Schwarzkopf & Schwarzkopf, 1999), 6.

49. Klaus Michael, "Macht aus diesem Staat Gurkensalat: Punk und die Exerzitien der Macht," in *Wir wollen immer artig sein,* 72–93, here 91. Elsewhere Michael highlights the threat posed by punk and its "symbolische Tötung des Staates" (73) as well as its ability to create a different kind of Öffentlichkeit.

50. I discuss some of the bands and fans whose biographies diverge sharply from those of the GDR professional bands in "Punk and the Genre of Politics," in *German Narrative Music,* ed. Ed Larkey, forthcoming.

51. *flüstern & SCHREIEN,* (DEFA 1988), Dir. Dieter Schumann.

52. *Feeling B. Mix mir einen Drink. Punk in Osten. Ausführliche Gespräche mit Flake, Paul Landers und vielen anderen,* ed. Ronald Galenza and Heinz Havemeister (Berlin: Schwarzkopf & Schwarzkopf, 2002). This volume covers the life and death of Aljoscha (Arthur Alexander Rompe) through extensive interviews with friends, family, and intimates, as well as photos, song texts, and other documents, including Stasi reports. The resulting study takes the form of a eulogy for Aljoscha, but also opens insights into the life that was possible for those marginalized in the *Nischengesellschaft* ("niche" society) of the former GDR.

53. Aljoscha to Michael Stappenbeck in Galenza and Havemeister, *Wir wollen immer artig sein,* 338.

54. Galenza and Havemeister, *Wir wollen immer artig sein,* 148.

55. Galenza and Havemeister, *Wir wollen immer artig sein,* 148.

56. Paul indicates an awareness of the hierarchy of critique among bands; he includes Pankow in the "conformist critical"; among the hard-core punk bands that had constant problems with the police Paul names Wutanfall, Schleimkeim, and Namenlos. He explains the ways Feeling B avoided such fates (145).

57. *Junge Welt,* 28.3.98.

58. The text is quoted in the appendix to Galenza and Havemeister, *Feeling B. Mix mir einen Drink,* 438.

68. Interview with the author, Schönhauser Allee 5, 7 June 1995. I remain grateful for his assistance. My status as an outsider, an American interested in the demise of the GDR and its music scene, may account in part for Aljoscha's adamancy about the superiority of the East under the shadow of the capitalist West. He does, however, in other interviews, echo certain opinions, especially his critical attitude toward the West. See *Feeling B. Mix mir einen Drink,* 167, 169f., 180, and 183 (here he describes the "hysteria about Groß-Deutschland" in 1989). Elsewhere he insists that the music was not directed at the state, the Wall, Honecker (230), and that the really "red" political band Die Firma turned out to be infiltrated by the Stasi (232 f.).

70. See also my "Germany and Its Discontents: The Skeptiker's Punk Corrective," in *German Matters in Popular Culture,* Special Issue of *Journal of Popular Culture* 34.3 (Winter 2000), 129–140. This reading departs from the conclusions of that earlier piece, though some of the background information is necessarily repeated here.

71. See Birgit and Michael Rauhut, *AMIGA. Die Diskographie aller Rock- und Pop-Produktionen 1964–1990,* (Berlin: Schwarzkopf & Schwarzkopf, 1999). 133, 258, 295, and 327.

72. Hofmann also worked on the Rock-Bilanz album referred to above.

73. Galenza and Havemeister, *Wir wollen immer artig sein,* 255.

74. The Stasi made similar efforts. See interview with "A.Z. Offizier und hauptamtlicher Mitarbeiter im Ministerium für Staatssicherheit," *Rockmusik und Politik,* (Berlin: Chr. Links Verlag/Berliner Zeitung), 189f.

75. Galenza and Havemeister, "Spule, Feedback und Zensur," interview with Lutz Schramm, *Wir wollen immer artig sein,* 288.

76. See Jasper André Friedrich and Ray Schneider, "Leipzig von unten: Punk- und Independent-Szene, Aktionen, Zeitschriften und Bands," *Wir wollen immer artig sein..,* 102–145, here 116.

77. Rainer Börner, interview with Christina Kurby and Martin Miersch, "Das Mißtrauen hat mich krankt gemacht. Ein FDJ-Funktionar zwischen Kulturforderung und –verhinderung," *Junge Welt* (19.12.92): 12–13, here 12.

78. See André Greiner-Pol, *Peitsche Osten Liebe* (Berlin: Schwarzkopf & Schwarzkopf, 2000), 217–220, for a concise rehearsal of violence at this event.

RE-MIXING IDENTITIES:
'OFF' THE TURN-TABLE

Shirin Housee and Mukhtar Dar talk to Bally Sagoo and Radical Sista

▣ Much talk about the hybridity of cultures and transnational cultural exchanges has occupied cultural commentators in the 1990s. In a discussion conducted in August 1995, Shirin Housee and Mukhtar Dar talked to Asian dance music producer Bally Sagoo, recently signed to Columbia Records, and Radical Sista (Ranjit Kaur), one of the more successful Asian female DJs in the country. Together, they explored some of the issues of how the crossing of boundaries and constant re-making of identities takes place on the dancefloor within the context of contemporary multi-racist Britain. In particular, the interview also examined the practices of the music industry and issues of entry into the mainstream, and looked towards future developments in Asian dance music inside Britain, and more widely.

Shirin   Let's start with a conventional but very important question, which is about how you choose to locate your "origins", since this is a significant issue when we begin to think through questions of identity, belonging and artistic production. What do you think led you to the position you are in now? Your background and the role of music in your life and the ways you think your family background has informed you musically?

Bally   I've been brought up here in this town [Birmingham] even though I was actually born in India, in Delhi. We emigrated in 1964 . . . and we were one of the first Asian families to set up in Birmingham. My father was in one of the first ever Indian bands in this country, way back in the early sixties. What they used to do was film tunes, and they were like the Shadows, there were four guys with these black suits and black ties. Obviously that was the era they were in, it was the way they were thinking and the way they were dressing. There's a record sleeve that's worth seeing, they looked like the Beatles—they were called the Musafirs. Some people will know about their tunes, like your parents, those kind of people, and they'd do famous film tunes on accordions and things, so music has always been in my family really.

   My mother is a priest in the temple, she's doing shabads and gurbani all the time. She's very religious. She plays the harmonium all day long, so knocking about around the house all the time is the keyboard, which excited me when I was a kid. I used to play the harmonium, and copy people; if I used to see people playing a tune I could pick it up very quick and then I'd start playing it. In our house there was always Hindi and Punjabi music, all this was the background that has influenced me today.

Mukhtar   Ranjit, Can you tell us a little to start off with about your background, where your parents came from, whether you were born here or born back in the subcontinent; what kind of things were happening at the time? Was there a strong influence of music in your background too?

Ranjit   Well, I was born in 1969 in Huddersfield, a town in the North of England, and my parents are both from the Punjab in India. When I was young I spent most of my life, literally every day of the week, listening to pop music, you know stuff like that. I used to watch my dad with a group of guys do dancing and stuff. That was my first real taste of Bhangra, as it were, but I wasn't really into it then. I liked the dancing but I didn't like the Asian music.

Shirin   Why do you think you didn't like it?

Ranjit   it was really old and staid for me. It was really old-style Bhangra and you know we didn't relate to it 'cos it wasn't ours, do you know what I mean? It clashed with the influences I had in my teen years when I was listening to Punk and Disco, and stuff from the era of Gloria Gaynor. I really loved that and I never listened to Asian music much at all, until I was about fifteen.

Mukhtar   What do you feel changed?

Ranjit   I started listening to Lata Mangeshka at home and I thought, 'this is quite funky, this is all right,' and developed a real taste for it. That was 1986, that was when the daytime dos started as well. I liked daytime gigs and stuff but they weren't Bhangra then, they were like folk parties. So I used to go to them and to college gigs and stuff. We didn't have Bhangra then, no one used to play it, so I used to dance to Funk and Hip-Hop and Breakdance. Breakdance was the thing that came out and really changed my life, I loved it. Then Bhangra slowly started coming in and some DJs started playing that at gigs.

Bally   I used to go to Handsworth College in Birmingham and I was hanging around with a very heavy Reggae crowd, as well as an Electro crowd, 'cos back in the early eighties really Electro was so big. It played a very important part in the way I was brought up. Break-dancing and all this was around and so I was really heavily into that, completely forgetting about the Asian roots and culture.

Shirin   What do you mean by this? Did the Reggae scene get you interested in your 'own background'?

Bally   Well not right then; Indian music was Indian music. So I just left that side of things and I moved into the Western side of things and I was getting into English and American music. I was spending a lot of money on American imports.
   I was a typical example of someone who didn't know what Asian people were about. I was too much into the Western society business. My friends were mainly black and I didn't have many Asian mates because of, talking fifteen years ago you know, we didn't have funky Asian music, you know . . . Asian music was the kind of gushy records that my dad plays at home, that are just crackling and you can't hear the vocals, there is no drum beat and it's always got

this dramatic string drawn all over it, and I'm like, 'I can't relate to that.' I'm watching *Top of the Pops* 'cos that show is the in thing. I want that music and I want to hear those records that I'm listening to in the clubs. I wanted that kind of beat, but I was completely forgetting about Asianness. Then all of a sudden things just changed, I just got so much into it and my mates were like "my god Bally Sagoo's doing Indian music." They couldn't believe it, it was like the talk of the town, 'cos I was so much heavily into black music. But I'm glad I went through that stage 'cos that's why I can make my music.

Ranjit   You appreciate it, having gone through that . . .

Shirin   When you say "Western side of things" what do you mean?

Bally   Back in 1980, I remember messing around with early records like the Afrika Bambata stuff and the Soul Sonic Force and those kind of tunes 'cos my record collection today is a full room of those Electro tunes. I'm glad that I was around in that era 'cos they form a great influence on my thinking my kind of production today. Hence the reason I can make a track sound very appealing to all sorts of crowds is because I've lived that era. I've had that kind of music upbringing. About six years ago, I decided to make Indian music sound funky like the kind of tunes that I was playing and listening to in clubs. And I think it was popular because everybody wanted this flavour of "East and West" in a heavy way.

Mukhtar   So in some ways there was a vacuum when you were growing up and listening to Soul, Funk, Reggae and those kind of tunes. Asian Bhangra groups, like Heera, were only doing the wedding circuits, and then along came a massive young Asian population looking for something they could relate to, so this Bhangra scene exploded with daytime discos.

Ranjit   Right. At that time, in the mid to late 1980s, there was a large increase in Asians, especially going to college, before then they weren't encouraged—guys were, but girls weren't. Girls were encouraged to stay at home, learn how to cook and get married. It's back down to the traditions and it's slowly moving out of that and developing an Asian-Western kind of lifestyle. So there were more Asian women at college and they were going to the daytime gigs. As a natural development from that, they went to universities and these same kids were saying. "What wicked times, but there's nothing afterwards." Some of the promoters, the new ones, started off as students spending next term's grant money to put on a Bhangra gig on a night, and that's how it all started. There was a whole scene evolving from the mid-1980s onward. Now it's really established.

Bally   In the 1980s when Bhangra really hit off there were groups like Alaap on the circuit, the Pardesis and the Prem Naraj. The ball was mainly in London anyway and everyone was all excited about this thing all of a sudden, it was a new craze these Bhangra gigs, and there was a massive community of Asian people clubbing together all of a sudden. You were getting clubs purely for Asian gigs, which was exciting for us 'cos we'd never had that before. The bands were getting so popular and in demand that they now played day and night.

Mukhtar   Describe the scene at these places; what was going on? While we needed our own spaces, these Bhangra dos weren't always fun. There was also friction taking place, with Asian parents saying, "Our kids are going to discos and in those discos there's a lot of tension between the guys, fighting each other and stuff."

Bally   Obviously it did cause problems 'cos kids were wagging school and pretending they'd gone to school and instead they were clubbing and the parents were going wild. It started getting out of hand, with gang fights and drinking and things. But I think wherever there is alcohol, you will always get that kind of problem. And Asian people are famous for drinking and fighting too, you know. Bhangra then was something totally new, but now it's no big deal.

Shirin   How did *you* feel about the club scene back then, Ranjit?

Ranjit   When I went to my first Bhangra concert I had to sneak out and I think I was one of four girls in a hall of about six or seven hundred guys. Boy did I have hassle man, big time. I was really lucky 'cos I went with my cousin and he stayed with me all night and I just said, "Don't leave me, man, whatever you do don't leave me." I made sure he stood next to me all night. It was scary, they were all leering and I was getting hassled because I was standing near the front. One guy was singing to me and I was going "Go away, please, creep." So I had all these guys chasing me about because I happened to be there. It was kind of like "Well, she must be a loose woman because she's here." Or "She's run away from home and that's why she's here 'cos there's no way her parents would've let her out." Which is right, 'cos I did sneak out but, I sneaked out with my cousin, you know what I mean? It was that kind of attitude, that was 1986 and I've had to kind of fight it all the time, I did that for about four years, but wherever I went I made sure that I was always with somebody that I knew, no matter what . . .
   Later on, because it got so popular the elders in the community got really concerned, and they were having meetings at the mosque and gurdwara talking about how they were going to stop this, blah blah blah. They'd spend a lot of time standing outside the gigs with cameras. I used to be really cheeky 'cos I'd go up and say, "Are you all right?" and I just used to walk inside. I remember one guy, he looked at me and said "it's all right 'cos she's a Sikh" 'cos he saw my kara and I thought, "Right it's acceptable for Sikh women to go there 'cos it's Punjabi music that's playing, you're allowed to drink etcetera." A lot of assumptions were being made and I thought what a cheeky thing because it doesn't matter what you are, if you want to go in you should be allowed to go in. When I started to DJ I used to make a lot of noise about it.

Bally   If you want to be involved in music, you have to be involved in the whole environment, the whole shabam that goes with it. It's like saying, "I want to be an actor but I can't go in front of the camera." If you're going to be involved in this kind of stuff, part of the package is—and this is most important—the audience. So you are going to get arseholes as well as good crowds, you will always get some idiots that want to spoil it. You have to accept it.

Shirin   What was the good side of Bhangra?

Ranjit   I remember the best buzz was when I was playing Bhangra music to two hundred white kids in Liverpool, they loved it, they listened to it for about two and a half hours. One of the women from *Brookside* [the TV soap serial] came in and said [puts on a Liverpudlian accent], "Ay ay, this is brilliant, what is it?" I said, "It's Bhangra." She said, "It's wicked," and walked off. We're getting there slowly.

Shirin   Moving on from the 1980s, do you think Bhangra has lost its original impact and popularity?

Bally   Yes, definitely, the Bhangra scene has gone stale now. All of a sudden there's a massive fusion of Hindi songs coming out now and everyone is jumping onto a different bandwagon and traditional bands are struggling. Even on the wedding scene now, DJs are more popular than live bands. Both because the live bands charge a lot of money and people can't afford that kind of money. You can get a DJ to play any kind of record any time which sounds as good as the original recording.

Shirin   You'd have to say that, though, wouldn't you?! But this brings me more specifically to the point about your particular career development, Ranjit. How did you get into DJing?

Ranjit   At the daytime gigs I had a really good time and used to muck around on the decks. Not with the intention of being a DJ, but just 'cos it was fun, it was nice, and to get enough respect from my friends . . . I went to a conference in Leicester, came across a record shop that sold Bhangra records and came out with about £300 worth of tunes. I thought "Shit, what am I going to do with this now?" Then I started Djing—it was purely by accident.

Shirin   How did your family take to you being a DJ? After all, this certainly breaks the conventional stereotypes, from all perspectives, of what young Asian women do.

Ranjit   Well, on the family front it was kind of like, "We've lost her now, we've lost her to the world of music. She's gone. No one's going to marry her," all that kind of thing. Marriage ratings have gone down, extended family dismayed. But if I'd wanted to get married then I would've ten years ago, so leave me alone. Slowly they came round and slowly it got easier. But when I was in the clubs and stuff I still used to get a lot of attitude from men 'cos I was the only Asian woman, in fact I was the only woman full stop, apart from those who worked behind the bar.

When I first came home and said to my mum that I was going to start a radio show, she just looked at me and said "OK." She was cool about it, 'cos I wasn't out in public, all people could do was hear my voice so that was all right and kind of low-key. But when she was told I was going to go to Maestros and DJ she freaked. She chased me round the house with a rolling pin! Calling me all of kinds of stuff. Then after a week of absolute silence and the doghouse, she spoke to me and said, "Are you going to do it?" and I said, "Yeah, I am." I'm very stubborn and if I want to do something . . . so, she wasn't happy about it, but she didn't stop me from doing it. Then, about a year later at the engagement party of one of my cousins, I was DJing while she was sitting in the audience, and when I finished she said, "Is that all you do?" I said, "Yes, I just play records." She started taking bookings for me then, and telling everybody what I did. Even my Grandma found out that day.

Bally   It's the same with me . . . It's funny how attitudes change though; all of a sudden if you start doing something and it's worth it. I've been through the hard times when my parents screamed at me for buying records and not becoming a doctor or a lawyer like my next-door neighbour. "What are you buying double records for?" They couldn't understand it. "Why have you got two record-players when most people have one record-player?"

But now they realize what I'm doing and now it's good, 'cos it's like: "Do you know who my son is?" whereas before they were ashamed. I'd come out of college with no qualifications, driving down the road full blast with my music on. It's the impression you give. I don't blame my parents for saying [hushed], "My God, there's my son," but now it's [loud] "There's my son guys!"

Shirin   Ranjit, do you think that things have changed for you too? Have the whole family accepted your career?

Ranjit   Yes, 'cos it was really working. Like my grandma was saying, "Hey, this is really good" and she started listening to my radio show which was nice. Once I DJed at a mela in Huddersfield, it was the first mela that they'd had and family from all over the place came to see me. They were all in one corner going "bhurra bhurra." I looked up and all the women of the family were there cheering me on. They made a real special effort to bring other members of the family.

Shirin   Aside from the dilemmas of family life, how have other spheres of society come to terms with you as a women being involved with DJing. What do the men do? How do they react? It's not a usual thing, there's only really you and DJ Ritu out there.

Ranjit   At the beginning when I first started, it was kind of like a novelty thing, it was like, "She's got to have a boyfriend that DJs or something and she's learnt it." I used to get really annoyed when I was classed as "the 'DJ's girlfriend" when I got to the door. The guys on the door would be like, "Where's the DJ?" They thought I was winding them up.

Bally   I know a couple of the Indian girl singers and they always say the same thing . . . but I think you have to expect that because you don't get hundreds of girls on stage. We don't get hundreds of girl DJs. If you get more girls doing DJing it won't be such a big deal. I mean it might be now because we don't see an Indian girl playing records and stuff . . . [to Ranjit] You had to go through that struggle to put it where it is now . . .

Ranjit   I had to really fight with them . . .

Bally   . . . because, like you said, no one was doing it. If you didn't do it, no one was doing it.

Ranjit   Nobody did it.

Shirin   Do you think it's easier now for women?

Ranjit   Definitely . . . because when I first started at Maestros I got a lot of hassle there and that was like in 1990. Now there's more girls that go to that club than guys. Today when I go to clubs I can guarantee that not one guy will hassle me. Its because they all know who I am and they also know that if they do anything the other guys in the club, whether they know me or not, will not stand for it. Because it lets down the whole community, do you know what I mean? We've been through that phase of guys fighting over girls and guys getting into drunken brawls; like: "you're taking our Sikh girls" and "you're taking our Muslim girls," "you're doing this" and "you're doing that" and the "Shere-Punjab" and all that kind of stuff that happened years ago. We've kicked that out, we've managed to get rid of it. Hopefully it won't come back, but there's no guarantee so we have to constantly challenge any kind of attitude like that.

The promoters are better as well. When women go in and the promoters see guys hassling women or someone, the promoters jump on the guys and say "pack it in." I had one guy, dancing right next to me, really close, last year, and he was really winding me up, I just slapped him and he fell on the floor. When he got up he was going "Kuthi, Kuthi, you bitch, I'm going to kill you" and I was getting really angry and I was saying, "Not if I kill you first!" and the security guard had to drag me away from him because I was getting so angry and there were all these other girls behind me waiting to beat the shit out of him. So the girls are saying, "We're going to come here and have a good time, we're going to come out with our sisters and we're going to have fun just like you guys. If you hassle us we're going to kill you. We ain't taking it anymore."

That's why now, it's kind of like fifty–fifty when you go to clubs. Even at night time 'cos the student scene is so big and most of the girls that go out now are at the university and stuff . . . or people that have had to fight really hard to get out of the house. I had to constantly fight, even now, if I know I'm going to be away for about a month it's like "please mum, don't give me a hard time, I have to go," stuff like that. But we have to constantly work at it. It's better for me and it's better for everybody 'cos if we develop some kind of a scene then it's easier for others to follow.

Shirin   You both seem to say that the scene at clubs has certainly changed, and for the better particularly for women. What about in terms of changes in the music itself?

Ranjit   Well, most of the time I play to young kids in clubs whether it's the daytime parties or the Bhangra at night. When I play to a mostly white audience, like when I've played the Mambo in London or the Bass Clef or various places like that, I've played a lot of remixes 'cos they tend to relate to that better than they do to traditional stuff. But, in the mixed club environment, I play predominantly Asian, and I can mix both quite happily and get a good reaction.

Mukhtar   Bally, you said somewhere how one of the things you wanted to do was, in some ways, to Westernize the music. Did you feel that the kind of music being played by bands like Alaap and that, that they were very much rooted back in the subcontinent, that the lyrics were desi, and that whilst people were dancing to it, their own life experiences of growing up here weren't really reflected?

Bally   Well, yes. I'm saying to people that the reason I want to make my music sound like this is because the stuff that the traditional bands were doing was talking about their days and the way they were growing up. Every single song was always on a similar line, and based on this typical boy-meets-girl song. They've always got to have loads of "*hoi's* in there, and so on. Like most of the Western youth, Asian kids brought up here also wanted the punchy, racy bass lines, the great drum beat and the powerful female vocals coming across. I wanted to hear, probably, more melodies than lyrics. I just wanted a good beat and a good vibe, a good song on the dancefloor. Because, obviously, that's what makes everybody get up and dance.

Shirin   Why do you think these remixes are so popular?

Bally   Because we never had that before, Asian people had Asian music or we had Western music. We could never compete with the Western market because their music was so much upfront. That's why people like myself, Indian producers, Asian producers who started making that kind of a tune, started getting Asian people back into the Asian music. Now people listen to the traditional as well as Western/Asian music. The best thing that I get is parents saying to me at least sons and daughters are listening to some Asian music, because before they didn't, etcetera, etctera. I'm the new proof of it. I listen to a lot of Indian music now and it's booming out my car and I wasn't before. Now the music is sounding the way I want it to sound.

Shirin   I think the pride issue is really important. Particularly with the youth. I remember growing up as an Asian kid in the 1970s. I'm a bit older than you, but I used to listen to Reggae and my parents couldn't understand it. I'm from Mauritius which makes it even more complicated, because we came out from India about three or four generations ago, so the only thing that I was exposed to that wasn't Western was Hindi film songs, and my parents were trying to shelter me from too much Westernization. When I was about eighteen or nineteen it was Reggae that I would listen to. I saw that as different to English or Western music. I know if I was growing up now I'd say, "Well there's Reggae and that's still good, but now there's something else" and I think it's important to have that pride in Asian communities. It speaks a language whether you're from Mauritius, Pakistan, India and so on.

Bally   Now, music today is influenced by Western as well as the traditional Asian styles. I don't go with the people who say you shouldn't tamper with Indian music. I want to know who makes up the law about how music should sound? Why can't you have hundreds of different styles? Imagine going into HMV and having only one style of music. You want to be able to have hundreds of styles for every kind of listener, because this is the way we'll open Asian styles out into the Western market and out to the world masses—because some people don't like traditional music, some people do like traditional music and vice versa. So why not cater for all of them? This is where I stepped in and obviously hit on to something big, hence the reason why I've done so many albums and got a deal with Columbia and stuff, they want to hear something like this, the mixing of "East and West."

Mukhtar   Why do you think they want these kind of music mixes?

Bally   It's new, it's exciting, it's refreshing and people are sick of hearing the same old crap over and over again. Before you were embarrassed to blast an Asian tune in your car 'cos the people were looking, and now you want to blast that tune out and show people, say "listen to this beat line" and "listen to this track." You know, I had to wind up the windows when I was blasting an Indian track a few years ago because it was, "What's that sound?" Now it's like "Wow, what's that sound?"

Mukhtar   You were saying that most of your music originates from your life in Britain. Having grown up here you saw something lacking in the "traditional music" and that you could produce more funky Asian music here. But there is a long history of very rich expertise in producing music in India, by people who are best placed to produce it. Often the music in Hindi films was better than the films themselves. Great music. Don't you feel that by Westernizing your music and it becoming so popular back home in India, some of our musical history is being lost at the expense of people looking towards the West and Western music? Or do you feel that you're combining the best of our traditions with the music here?

Bally   That's exactly what I'm doing, I'm taking the best of both worlds and putting them together for the songs and bringing everyone together through the music. Most people probably wouldn't have ever recognized a Raj Kapoor song before and probably couldn't even relate to it. Whereas, all of a sudden, if it's sounding different, a bit of both, they might get into it. Classic example, when people first heard Churaliya on the *Bollywood Flashback* album, a lot of people didn't even know it was an old song. The youngsters who bought the song didn't know it was from a twenty-year-old movie. And so all of a sudden they were playing both versions on the radio alongside each other, and the kind of responses we were getting were amazing. Most of the youngsters were saying. "We like the new version," a lot of the older folks liked the original version. I always liked the original version because it's my favourite—that's why I had to do a revitalized new version. Now kids are listening to the old version as well.

People are listening to it, not just our kids, I'm talking about Western kids as well. English kids, whatever, are watching Hindi movies all of a sudden, and people are asking what is "Bollywood," the word is getting big. Of course everyone wants more exposure to their material. Every movie guy in India would dream of goras watching their movies too. I heard some people say, "Goras shouldn't come into Indian movies." What the hell are they talking about? They say "Indian movies are about Indian people." I say, "But you want to do what goras are doing man." I mean doesn't it give you a great boost when you see a gora speaking in Indian, it's so exciting. It's like when I see a Chinese girl speaking in an Indian language, like when we did our show in Calcutta: I was like, "Fantastic man, this girl is Chinese." I find it so exciting . . .

Shirin   You seem to be saying that music is becoming more global. If so, how does the issue of language feature in this?

Bally   I've done so many different languages, I don't have to understand the language, people don't have to understand the language. People say, "We don't understand your songs," I will say, "Listen man, can you tell me half of the songs that are in the charts, what they're about?" I've done Japanese, French, Arabic, Italian; I've done Urdu and Bengali, Punjabi, Hindi, and I don't understand all those languages. It just goes to show that if I'm making a song like that and it sounds good, hopefully you can get into it as well.

   The Asian scene is advancing, it's good and it's about time, and it's just because people like myself and other people who are in the business have got off their backsides and said we are not just good for making rotis, we don't just make balti chicken for a living, we can make this, we can act, we can sing, we can dress as trendy as you or anyone else in the world. Asian people are more proud now. You have to give to take as well, you know we've taken a bit of their stuff and we've given them a bit of ours. We're combining it in our own thing, and it's nice to have people like us doing something and it shows the goras as well, 'cos it's getting the non-Asians into what we are doing. My goal, my dream, is still to get an Indian song in the charts . . . whether it's me or not, I want to get an Indian language song in the charts and play it regularly in there and it's no big deal, but it hasn't happened yet. I think it's going to happen slowly, when regularly in the top forty we have got Indian singers, girls and boys, whatever, singing Indian songs. It's going to happen sooner or later because things are changing, major companies are picking up on what we are doing.

Shirin   Why do you think this kind of cut'n'mix hasn't happened in the past?

Bally   I think we have not been recognized because of the way our tapes get sold. We are selling more records than people in the charts, we are more than qualified to get in the charts. But in this we are being victimized, it's racism too. Everything is coming into it because Radio One and other radio stations don't want to play our songs. And as you know without major radio you're not going to chart. You need their support, you need their help. Because they're going to play your records during the day—you need more than just club play.

Mukhtar   Why is it important to get your records in the charts when they are already selling and the community is enjoying them? Isn't there a danger that commercialism will make our music bland and meaningless?

Bally   It is very important to get your record in the chart. People say it's the same for any artist, but why does any artist want to get their music in the chart? Mass exposure, nothing to do with money, it's all to do with mass exposure and obviously your cred. So that whenever you do something you'll have a big following and you'll sell a lot of music and so on . . . and pow— going all over the world because the chart in this country plays a very important part to people abroad.

I am now working with a major label and I'm getting treated like an artist. I'm not knocking the Asian record companies down but it's just like, what they don't know they won't miss, you see. These are the kinds of things that Asian artists have missed out on 'cos they aren't getting the treatment. Top Punjabi singers, your Malkit Singhs and your Alaaps and all these other people, they really haven't had the exposure, the treatment that they should've got being singers of that calibre on the Asian market. They've been on the Asian music scene and sold so many tapes that if they'd been on Western mainstream status they would never need to work for the rest of their lives.

Ranjit   They don't get the respect they deserve basically . . .

Bally   They've conquered the Asian market, they've been big and now they want to go into the Western market. They want to show everybody our music, to show their music to every colour, every kind. We want to do that with our music.

Ranjit   It's like we've had the sense of pride in the Asian community and now we want to show it all over the world. It's like "Hey! Look at us! You can check it out too."

Bally   Everyone wants to taste that glory of going into the mainstream. Things are slowly changing, but we haven't really done it yet and until you're sitting at number one in the UK Chart—well, then you can safety say that we have an Indian song in the UK chart!

Ranjit   It's like when I did four shows on Radio One in the evening session. The first track that I played was "Bhabiye Bhabiye," and like over four days we had like eight hundred calls, faxes and letters and stuff from Asian kids saying "yeah, man, this is really wicked, it's about time."

Shirin   Did you get mail from . . . white folk too?

Ranjit   Quite a lot of them were English but most of them were Asian saying "Yeah, man, we want stuff like this on One FM . . . we pay our license like any one else."

Bally   I think every Asian wants a piece of their pie on a gora station. It's no big deal having it on a local Asian radio station like Sunrise, 'cos you expect it, but . . .

Ranjit   . . . it's our own, isn't it?

Bally   I always think that if I want to make it in the West, I have to follow what is happening on the Western scene. I have to constantly keep up with all the Mix-Mags and all the magazines that are coming out to see what is big, why it's big, why is it big in Sweden, France, Germany and Italy, America and Canada and so on? England is a very limiting country anyway and so we are talking about something that's got to be worldwide. I think there's a lot of racism when it comes to music in this country. It's very difficult to chart "foreign tunes" in this country 'cos you've got arseholes like Take That, who can't even sing, selling to teenagers that are fifteen years old. More serious music doesn't even get sold 'cos these fifteen-year-olds want to see good-looking guys on the stage prancing around . . . So that's why good songs go bigger in other countries like America and Canada, Germany and Italy.

Shirin   Would you say that the racism, particularly in the music scene, but generally anyway, is greater here in Britain?

Bally   There is a lot of it in this country; it's plain to see. A lot of clubs will refuse to pick up your record if it's got a slight Asian tone on it. They're appealing to Kevins and Tracys, you know, appealing to that kind of crowd. But if you go to Germany, France, Italy, Belgium, they will throw any language on a Saturday night, and people just freak out. It's good having that kind of atmosphere, because you want people to dance to your tunes. And it doesn't matter that they don't always know what they are singing about, I mean no one in the world knows what Enigma sing about, yet everybody loves it. I mean what the fuck do those people sing about? So how can people turn round and say, "We don't understand your language so we can't play your music." What? Is it going to offend the daytime listeners? If that isn't prejudice or racism, whatever you want to call it, I don't know what is.

Shirin   Would you agree, Ranjit?

Ranjit   Yes, I do, 'cos Yusuf D'Amour's right. The only reason his stuff charted is 'cos he did the duet with Maina, that's the only reason, and got played on the One FM "A" list. It's for reasons like that that our stuff will never get there. The only people that play our stuff is people like John Peel or Andy Kershaw.

Bally   At 3 o'clock in the morning . . . There was a time when if you heard an Indian tune you had to check the radio frequency 'cos it wasn't the usual Radio One stuff—and it was Radio One! So we've obviously slowly opened the doors, but to get a record in the charts, like I keep saying, you've got to give the gora what they want to hear, but they can never ever relate one hundred per cent to a traditional anthem for the Asian people. They can't relate to it, but you have to go into their market at the end of the day.

Shirin   Why do you think that's more of an issue here than in France? Because the racism, historically, and in modern times, has always been as bad if not worse?

Bally   Yes, but the main issue here is, the UK is the leading trendsetter for music worldwide. Foreign countries look at the UK chart and then follow suit. So whatever is happening in the charts here, they normally like to follow suit in their chart. That's why if Indian songs were coming in the charts, you could guarantee they'll be going all over the world, big time.

It's not as bad now, you can go to HMV and buy an Indian track that's not in the corner of a dusty World Music section that nobody looks in. You want to go to that trendy dance section where all those cool, good-looking kids are hanging out. This is why we're forcing our records to be sold in those sections of the store. If you put good dance music in a corner that nobody ever looks in, it won't get sold. So it's the same with our records, we don't want them in the dusty corner with a Buddha standing there. We want our music to stand up as big as your other dance crazes, other dance styles and music scenes. But we want, not one classification, like Bhangra, we want hundreds of classifications. Like Country and Rock and Soul and Hip-Hop, because what we are doing is not just Bhangra music, we all know what Bhangra music is, it's a different thing, it's a traditional thing which is done in India with dohl and Boliyaan, but we've taken it more than one step to a different league. We've taken it to the same league as what's happening on the Soul league, the Ragga league. We're making the tunes as good, as fresh as those tunes, but with one major important difference and that's with our kind of a lick, with an Indian vocal and so on.

Ranjit   But the best we can do is make majors more aware and say "Hey look at us." But we need more than that because the record companies may have the best intentions in the world and want to get an Asian artist, but if you haven't got anybody in there who knows how to marker that type of music . . . in terms of A&R, talent scouts, marketing, people who understand the scene. We need Asian people in there, we need record companies to employ Asian people with a specific aim of bringing in Asian artists and developing it.

Mukhtar   The people who are buying your music are our people. You'll hear it all over India and so on. Do you not feel that the music entertainment corporations are creaming off a lot of the money? And that it's not really going back into the communities. What do you feel about things like that?

Ranjit   Like Bally, I want to see Indian stuff in the charts and I'm always looking at ways we can do that feasibly, without the money being lost from the community. The danger is that the majors are going to take a big cut and all the Asian record shops are going to lose out. They're going to go bankrupt basically.

When we set up, we set up the band and we set up the label to go with it. So, what we did as a label was that we licensed our product to the majors, saying you give us money to distribute it and promote it. When we did the promotion we did it with them, like Big Life did the promotion for the last track, and I worked at Big Life Records, and I dealt with the Asian market myself. I sent the product to the Asian record shops. I said "Here, have product, sell it, make money." I wasn't so worried about charting but I just wanted the exposure and all the other products were sold through HMV, Our Price and all. You have to have a parallel, you can't just expect one kind of market to sustain total sales and get you recognized on both sides, on the Asian market and on the European market. You have to do both at the same time and that's when you need your own specialist people going in there and doing it on your behalf.

I get a lot of girls writing to me and stuff about how to get started. The only mail I get from guys is "Are you married? Do you want to get married?" Most of the girls are saying like, "How did you get into it?" 'Cos it's really hard and they worry whether their parents will throw them out and disown them for even thinking about it . . .

When I DJ I go on with Asian gear on. It's really weird 'cos it really freaks people out! But, it's also great when people see you as a role model. There's a group of people now, wherever I go, a group of women and there's even like four guys that follow me all over the country. I don't even have to tell them where I am, they find out. Like one time I was at Lambeth and I just kind of stuck my head out to look and I could see these guys at the back going, "hoi hoi," and they'd followed me from Huddersfield to London just to see me with the band, KK Kings. I was like, "this is mad, this is really freaky." And I've got a group of girls, about thirty women, who just follow me all over the country. One of them followed me to Vienna. She is an Asian woman and she was there—you know it's wicked, and it's not very often that you see people like that because it is a really hard environment.

Mukhtar   We live in a hostile society and you can have a club and in the evening everybody is in there having a really good time dancing away, but right outside you could have somebody being racially attacked or murdered. Now you've chosen to call yourself Radical Sista—all this shows consciousness that whilst we know how to celebrate, have a good time, at the same time we are not divorced or isolated from the reality of racial violence in the ghettos where we live. How important is that to you, to be conscious and aware of that?

Ranjit   To me, it's all-important. When I did first start out I was doing quite mainstream clubs in London and Liverpool and stuff. I got a lot of letters from the BNP [British National Party] and the NF [National Front] and stuff. I used to get death threats literally every week. It's kind of like, "oh another death threat, put it with the others" kind of thing. It got to the stage where I was like that and I was getting religious fundamentalists trying to kidnap me and stuff in London! I'm used to it and I know it's a political thing—the very fact that as an Asian woman I am actually "out there" for a start, and the fact that I'm wearing Asian gear just makes the point in itself in a way. Because people look and go "What's she doing there?" You know if I was wearing Ragga shorts and a little bra top, they would hardly bat any eyelid. Asian guys would, they'd look "phwaar, hey," but other people wouldn't really give a damn. But, seeing someone in full "traditional dress" doing something that's like a Western concept doesn't correlate with the expected images of Asian women.

Mukhtar   We've talked about the struggles in the families and the communities to do what you want to do. But also what about other obstacles that exist, the doors that are closed to you by racism? It's present in every sphere of society, and surely there in the music industry, despite the long history of black music. The impression you get is that it's very much managed and controlled by the whites who make most of the money. And with the kinds of stereotypes that you've had to break down, you know the stuff about "a bunch of Pakis who can't really sing, can't do more than just make vindaloos" . . . What about struggles against racism in this industry?

Ranjit   Well, there's a great assumption that we don't know anything about business, we know about corner shops and groceries, but when it comes to the music business they think we don't know anything. As if we're just good at making tunes in traditional Punjabi style and that's it. They don't realize that we do know about contracts, we do know about publishing, we do know about the MU [Musicians' Union], we do know about things like that. So when Sony got into the Bhangra scene artists were actually joining the MU and getting themselves more protection. Even our own companies are ripping off artists big-time [to Bally], well, they aren't they? . . . They're all at it, and it's like only when our own record companies start respecting artists that the major record companies start respecting Asian artists. And the only way they're going to do that is if the artists start taking control themselves. Start saying, "Hey hang on a minute, you can't give me £10,000 for an album and expect me to live off that and leave me to earn the rest of my living by doing live gigs four or five times a week."

Bally   Just to show how difficult it is: there are hardly any Asian people who are full-time in the music business because they've all got their own accountancy jobs, or work for British Gas. This is the top Asian singers I'm talking about. The Asian music business doesn't work the way that the English record companies work. I don't think that any top Western artist works for British Gas while they're doing gigs in the evening or they're singing songs in the charts. One main reason is because they have proper companies looking after them. They have a budget to produce a recording, they have a publishing company that does all their work for them; they are members of other unions as well. Everything is protected so when their record is played it's all logged, it's done properly. Whereas our stuff doesn't always get that kind of treatment. Even the lyrics aren't protected properly, the guy who wrote the song gets ripped off. Someone says, "Here's £100 and you go and do the lyrics" and the poor guy is probably never going to hear the thing again. So, it doesn't work the way that the white companies work. I'm getting to know that now 'cos I've been learning a lot about what happened with me when I was with my old record company.

Shirin   Now you've got this deal with Columbia, what are your concerns? Talking about the blockages by racism, are you worried that you won't have that much autonomy over your work? That you might have to compromise; are you worried about any of those things?

Bally   No, not at all, 'cos I've been signed up for what I'm good at doing . . .

Shirin   . . . and you're confident that you'll be allowed to do that?

Bally   . . . yes, that's the most important thing; I've got a great A&R guy as well and I've got a great relationship with Columbia. I am what they call their "touch with the East," they've seen my track record. We talked loads in detail with Columbia—they are very good for breaking black artists abroad. One important thing that I agreed with the company is that I don't want them ever to tell me that I shouldn't have Indian singing in my songs; or I shouldn't have tabla playing, or I shouldn't have an Indian sound etcetera, and they said that's the last thing they want to do because what I'm doing now obviously works.

I don't want to be limited with "you can't do this, you can't do that." Obviously there are parts in any contract which say you can't do this and you can't do that, within reason, but I think I've been fortunate. But the most important thing is that they said to me, "Just do whatever you've been doing and let us do the rest."

Ranjit   I think it's payback time basically, you know, 'cos Asian communities have lived here for thirty-odd years now, and longer than that, and they've shown some serious commitment to the country. We built it, the health service amongst other things . . .

Bally   Yes, you can't leave the country now without being searched by an Asian at Heathrow . . .

Ranjit   If all the Asians went to India, the health service would be destroyed. That's how important we are here, and in every area. It's how, "OK, you've got our legal expertise, you've got our medical expertise, you've got every kind of expertise that you want from us. You've got engineers, our dentists, our accountants, doctors," what I call the "dead posse," right? . . . Now like what about us as artists, 'cos we have got that down too. Its like, India's the largest market in the world in terms of music. They sell billions there every year.

Bally   . . . Big things are happening now for India and it's about time, that's all I can say. A lot of majors, big record companies, are going there, proper franchises of restaurants, lots of things are happening in India and at the end of the day, the best place in the world is India.

Mukhtar   You were saying before that in some ways what you are more interested in is the form: the sound and the lyrics aren't that important. Don't you think that the message is just as important?

Bally   Depends what you're listening to, though, doesn't it? I'm talking about hundreds of categories, hundreds of stars and stuff. If you're listening to a mellow song or something, you're obviously listening to the lyrics, you're not listening just to the music are you? If you're listening to a dance track that really gets you up and going on the dancefloor—"Everybody Dance Now"—what kind of lyric is that? That's one of the biggest dance records ever and its just three words spoken. Certain songs are for certain kinds of categories. Dance music really doesn't have to have the best lyrics in the world, what carries it is the beat and the groove. Period. But if you're talking about a love song, or a song that's got meaning, like a political song or a Rap song, then yes, the lyrics are important. There's every kind of thing for every kind of listener. Lot of times, kids don't really know everything about the lyrics in a song. When it comes to Indian songs mainly 'cos a lot of kids don't understand traditional Punjabi talk. Even if you are Punjabi, even if it's a

Hindi song, they still love it and buy it, mainly because of the music. They love the music. Why do goras buy our music? Can't be because of the lyrics, impossible. Obviously music is a very, very important part of it. Lyrics play an important part in a different way, at a different level . . .

Shirin   Ranjit, do you think about the lyrics and the choices of records you play as a DJ? Are you consciously thinking, "Well I won't put this on because of some of the rubbish that this guy's on about"? Do you think about these issues when you're DJing?

Ranjit   Yes I do. There's one track especially that I really, really hate. It's absolutely obnoxious, that "Patel Rap." I banned it from the word go. When it came out I scratched it all over the vinyl . . . I thought, "There's no way anyone is playing this. I don't care."

Shirin   Tell us why.

Mukhtar   . . . for promoting stereotypes?

Ranjit   Yes, for promoting stereotypes, and for just killing any positive images of Asian people. If we really want to get anywhere in the music industry, in the mainstream, we've got to take ourselves seriously before we expect anybody else to do it. Tracks like "Patel Rap" are just shit.

Bally   It would've been worse if was a gora done it; 'cos an Indian man done it . . .

Ranjit   . . . they accepted it.

Bally   Yes, if it was a gora then nobody would've put up with it, you know.

Ranjit   They'd have banned it . . . That kind of stuff doesn't wash with me at all. And like lots of the Bhangra songs, I used to think about the lyrics and I realized I hated those tracks. The music's nice, the voice itself is really beautiful, but the content is really winding me up. You get guys that were really pissed singing it to you. There's that kind of level of harassment.

Shirin   So they were internalizing the lyrics when they sang them to you? It probably meant something to them. Are you saying then that lyrics do matter?

Ranjit   Yes, if they're singing that crap to you, you know it's a wind-up, man. Now some Bhangra bands are jumping on the Hindi band-wagon and singing love songs and stuff which is fine, but in terms of creativity in the Punjabi lyric, there is none. A lot of it was sexist rubbish.

Bally   And it does not work. Even the public out there think that those on stage must know it's not working. But they do it 'cos everyone else is doing it.

Shirin   Finally, I want to talk about both your futures, and the developments in Asian dance music that you imagine happening.

Bally   Big things are happening for myself and what I've always wanted to do is to get my music into major mainstream audiences such as movies and it's happening now. It's only happening now simply because of the hardships I went through for so many years. It's just going to show that all that bloody frustration and all that banging down of all those doors of the major companies has finally come around, so now everybody is finally listening to our kind of music. And obviously the help of a major record company pays off, that's helping me do things, like working with Mariah Carey, that I've only dreamt about. You wouldn't have got that before. Now things are changing.

Ranjit   The stuff I do is predominantly dance. It's not often Bhangra. I've been asked to do Bhangra, and to remix Bhangra, but I'm not that interested 'cos of the lyrical content of the product. I thought, "No, that's not me" . . .

Bally   So you do remixes, yeah?

Ranjit   No, I've been asked to do remixes, but I won't do them 'cos I want to do something from scratch, I want to do something completely original . . .

Bally   To write new songs, yeah?

Ranjit   . . . from bass line on and just work my way up.

Bally   Have you done new songs like that?

Ranjit   I've done dance music. That's what I do. I do dance music, with Rap, with Hindi vocals, Punjabi vocals, English vocals.

Bally   Which company is it coming out of?

Ranjit   Well I've done it through Time Recordings, Hollywood Records and Big Life, that was the last one that I did, and Sony Japan, the Jungle tracks.

Shirin   Do you have an audience in mind when you're actually doing this?

Ranjit   No, it's just something that I like doing, you know. I will get into Punjabi stuff, but that's not until I feel it's worth getting into again 'cos at the moment it's just very staid. A lot of our stuff is sold in the UK, but Italy's got a lot of our stuff, Japan as well—we've got a really large following there and Japan's a massive marker. We've been featured in the major press in Japan. I'm catering for a specific market. I do dance music, and I am able to sing in three languages, and I happen to know how to write all these languages, and my musical influences come from Funk and early Techno, that's the kind of stuff I grew up on. So my influences aren't all completely different to those on the kids that are growing up now. Obviously my style's going to be a little different. It's just a natural progression for me. It'll happen slowly, getting into the charts, but someone's got to do it somewhere along the line.

Bally   I think slowly things are changing, people are going to come in, people are getting into those places now. It's early days yet still for Asian people 'cos we haven't really tasted the success of being mainstream and at the top of the charts. We've only witnessed and seen and felt the whole potential of the Asian music scene 'cos we've been there for so many years. But it's also all new and exciting and everyone wants to be a part of it and slowly but surely people will be doing proper jobs and doing things in proper companies.

Ranjit   But then it goes back to what you were saying before, Bally, about lots and lots of styles—whatever you do there'll always be a traditional circuit anyway. Mainstream success won't really kill it, it'll just kind of enhance what already exists. There'll always be people like the Alaaps and Heeras—they'll always be there because there's always a market for them.

Mukhtar   I think it's definitely positive. Like we said in the beginning, we had a vacuum, there was nobody there and we were dancing to different rhythms. At least now, Asians are making a positive space out there and doing their own thing, producing their own music, making their own dance moves. And as we've heard today, it's all related to the issue of identity in many different ways.

Bally   And now at least the kids are paying some attention to their roots and their culture, and their music, listening to the originals, as well as to what we're doing now.

Ranjit   Yes, and they take more interest as well. It's about identities at the end of the day, 'cos now, when we listen to Alaap it's like, "Yes it's good, it's nice, it's from back home, but we can't relate to it 'cos they're only talking about life in the Punjab." You know, I've been born and brought up here in England. I can't sing about that and feel that it's a part of me. Now we are creating our own stuff, which is relevant to British life.

Bally   We are the generation now, they were the generation in that time, so we are representing what is happening now. Maybe in twenty years' time, our kids will be saying, "God, our folks used to listen to all that kind of stuff' . . . you know, way back in the 90s!" You have to go through all the stages, everybody does it. Just like how the English people have Disco and Rock and other styles going in and coming out, and then something else comes in. Our music does the same and it's doing it now . . . Who knows what's going to happen tomorrow.

Ranjit   Whatever happens, whether I'm behind the scenes or on the stage, or managing or something, which is what I've done before, I will always be doing something in the music industry. I'll probably still be spinning records at fifty! That's how I see it 'cos that's where I started off. It's like I'm going to be "Radical Mother," you know! Or "Radical Grandma," you know what I mean?

Thanks to Laura Turney for transcribing the tape of this interview.

THE ASIAN ROOTS OF ASIAN MASSIVE

Karsh Kale and the Midival Punditz create rich orchestral textures

TEED ROCKWELL

BROKEN ENGLISH by Karsh Kale. MIDIVAL TIMES by Midival Punditz. Available at www.sixdegreesrecords.com

When I first asked Karsh Kale why he called his music "Asian Massive," he said, "Talvin Singh called his music 'The Asian Underground.' I wanted to say that we were no longer underground, we are now massive." But Kale's music is not just massive in the sense of reaching a mass audience. There are intrinsic characteristics in the music itself that are best described by the word "massive," and these qualities spring from Indian roots.

Indian classical music is rich and complex, and filled with references to an intricate network of traditions and meanings. But all of that information is expressed in a single melodic line, which 1) both follows and breaks melodic rules, 2) layers cross-rhythms against a foundation which is mostly heard in the audience's and performer's minds, and 3) is ornamented by sruti (microtones) and other instrumental techniques, which color and change each note with the same kind of complexity that is produced in the West by orchestrations. Despite its complexity, such music will sound "thin" to people who are used to listening to the "massive" textures of a Wagnerian symphony orchestra.

However, it is not just Westerners who have been trained to hear in thick textures. For many years, Indian film songs were supported by large Western orchestras supplemented by a few Indian instruments. The arrangements accompanying these songs weren't (and still aren't) considered to be "serious" music. But as time has gone by, they have evolved their own kind of artistry which is both original and uniquely Indian. The earlier Indian film orchestrators had to write out arrangements for both Indian and Western instruments, and have them all played together in one take. These conditions put the improvising Indian musician at a disadvantage. Contemporary film composer A.R. Rahman, however, introduced multitrack recording, sampling, and synthesizer programming. These new technologies enabled him to capture improvised musical performances at their most spontaneous, and then later build the arrangements around them. "You can't expect an Indian classical musician to read a hundred measures of rests, and then play 20 notes," Rahman said when I interviewed him in London. "They're like free birds, and you can't cage them up that way." Multitrack recording made it possible to combine the spontaneity of improvised music with the massive textures that could once be produced only by written arrangements.

The music of both Karsh Kale and Midival Punditz grew out of the orchestral textures that have been created for these contemporary Indian films, and the work of expatriate Indian Club DJs in London. Those DJs first used multitracking to create rich textures on top of traditional Indian foundations. What is now widely known as bhangra was first created by adding electronic drums and bass to recordings of Punjabi bhangra folk music. The Asian Massive sound continues this tradition of "cutting and pasting" contemporary and traditional music into a sonic collage, but uses a much broader palette of musical colors. Indian folk and film music goes into the mix, and so does classical. However, it is obviously impossible to fully develop a raga when it functions like a single stone in a musical mosaic. If listening to a classical raga is like dwelling in a cave with a yogi, then listening to an Asian Massive recording is like wandering through the Taj Mahal. It might not be as profound, but it is overwhelmingly ornate and dazzling.

However, this new technology is not a substitute for craftsmanship or creativity. There are still techniques that must be mastered by the DJ/engineer, and artistic decisions that need to be made. If these diverse elements are not combined in such a way as to be both related and distinct, the result could be an incomprehensible sonic mush. Proper placement of tracks in the stereo image is essential, which is why Kale's and the Punditz's artistry are only fully revealed in headphones, or when one is standing between two massive speakers on a dance floor. Skilful equalization is also necessary, because too much volume within the same frequency range can cause sounds to cancel each other out. And the use of multiple reverbs of different depth and sustain creates a sense that certain tracks are nearer and further from each other, giving a sense of a truly massive sound.

The Midival Punditz were, ironically, the first Indians actually living in India to create music in this style. The Gaurav Raina and Tapan Raj duo patterned their "Cyber Mehfils" in New Delhi after The Asia Underground club scenes, and attracted young Indian professionals who heard the techno-aspects of this music as being exotic evocations of faraway London, and the Indian elements as accessible reminders of home. For my taste, their self-titled first album relied a bit too much on machines and not enough on human performances. In *Midival Times*, however, they have produced a beautiful balance between programming and musical performance, providing an original and effective showcase for the talents of traditional masters like Sultan Khan, Anoushka Shankar, and Vishal Vaid. The electronic textures add a rich grandeur to the classical performances that is both appropriate and innovative.

In Karsh Kale's newest album, *Broken English,* he brings forth even more of his many talents to make the transition from DJ and producer to full-fledged rock star. The producer as the "front man" in a rock album will seem strange to American audiences—as if the Wizard of Oz were shouting, "Pay more attention to the man behind the curtain!" But the production is what is truly stellar about this album. Kale stamps every song with his distinctive style as he showcases different rap, rock, and folk vocalists, while weaving in his trademark Indian and techno elements. You don't really want to hum the tunes or think about the lyrics when you listen. You just want to bathe yourself in the massive universe of textures that only he could create.

Teed Rockwell has studied Indian classical music with Ali Akbar Khan and other great Indian musicians. He is the first person to play Hindustani music on the Touchstyle Fretboard.

A Quick Guide to Asian Fusion, Part 1

Darragh Brady

There was a time when the only exposure to Asian music was on a Saturday night after you stumbled into your local Tandoori or on the late great George Harrison's incredible output of Indian inspired records.

In the past ten years, however, that has all taken a dramatic turn with some pivotal movements in the so called Asian underground.

The term Asian underground has been a double-edged sword just as Britpop turned, with its rise and now its fight for survival, in the fickle world of fad culture. As urban myths go, the term Asian underground came from the legendary Anokha nights at the Blue Note club in London. The night was put on by one of the main players on the Asian scene, Talvin Singh.

Born of Indian descent in Britain in 1970, Singh shared the cultural confusions of being seen as Indian in Britain, and British in India. The spark of his musical awakenings, however, came from listening to British bands such as The Jam and The Clash, which got him dismissed by Indian promoters as a punk who was being tarnished by western influences.

Defying the criticism and conformity, Singh went on to work with luminary forces in the musical world coming into the fray with Massive Attack, Madonna, Sioxusie and the Banshees and numerous other heavyweights.

The album that launched the well used term was *Anokha: Sounds of the Asian Underground*, which gave the media a convenient box to place this new movement in. The album featured some groundbreaking artists who where experimenting with traditional and electronic sounds on the decks and live at the Blue Note Club. The sound of Asian Fusion subsequently caught global attention and put State of Bengal, Amar, Future Sound of India and Singh himself firmly in the spotlight. With the floodgates opened Talvin was able to release his own solo experimentations, which can be heard on the *OK* and *HA* albums.

Another British Asian artist also working in the same ball park is Nitin Sawhney, currently riding high above the Asian underground tag, with his sixth album titled *Human*. Born in Dulwich in the mid-nineteen sixties Sawhney experienced, like Talvin Singh and most other colonial immigrants growing up in Britain, that uncertain feeling of alienation. However, great diversity often leads to great art, and Sawhney's releases are a good argument for the fact.

All artists need their advocates and Outcaste and Nation Records have been instrumental in giving Asian artists a voice. The Outcaste label was formed in 1995 by Shabs and Paul Franking to create a home for world music making artists and releasing some awe inspiring records in the process. It's a partnership that has risen from humble beginnings to being a major force in world music, winning the outstanding achievement award in 1998 and getting a nomination for a mercury music prize in 1999 with Nitin Sawhney's *Beyond Skin* album.

Martin Morales head of A+R at Outcaste explained his reasons for setting up the label was to represent Asian music to a wider audience. "The key to a successful label is having great artists, which we've had with Nitin Sawhney, Badmarsh And Shri and now with Oi Va Voi." Morlaes is clear to point out that "Outcaste is run by people who love music; we treat our artists as stars. We sign future stars, treat them with respect and then tell the world." He sees the current climate of economic problems suffered by the entertainment industry as an opportunity for smart labels to rise above the competition from other products like DVD's and computer games. Creating exciting music, making original-sounding records that people want to buy and not copy, and offering value for money is Outcaste's policy and it seems to work. As I write this, another Outcaste release is delivered by the postman; the album is *The Classical Indian Selection.* No beats this time, just amazing sound-scapes and arrangements from the legendary Ravi Shanker to new school producers Medival Punditz and heaps more. Diversity is part and parcel of what the label puts out, making them more accepted today than the label name suggests.

Nation Records has also played a massive role in placing this genre on the map, with a slightly harder sound and political slant being exemplified by its connection with bands like Asian Dub Foundation and Fundamental. The concept of the label was coerced back in 1989 with the intention of transferring the energy of a Sex Pistols gig circa 1977 to the Asian back-beat of Bhangra. The vision, however, wasn't shared by the rest of the music industry, and the obvious plot was to go it alone.

Aki was one of the founding members of the label and the ever growing sound of the band Fundamental. The spark began with an eight track album called *Fuse*, which got the ball rolling as Rich from Nation explains, "we knew something was going on once the genres of hip-hop and Bhangra started to merge, creating a sound that was new and fresh from the streets of Britain."

While I spoke to Rich, doing this interview, a guy knocks at the door with a demo; the interview stops and Rich welcomes him in the door and offers him a tea before recommencing the interview. You get the feeling from the way they operate that it's not rhetoric but action that creates new breakthrough in music and the arts. Nation has always been ahead of the game because it came from the soul in the first place. In a reserved and not boastful manner, Rich states, "we don't have a problem with piracy; in fact, it shows you that what we do is wanted by people. We don't have to downsize cause we only ever had 3 people running the show here."

Fourteen years on, their mission has launched the careers of Talvin Singh, Natacha Atlas, Loop Guru, Transglobal Underground and a host of others. They look towards the future with a crew from France called Recycler who is busy producing its first album for the label after being huge fans of what Nation did. Aki's band Fundamental is also in the studio recording tracks for its new album due out next year.

A big forerunner in this genre of world groove who paved the way for this merging of cultural sounds is UK based Indi-Pop Records. Set up by Steve Coe, a musical visionary and discoverer of Shelia Chandra, who provided the vocals for the 80's hit *Ever So Lonely* and countless other groundbreaking releases.

Indi-Pop is not ashamed to take the credit for creating the whole fusion style, which is still influencing now-established names like Nitin Sawhney and Talvin Singh and other composers. Its legacy can be heard on its recent retrospective *Compil-Asian* album, which gives you a taste of the boundaries it has crossed.

The new players, however, are coming on the scene quicker than you can write an article on them. The world is getting a taste of this music from people like Punjabi MC, who broke the nationals with Mundian To Bach Ke recently; New York's Dum Dum project with Punjabi 5-0; and the Bhangra Knights Vs Husan track, which accompanied the Peugeot 206 TV ad.

Less conspicuous artists making outstanding records are Thievery Corporation, their album *The Richest Man in Babylon* is well worth looking out for, and San Francisco's DJ Cheb I Sabbah on Six Degrees records is writing and remixing anything that moves on the world groove scene.

Closer to home and about to make waves is Visionary Underground, a collective from London who does everything as a close-knit community with a visual break beat concept. DJ Feel Free and visual artist Coco put together a live act and sound system with the help of Mc Navigator, Tc Izlam (Zulu Nation) Aref Durvesh who plays the tablas, Sonia Methta, a Hindi vocalist, and Dr Das from Asian Dub Foundation. Their recent release and live shows have received warm accolades from the break-beat raga fraternity.

The BBC has also caught up with this explosion by creating BBC Asian, a kind of Radio One for Asians, which unfortunately at times like its counterpart, falls short of the mark. The hiring and firing powers at the BBC have recently given Bobby Friction a graveyard slot on Radio One and, to its credit, supported world music through its Radio Three world music programs.

Another station to give air time to this music is Totally Radio, who is based in Brighton. It now broadcasts a hugely popular show around the world called the Kundalini Dub Lounge on www.totallyradio.com/kdl. The program is an online interactive show, which is listened to by an ever-growing global network. The station, together with the producers of the show Kusha Deep Productions, is currently putting together an album of music that has featured on the Dub Lounge. It is also running a competition for new artists working in this genre to submit their work for inclusion on this release. Chosen artists and producers will feature alongside some of the cutting-edge names on the UK fusion scene with the idea of greater cultural musical exchange by dismantling the musical boundaries.

The future of this scene will depend on the innovation of labels and artists to create a genre that is received by the world like other styles such as rock and RnB and not filed away in the novelty section of the musical spectrum.

BLACK AND WHITE (LYRICS)

WRITTEN BY DAS / PANDIT / SAVALE / TAILOR / ZAMAN
PUBLISHED BY MCA MUSIC LTD /
PRODUCED BY ASIAN DUB FOUNDATION /
& RECORDED BY REX SARGEANT ASSISTED BY JON MUSGRAVE /
ADDITIONAL PRODUCTION AND MIXING BY LOUIS BECKETT & BOBBY MARSHALL
ASSISTED BY JON MUSGRAVE /
RECORDED & MIXED @ THE ROUNDHOUSE STUDIOS /
℗1998 LONDON

J AND D HERE UNITED

BLACK AND WHITE HERE TO SHOW YOU HOW WE'VE BEEN DELIGHTED

THE NEW GENERATION SINCE THE MID NINETIES

SHOWING YOU HOW IT'S DONE IF YOU THINK YOU ARE A SMARTIE

TELLING YOU THE TRUTH SINCE WE SPOTTED EACH OTHER

WE'D LIKE TO BIG UP OUR ELDER SISTER AND BROTHER

BECAUSE THEY ARE THE LEGEND AND THEY ARE LIKE NO OTHER

TRAINED BY THE GREATER LEGEND MOTHER AND FATHER

NOW WE THINK JUMP UP LYRICS ARE ALIGHT

BUT WE'D LIKE TO BROADCAST A SUBJECT WE KNOW IS NOT RIGHT

LOOK AT US—BUT DON'T LOOK AT US IN DISGUST

BECAUSE YOU KNOW THE REALITY AND IT'S TIME TO ADJUST

THINK TO YOURSELF—DON'T BE FOOLISH ABOUT IT

FIX UP YOUR BRAIN OR YOU'LL BE THE TARGET

A BLACK MAN AND A WHITE WOMAN LIVING TOGETHER

FACE THE FACTS YOU FASCIST PERPETRATORS

AND AS THE WORLD IS GETTING SMALLER

WE CAN ONLY GET CLOSER AND CLOSER

BUILDING THIS COMMUNITY OF SOUND

CELEBRATING THE UNITY WE'VE FOUND

AND WE KNOW THIS IS THE MODEL TO FOLLOW

FOR ALL THE DUB CHILDREN OF TOMORROW

AS THEY GROW UNDER SHIFTING SKIES

WE'LL SEE EVERY NATION IN THEIR EYES

BLACK AND WHITE HERE HAS UNITED

WE'RE HERE TO SHOW YOU HOW WE'VE BEEN DELIGHTED

BLACK AND WHITE HERE HAS UNITED

BUILDING THIS COMMUNITY OF SOUND.

Hypocrite (Lyrics)

Written by Das / Pandit / Savale / Tailor / Zaman /
Published by MCA Music Ltd /
Produced by Asian Dub Foundation /
Engineered & Recorded by Rex Sargeant Assisted by Jon Musgrave /
Additional Production & Mixing by Louis Beckett & Bobby Marshall /
Recorded & Mixed @ The Roundhouse Studios /
Ⓟ1998 London

HYPOCRITES! WE GONNA GET INSIDE YOUR MIND

HYPOCRITES! YOU WILL PAY FOR YOUR CRIMES

HYPOCRITES WE'RE GONNA BLEED YOU DRY

YOUR POCKETS WILL BE EMPTY BUT YOU WON'T KNOW WHY

REDISTRIBUTION IS THE NAME OF THE GAME

ALL THE CASH THAT YOU STASHED MAN

WE'RE GONNA GIVE AWAY

LIZARD MAN BEWARE THIS IS THE DIGITAL UNDER CLASS

COMING FROM PLACES YOU'VE ONLY SEEN FROM YOUR CAR

ACCOUNTANT, LAWYER, FINANCIAL ADVISOR

PR CONSULTANT, JOURNALIST, ADVERTISER

WE KNOW YOUR GAME AND YOU THINK THAT WE'RE PLAYING IT

WHEN THE BILL COMES THROUGH THE DOOR YOU'RE GONNA BE PAYING IT

HYPOCRITE! WE GONNA GET INSIDE YOUR MIND

HYPOCRITE! YOU WILL PAY FOR YOUR CRIMES

HYPOCRITE! WE'RE GONNA BLEED YOU DRY

YOUR POCKETS WILL BE EMPTY BUT YOU WON'T KNOW WHY

ADF DEFINITELY WITHOUT A DOUBT HAVE THE SKILLS TO PAY THE BILLS

THE WORD IS COMMUNITY

WE SHOUT IT WITH IMPUNITY

IT'S SO UNCOOL

IT'S INCENDIARY

NO SLOGANS, NO SOUND BITES, BUT A LONG TERM PLAN

TEACHING IS THE FRAME WORK

BUILDING CHAINS OF COMMAND

SO WHEN THE LIZARD MAN STICKS OUT HIS TONGUE

WE PULL OUT OUR SCISSORS AND DO A HIT AND RUN

THIS IS THE DIGITAL UNDERCLASS

YES THIS IS THE DIGITAL UNDERCLASS

ADF DEFINITELY WITHOUT A DOUBT HAVE THE SKILLS TO PAY THE BILLS.

Free Satpal Ram (Primal Scream and Brendan Lynch Mix) (Lyrics)

Written by Das / Pandit / Savale / Tailor / Zaman
Published by Mca Music Ltd/
Produced & Mixed by Primal Scream & Brendan Lynch /
Engineered by Max Hayes /
Recorded by Adf & Rex Sargeant /
℗1998 Ffrr

BACK WAY TO ALL THE TROUBLE MAKERS

BETTER FIX UP YOUR BRAINS BECAUSE YOU'RE THE BIGGEST FAKERS

COME IN THE PLACE BETTER KNOW WHO YOU ARE

SELF DEFENCE IS NO OFFENCE

THE SCALES OF JUSTICE ARE WEIGHED DOWN ON ONE SIDE

FREEMASONS ON THE CASE YOU KNOW YOU'RE GONNA GET A ROUGH RIDE

HOLD TIGHT EVEN IF YOU KNOW YOUR RIGHTS

IT'S JUST A PIECE OF PAPER UNLESS YOU'RE PREPARED TO FIGHT

FOR TEN YEARS ONE HELL OF A LONG TIME

TO ROT IN A CELL WHEN YOU'VE COMMITTED NO CRIME

ANOTHER INNOCENT MAN FORCED TO CARRY THE CAN

FREE SATPAL RAM

FREE SATPAL RAM

ANOTHER INNOCENT MAN

WHOSE WORD AGAINST WHO?

WHOSE WORD AGAINST WHO?

THE DEGENERATE CREW

OUT ON THE TOWN THOUGHT THEY HAD SOMETHING TO PROVE

SELF DEFENCE—ONLY OFFENCE—HAD TO PROTECT HIMSELF FROM ALL THE MURDERING FOOLS

CUTTING REMARKS ON ACOUNT OF HIS RACE

A BLADE TO HIS CHEST AND A GLASS TO HIS FACE

AN ASIAN FIGHTS BACK CAN'T AFFORD TO BE MEEK

WITH YOUR BACK AGAINST THE WALL YOU CAN'T TURN THE OTHER CHEEK

AND ITS BACK WAY TO ALL THE TROUBLE MAKERS

BETTER FIX UP YOUR BRAIN BECAUSE YOU'RE THE BIGGEST FAKERS

COME IN THE PLACE BETTER KNOW WHO YOU ARE

FREE SATPAL RAM

ANOTHER INNOCENT MAN

BIRMINGHAM SIX

BRIDGEWATER FOUR

CROWN PROSECUTION TOTTING UP THE SCORE
KINGS CROSS TWO
GUILDFORD FOUR
WINSTON SILLCOT—MAN HOW MANY MORE?
SATPAL ATTACKED IN A RESTAURANT BY RACISTS
NOW THE BROTHER'S LOCKED UP ON A LIFE TIME BASIS
CONVICTED OF MURDER BUT WHAT'S NEVER MENTIONED
SELF DEFENCE WAS HIS ONLY INTENTION
ADF ONCE AGAIN TAKING TO THE STAND
WITNESS THE JAILING OF AN INNOCENT MAN
KICKING UP A FUSS BECAUSE IT COULD HAPPEN TO US
TIME TO JOIN IN THE FIGHT BACK
BECAUSE ENOUGH IS ENOUGH
AND ITS BACK WAY TO ALL THE TROUBLE MAKERS
BETTER FIX UP YOUR BRAINS BECAUSE YOU'RE THE BIGGEST FAKERS
COME IN THE PLACE BETTER KNOW WHO YOU ARE
FREE SATPAL RAM.

Operation Eagle Lie (Lyrics)

Written by Das / Pandit / Savale / Tailor / Zaman
Published by Mca Music Ltd /
Produced by Asian Dub Foundation /
Engineered & Recorded by Rex Sargeant Assisted by Jon Musgrave /
Additional Production & Mixing by Louis Beckett & Bobby Marshall /
Recorded & Mixed @ The Roundhouse Studios /
℗1998 London

Lies! Damn lies and statistics
Fitting up and stitching up down at ballistics
The back of the van it ain't used for seating
Just check through the window the youth them get a beating
Meet P.C. P.R. the designer policeman
Putting up a smokescreen with his multi coloured truncheon
Shake a few bad apples off the long arm of the law. But he knows and we know
    that it's rotten to the core
Black man on a double yellow he's a criminal
A racial attack—investigation minimal
You'll always find us on the end of a baton
When the black meets the blue you know who's getting spat on
Now I'm giving to you and I'm driving into you
The truth—no number crunching—it's just your mind that we are mugging
ADF taking them on at I-Spy
Watching them watching us Operation Eagle Lie
Unity is strength and strength is unity
IC1, IC2 and also IC3
All together we can defend the whole community
One people, all nations to reach their destiny
Before the devil man used to use the truncheon
To kill the black man is still his dream ambition
Now they have swat batons and CCTV
For unusual people just like you and me
Young sisters and brothers dying from heart attacks
But how can we breathe when the beast is on our back
CS gas in your lungs, eyes and your mouth
Just another police murder without a doubt
CPS is the piggies alibi
None of them ever prepared to be the fall guy
ADF taking them on at I-Spy
Watching them watching us Operation Eagle Lie.

CHANGE (LYRICS)

WRITTEN BY DAS / PANDIT / SAVALE / TAILOR / ZAMAN
PUBLISHED BY MCA MUSIC LTD /
ENGINEERED & RECORDED BY REX SARGEANT ASSISTED BY JON MUSGRAVE /
ADDITIONAL PRODUCTION & MIXING BY LOUIS BECKETT & BOBBY MARSHALL /
RECORDED & MIXED @ THE ROUNDHOUSE STUDIOS /
℗1998 LONDON

LOOK THROUGH THE SQUARE OR ROUND WINDOW
NOW A CHANGE GONNA COME
WHETHER YOU COME BY BUS OR UNDERGROUND
STILL A CHANGE GONNA COME
IF YOU'RE NORTH OR IF YOU'RE SOUTH
YOU KNOW A CHANGE GONNA COME
WHETHER BY FAX OR WORD OF MOUTH
STILL A CHANGE A GONNA COME
METERS PEAKING
TRUTH IS LEAKING OUT INTO THE STICKS
TOO LATE NO TURNING BACK NOW
BECAUSE THE SWITCHES HAVE BEEN FLICKED
GOAL POSTS MOVING
SIGN POSTS POINTING YOU THE WRONG WAY
THEY'RE SCREWING UP
YOU'RE QUEUING UP
COME BACK ANOTHER DAY
IF YOU'RE OLD OR IF YOU'RE YOUNG
YOU KNOW A CHANGE GONNA COME
NO MATTER WHERE YOU COME FROM
WHAT COLOUR BLACK, WHITE OR BROWN
GOVERNMENT MAN PLAN
MASH UP IN A BRITAIN
CRIMINAL JUSTICE BILL ME BAWL
WHERE THEY GET IT FROM?
THEM CAN'T UNDERSTAND
JUST WANT TO BUILD UP TENSION
BUT JUST WATCH THE FUTURE
BECAUSE A CHANGE A GONNA COME
ADF IS HERE TO SHOW YOU HOW IT SHOULD BE DONE
AND WE KNOW THAT THIS STYLE IS IDENTICAL TO NONE
YEAH!

BUREAUCRAT AND FAT CAT
TOO LONG THEY'VE HAD THEIR WAY
A BREEZE OF SLEAZE COMING TO BLOW THEM AWAY
SATELLITES CRASHING DOWN ON INDIA
WE SAY NO WAY
ADF BROADCASTING
WE NO RAMP
WE NO PLAY
WE GET MAD!
WHAT THEM A SAY
WHAT THEM A CHAT ABOUT
THIS IS REALITY MAN
YOU CAN'T RUN ADF OUT
WHAT THEM A DO WHAT THEM A TALK ABOUT
ALL YOU POLITICIAN A RUN UP YOUR MOUTH
MAN YOU GIVE ME JOKE . . .

Copyright Acknowledgments

"The Art Scab," by John Heartfield and George Grosz, reprinted from *The Weimar Republic Sourcebook*, edited by Anton Kaes, Martin Jay, and Edward Dimendberg (1994), by permission of University of California Press.

"Program of the Staatliches Bauhaus in Weimar," by Walter Gropius, reprinted from *The Weimar Republic Sourcebook*, edited by Anton Kaes, Martin Jay, and Edward Dimendberg (1994), by permission of University of California Press.

"Art is a Weapon," by Friedrich Wolf, reprinted from *The Weimar Republic Sourcebook*, edited by Anton Kaes, Martin Jay, and Edward Dimendberg (1994), by permission of University of California Press.

"Photomontage," by Raoul Hausmann, reprinted from *The Weimar Republic Sourcebook*, edited by Anton Kaes, Martin Jay, and Edward Dimendberg (1994), by permission of University of California Press.

"Photomontage as a Weapon in Class Struggle," by Alfred Kemenyi, reprinted from *The Weimar Republic Sourcebook*, edited by Anton Kaes, Martin Jay, and Edward Dimendberg (1994), by permission of University of California Press.

"Germany: The Third Reich, 1933–1945," by Karl A. Schleunes, reprinted from *britannica.com*, June 1, 2007, by permission of Encyclopaedia Britannica, Inc.

"Modern Art and Politics," by Stephanie Barron, reprinted from *Degenerate Art: The Fate of the Avant Garde in Nazi Germany* (1991), by permission of Los Angeles County Museum of Art. Copyright (c) Museum Associates/LACMA.

"Beauty without Sensuality" by George L. Mosse, reprinted from *Degenerate Art: The Fate of the Avant Garde in Nazi Germany* (1991), by permission of Los Angeles County Museum of Art. Copyright (c) Museum Associates/LACMA.

"Hitler: Speech of 19 July 1937," edited by J. Noakes and G. Pridham, reprinted from *Nazism 1919–1945: A Documentary Reader, Volume 2: State, Economy and Society 1933–1939* (2000), by permission of University of Exeter Press.

"Soviet Literature" by Maxim Gorky et al., reprinted from *Soviet Writers' Congress, 1934* (1977), by permission of Lawrence & Wishart.

"Synopsis: Lady Macbeth of Mtsensk," reprinted by permission from *Opera News*, August 30, 2002.

"Program Notes: Lady Macbeth of Mtsensk," by Lisa Y. Christensen, reprinted from *laopera.com*, August 23, 2002, by permission of the Los Angeles Opera.

"Chaos Instead of Music, January 28, 1936," reprinted from *Seventeen Moments in Soviet History*, translated by James von Geldern and Lewis Siegelbaum, reprinted by permission of Lewis Siegelbaum.

Excerpt from *City of Quartz: Excavating the Future in Los Angeles* (2006), by Mike Davis, reprinted by permission of Verso Books.

Excerpts from *The Architecture of Happiness* (2006), by Alain de Botton, Peters, Fraser and Dunlop Group.